THE LATE BABYLONIAN TEXTS OF THE ORIENTAL INSTITUTE COLLECTION

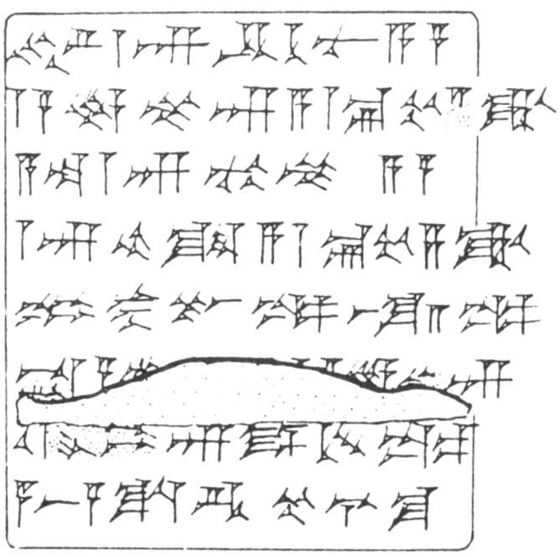

Bibliotheca Mesopotamica

Primary sources and interpretive analyses for the study of Mesopotamian civilization and its influences from late prehistory to the end of the cuneiform tradition

Editor: Giorgio Buccellati

Assistant Editors: John L. Hayes, Patricia Oliansky

Published Under the Auspices of
IIMAS
The International Institute for Mesopotamian Area Studies

BIBLIOTHECA MESOPOTAMICA

Volume 24

THE LATE BABYLONIAN TEXTS OF THE ORIENTAL INSTITUTE COLLECTION

David B. Weisberg

UNDENA PUBLICATIONS

Malibu 1991

ABSTRACT

This volume consists of 54 texts belonging to the Collection of the Oriental Institute of the University of Chicago. Originating from Uruk, these texts belong to the Seleucid and Arsacid periods. They date from 292 to 128 B.C. The types of texts included are: deeds of sale, gifts and dedications, divisions of property, quitclaims, other private transactions, a letter, and a literary document. These carefully prepared copies are supported by indices of personal and divine names, lists of feminine personal names, and Greek personal names. They provide valuable new data for Assyriologists and historians interested in the Hellenistic era in Babylonia.

Published with the assistance of the Henry Englander -- Eli Mayer Publication Fund of the Hebrew Union College Press, established in their honor by Esther Straus Englander and Jessie Straus Mayer.

ISBN 0-89003-300-5 (paper)
0-89003-301-3 (cloth)

Undena Publications, P.O. Box 97, Malibu, California, U.S.A. 90265

Dedicated to my wife,

Ophra

CONTENTS

PREFACE

It is a pleasure for me to thank the following people:

Erica Reiner, Editor-in-Charge of the Chicago Assyrian Dictionary;

John A. Brinkman, Curator of the Oriental Institute Tablet Collections;

Other faculty members of the Oriental Institute, in particular: Robert D. Biggs, Miguel Civil and Matthew W. Stolper;

The late I. J. Gelb and A. Leo Oppenheim;

Charles Jones, Trudy S. Kawami and Ronald Wallenfels;

Colleagues at HUC-JIR; Alfred Gottschalk, President of HUC-JIR, who arranged for grants that enabled me to work at the Oriental Institute; Michael A. Meyer, Chair of the Publications Committee;

HUC graduate students: Bill T. Arnold, Bryan Beyer, Deborah Bram, David Burge, Ruth Deemy, Sherry Walton Kingston, Joseph Shao, Joe M. Sprinkle and Paul H. Wright;

Giorgio Buccellati, Bernadette L. Fay and James H. Platt;

Dan S. Chill, Karol Hoffmann, Glenn K. Manacher, and Richard H. Weisberg;

Ophra and our children.

CINCINNATI, OHIO *D. B. W.*

JULY, 1990

ABBREVIATIONS

The conventions followed in this book are those of the Chicago Assyrian Dictionary. Abbreviations cited below are for the convenience of the reader and include commonly used sigla as well as frequently quoted bibliographic sources.

a. ancestor

A Text in Oriental Institute Tablet Collection

A.E. Arsacid Era dating

AHw W. von Soden, Akkadisches Handwörterbuch, Wiesbaden, 1959-81

AJSL American Journal of Semitic Languages

BiMes Bibliotheca Mesopotamica

br. brother

BRM 2 Albert T. Clay, "Legal Documents from Erech dated in the Seleucid Era (312-65 B.C.)," Babylonian Records in the Library of J. Pierpont Morgan 2, New York, 1913.

CAD The Assyrian Dictionary of the Oriental Institute of the University of Chicago, Chicago, 1956-

CAHU L. T. Doty, "Cuneiform Archives from Hellenistic Uruk," Yale University Ph.D. Dissertation, 1977, University Microfilms, Ann Arbor, Michigan.

desc. descendant

f. father

Falkenstein, Topographie Adam Falkenstein, "Topogaphie von Uruk," Ausgrabungen der deutschen Forschungsgemeinschaft in Uruk-Warka, Band 3, Harrassowitz, Leipzig, 1941.

ggf. great grandfather

gf. grandfather

JCS Journal of Cuneiform Studies

JNES Journal of Near Eastern Studies

Le.E. Left Edge

Lo.E. Lower Edge

McDowell Robert Harbold McDowell, "Stamped and Inscribed Objects from Seleucia on the Tigris," University of Michigan Studies. Humanistic Series, Volume XXXVI, Ann Arbor, University of Michigan Press, 1935

MLC Tablets in the collection of J. Pierpont Morgan

O. Obverse

Oelsner Joachim Oelsner, "Materialien zur babylonischen Gesellschaft und Kultur in hellenistischer Zeit," Az Eötvös Loránd Tudományegyetem Ókori Történeti, Assziriológiai És Egyiptológiai Tanszékeinek Kiadványai 40, Budapest, 1986

OITC Oriental Institute Tablet Collection (New Text Siglum)

Or. Orientalia

Parker and Dubberstein R. A. Parker and W. H. Dubberstein, Babylonian Chronology 626 B.C.-A.D. 75, Providence, 1956

PN Personal Name

R. Reverse

R.E. Right Edge

RN Royal Name

s. son

S.E. Seleucid Era dating

TBER Jean-Marie Durand, "Textes Babyloniens d'Époque Récente," Recherche sur les grandes civilisations, Cahier n° 6, Éditions A.D.P.F., Paris, 1981, and Francis Joannès "Textes Économiques de la Babylonie Récente," Éditions Recherche sur les civilisations, Cahier n° 5, Éditions A.D.P.F., Paris, 1982

ABBREVIATIONS

U.E. Upper Edge

VAS 15 Otto Schroeder, "Kontrakte der Seleukidenzeit aus Warka," Vorderasiatische Schriftdenkmäler Heft 15, Leipzig, Hinrichs, 1916

wit. witness

+ (indicates join)

INTRODUCTION[1]

This volume consists of 54 texts from the Seleucid and Arsacid periods of Mesopotamia, stemming from Uruk. The texts are in the Collection of the Oriental Institute of the University of Chicago, whose Curator is J. A. Brinkman. The time range (based upon the datable texts) spans 164 years, from Seleucid Era 20 (= 292 B.C.) to S.E. 184 (=Arsacid Era 120 = 128 B.C.).

Permission was granted to the author to work on these texts by the late I. J. Gelb, former Curator of the Collection and J. A. Brinkman. An arrangement was worked out to the effect that the present author would copy and index the texts while Joachim Oelsner and G. Sarkisian would transliterate and translate them. The present author has endeavored to stay within the bounds of that original agreement, hence the absence of transliterations and translations in the present volume.

Some references to the Late Babylonian material in the Oriental Institute have appeared in the literature such as in Olmstead[2] and Parker and Dubberstein.[3] The larger groups of material from the Collection have been cited in print in 1977 by L. T. Doty[4] and in 1986 by Joachim Oelsner.[5]

The Near East after the time of Alexander the Great was a place of profound change and transformation which affected language, religion, culture, and political and economic structures.[6] Yet, despite that change, there were elements of rootage in antiquity that also flavored the character of the age.

---

[1] Note "The Oriental Institute's Neo- and Late Babylonian Texts: A Progress Report," delivered at the meeting of the American Oriental Society in Toronto, April 13, 1978 and "Texts and Studies from the Oriental Institute Neo- and Late Babylonian Collection," delivered at the 29th Rencontre Assyriologique International, London, July 9, 1982.

[2] "Cuneiform Texts and Hellenistic Chronology," Classical Philology 32 (1937), pp. 1-14. Pp 10ff. refer to A 2518 (Text 13), A 3679 (Text 32) and A 3688 (Text 10). For a correction on Olmstead's reading of A 2518, see our comment in the Descriptive Catalogue at Text 13.

[3] Babylonian Chronology 626 B.C.-A.D. 75 (Providence, 1956), p. 23, citing Olmstead on A 2518 (see previous footnote).

[4] "Cuneiform Archives from Hellenistic Uruk," Ph.D. Dissertation, Yale University, New Haven, pp. 46 and 361 (n. 123).

[5] "Materialien zur babylonischen Gesellschaft und Kultur in hellenistischer Zeit," Az Eötvös Loránd Tudományegyetem Ókori Történeti, Assziriológiai És Egyiptológiai Tanszékeinek Kiadványai 40 (Budapest, 1986), pp. 158-160, 517.

[6] See Doty, CAHU, pp. 1-14, Oelsner, "Materialien," pp. 51-71, both with extensive literature and Amelie Kuhrt and Susan Sherwin-White, eds. Hellenism in the East: The Interaction of Greek and non-Greek Civilizations from Syria to Central Asia after Alexander, (London: Duckworth, 1987 [last reference courtesy of Getzel M. Cohen and Lee Fields]).

Babylonia during the period covered by this book, was, after Syria, a major Seleucid stronghold. The Greek rulers recognized the venerable traditions of this ancient land and bestowed special entitlements upon it.

> "Alexander the Great...had deliberately represented himself as the legitimate successor of the ancient rulers of the land [Mesopotamia]. Subsequently, Seleucus I Nicator, after victoriously asserting his claim to Babylonia against the other Successors, made a similar claim, respecting the country as the original nucleus of his rise to special power, and granting it protection and privilege.[7]

Though Babylonia's writing tradition went back to 3200 B.C. Uruk, its cultural legacy was still alive and well in that selfsame Uruk, now part of a brand new world. This heritage was venerated by the generals and politicians whose own roots were in distant Europe.

> "Babylonia had preserved, and was still allowed to retain, large parts of its own native, traditional, centralized governmental and social system. In particular, its ancient law - the most sophisticated legal system in the world outside Greece, Rome and China - was still very much alive, and represented a potent, unifying factor."[8]

As a glance at the Table of Contents and Catalogues of this book will reveal, the texts published herein reflect a vigorous economic and social life, in addition to the rich cultural heritage of which we have spoken. This was due in no small measure to the healthy connections that were cultivated between the State and local (especially religious) functionaries.

> "Lavishly reconstructed under the sponsorship of the Seleucids..., the temples of Marduk (at Babylon), Anu (at Orchoi or Uruk) and Nabu (at Borsippa) regained their prosperity and transacted their own business in their own language and according to their own code."[9]

A valuable source of information from this time is the seal impressions found on the clay tablets, sometimes neglected by Assyriologists. It is hoped that the inclusion of these drawings will represent a useful addition to the corpus of seals known to scholars.

---

[7]Michael Grant, From Alexander to Cleopatra. The Hellenistic World (New York, Scribner's, 1982), p. 59.

[8]Grant, p. 59.

[9]Grant, p. 59.

The 201 stamp seal impressions indexed in this volume reflect artistic motifs in use from the early years of the Seleucid Empire to the end of the second century B.C.[10] Most, if not all of them, were produced from engraved metal rings (rather than engraved stones set into rings).

One set of familiar themes involves passant quadrupeds, lions, bulls and sphinxes, often with a small star and crescent in the field above or before the animal. Such figures might reflect Achaemenid origins, as might the occurrence of the palm tree as a solitary motif.[11]

Another tradition is seen in the draped standing figures of Neo-Babylonian stamp seals[12] and Mesopotamian motifs such as the goat-fish,[13] merman,[14] scorpion-tailed bird-man,[15] the god with the flowing vase,[16] and in at least one case, a representation of the fish-garbed priest.[17]

A third artistic tradition perhaps may be seen in the sealings of pairs of antithetical animals, often sphinxes, sometimes separated by what appears to be a vertical line or pillar.[18]

On some of the seals there is an attempt to render the naturalistic figures of Hellenistic art[19] or to depict portraits[20]. However, these are not very competently done.

---

[10]I am indebted to Trudy S. Kawami and Ronald Wallenfels for their kind help in evaluating the seal impressions; the author, however, bears full responsibility for any errors that may be present in this formulation.

[11]Text 19, impression 73.

[12]Text 2, impression 12; text 13, impression 57; text 16, impression 66; text 42, impression 170; text 48, impression 196.

[13]Text 9, impression 32; text 17, impression 70; text 20, impression 88.

[14]Text 13, impression 55.

[15]Text 22, impression 96.

[16]Text 2, impression 12.

[17]Text 14, impression 64.

[18]Text 10, impression 40; text 20, impression 87; text 28, impression 132.

[19]Text 14, impression 63; text 22, impression 97; text 27, impression 123; text 29, impression 130 (duplicate).

[20]Text 12, impression 45, text 27, impressions 120 and 121, text 29, impression 129 (duplicate).

A motif that is not known earlier in Mesopotamian art, the crab, occurs in some impressions.[21] In addition, a fish resembling a dolphin occurs once.[22]

All motifs occurring on the Chicago tablets occur in other collections of tablets from this period as well. They present us with a unique visual document of the Hellenistic world and its impact on older Mesopotamian traditions, and give a welcome perspective on the rich and varied culture of the waning years of the first millennium B.C.

The following comments were excerpted from notes recorded during collation of the duplicates housed at the Yale Babylonian Collection:[23]

BRM 2	22 (MLC 2122)	= BiMes 24	1 (A 2527)
	37 (MLC 2137)		23 (A 2523)
	54 (MLC 2154)		28 (A 2525)

(1) On the Lo.E., R.E. and U.E. of MLC 2122 (=BRM 2 22) and its duplicate, A 2527 (=BiMes 24 1) both texts have the same Personal Names in the same order, whereas on the Le.E., A 2527's Tattannu is correctly read by the scribe of MLC 2122 and copied by Clay as ^{d}Anu-balaṭsu-iqbi. The same ten witnesses appear in both texts, though in a different order.

(2) In MLC 2137:7 (=BRM 2 37:7) at the end of the line, the phrase *u ma-a-du ma-la ba-šu-ú* is destroyed. It is possible this has flaked off since Clay's copy was made, or he might have copied on the basis of the familiar formula, as if nothing were broken.[24]

(3) Signs belonging on one line were copied by Clay onto another, for the purpose of saving space:

MLC 2137 R. 4 begins, as does A 2523 R. 4′ (=BiMes 24 23 R. 4′), with three signs: LÚ MU.GUB (rest blank). However, these were copied at the end of the third line of the

---

[21]Text 27 impressions 122 and 126; and text 29, impression 131 (duplicate).

[22]Text 10, impression 40.

[23]William Hallo and Gary Beckman have kindly helped me with readings which I requested while I was in Cincinnati.

Insofar as the comments relate to the work of A. T. Clay, research underscores the enduring quality of his fine copies. The few errors discovered here and there should be seen within the context of the remarkable accuracy of most of his text copies.

[24]This must have been a common technique in those years as I discovered when I collated the texts in Ivan Lee Holt, "Tablets From the R. Campbell Thompson Collection in the Haskell Oriental Museum of the University of Chicago," AJSL 27 (1910/11), pp. 193ff.

Reverse (in Clay's line count=line 18). Clay's fourth line of the Reverse (in Clay's line count=line 19) begins with the witness names.

(4) Additional signs, which are present in MLC 2137 Reverse, inadvertently were omitted from the copy of *BRM* 2 37 R. This sometimes resulted in the omission of the full Personal Name of a witness.

(5) MLC 2154 (=*BRM* 2 54) is a duplicate of A 2525 (=*BiMes* 24 28), whose signs match up exactly on the Obverse but not the Reverse. Contrast MLC 2137 (=*BRM* 2 37), the duplicate of A 2523 (=*BiMes* 24 23), in which the signs do not match exactly on the lines even though the signs and the words are the same.

Moreover, In *BRM* 2 54, Reverse, some Personal Names have been miscopied and some omitted by Clay, especially in lines 25-29 (note the lacuna in the column of ancestral names). Here are corrections to misnumbered lines on the Reverse:

BRM 2 54:30 should be	54:29
" 31	" 30
" 32	" 31 and
" 33	" 32.

The following method of line numbering has been utilized: Consecutive numbering continuing on the Reverse is used (for 16 of the 54 texts) unless there is a break whose lines cannot be calculated, in which case prime numbers beginning with 1′ are employed.

Text #	Method of Line Numbering
1.	consecutive
2.	R. 1′
3.	1′
4.	1′; R. 1′
5.	R. 1′
6.	R. 1′
7.	1′
8.	1′
9.	1′; R. 1′
10.	consecutive
11.	R. 1′
12.	R. 1′
13.	consecutive
14.	consecutive
15.	1′
16.	R. 1′
17.	R. 1′
18.	R. 1′
19.	consecutive
20.	consecutive
21.	consecutive
22.	R. 1′
23.	R. 1′
24.	(Rev. destroyed)
25.	consecutive
26.	R. 1′
27.	consecutive
28.	consecutive
29.	consecutive
30.	R. 1′
31.	(Rev. destroyed)
32.	R. 1′
33.	R. 1′
34.	consecutive
35.	consecutive
36.	R. 1′
37.	R. 1′
38.	1′
39.	R. 1′
40.	1′; R. 1′
41.	1′; R. 1′
42.	1′; R. 1′
43.	R. 1′
44.	R. 1′
45.	R. 1′
46.	consecutive
47.	(Rev. destroyed)
48.	consecutive
49.	1′; R. 1′
50.	consecutive
51.	R. 1′
52.	1′
53.	R. 1′
54.	1′; R. consecutive prime

CLASSIFIED CATALOGUE OF SELEUCID TEXTS

A. Deeds of sale

1. of an allotment (*isqu*)	1-12
2. of real estate	13-38
3. fragmentary texts with one possibly a bill of sale of a slave	39-41

B. Gifts and Dedications

1. deed of gift of real estate	42
2. deeds of dedication of children to temple	43, 44

C. divisions of property	45, 46
D. quitclaims	47, 48
E. other private transactions	49
F. letter	50
G. literary document	51
H. destroyed	52-54

Text	Museum Number	City	Seleucid Era Month	Day	Year	King's Name or Era	B.C.	Description and Comments
1.	A 2527	Uruk	Add II	14	77	Seleucus II Callinicus, or Seleucus III Soter	234	Deed of sale of prebendal income from a bow fief in the Irigal, Reš and ^{d}Innin-akītu house...monthly throughout the year...for 4 shekels of silver. Dupl. <u>BRM</u> 2 22, see ib. pp. 24f.
2.	A 3497	Uruk	Sim	29	108	Antiochus III the Great & Antiochus, his son	204	Deed of sale of fractional share in portion of ox-flesh of temple offering.
3.	A 3509	X	X	X				Fragment of Deed of sale of GÌR.SÈ.GA-ú-tú (=girseqūtu) isqu (a prebend whose "nature of function ...remains unknown" - CAD G 96a). This fragment has been filed down on each edge.
4.	A 3653	Uruk	Aya	5	X	Seleucus		Possible sale of prebend-note cp. Obv.: šalšu...UD.5 [KÁM]. Obv. mostly destroyed; scattered signs only preserved. Names of ancestors of witnesses on Rev. are preserved.
5.	A 3676	Uruk	Šab	X	X	Seleucus		Deed of sale of prebendal income (isqu) for (all? or portions? of) days 25 and 26 of the temple routine for each month, by one man, for the sum of 16 shekels of silver.
6.	A 3678	Uruk	Arah (<ITI.>APIN)	3	⌈121⌉	Antiochus III the Great	⌈191⌉	Deed of sale of prebend (or prebend income). Most details destroyed. For ^{d}Anu-uballiṭ-Kephalon, see also Texts 31 & 33, below.

Text	Museum Number	City	Seleucid Era Month	Day	Year	King's Name or Era	B.C.	Description and Comments
7.	OITC 2.2	X	X	X	X	(Antiochus)		Fragment of Deed sale of butcher's prebend (šalšu ina UZU tikki ša PN...).
8.	OITC 2.1	X	X	X	X	(Antiochus)		Fragment of Deed of sale of (prebendal shares in?) ra-si-en.
9.	A 3681	X	X	X	X			Deed of Sale of (prebendal shares in?) cuts of meat from the neck (IM.DUB.KI.LAM.MEŠ ša UZU tikki, Obv 6′).
10.	A 3688	X	X	10	141	Antiochus IV Epiphanes & Antiochus, his son	171	Deed of sale of 1/20th share in each day, from the 1st to the 30th day of the month, in the brewer's prebend (LÚ ŠIM×GAR-ú-tú = sirašūtu) before all the gods of the temple for ⅓ mina of silver.
11.	A 3693	X	X	X	70	Seleucus II Callinicus	242	Deed of sale of doorkeeper's prebend (GIŠ.ŠUB.BA LÚ NI.DUḪ-ú-tú = atūtu) sale price - ¼ of 1 day is mentioned - many details lost in break.
12.	A 3698	Uruk	Nis	X	162	Alexander I Balas	150	Deed of sale of ¼ of the sixth day of the month in the prebends of the office of person admitted to all parts of the temple (LÚ TU.É-ú-tú =ēreb bītūtu) and temple butcher (LÚ GÍR.LÁ-ú-tú = ṭābiḫūtu) for the price of 16 shekels of silver.

Text	Museum Number	City	Seleucid Era Month	Day	Year	King's Name or Era	B.C.	Description and Comments
13.	A 2518	Uruk	Add	10	137	Antiochus IV Epiphanes & Antiochus, his son	174	Deed of sale of an empty plot of land, "property of ^{d}Anu," in the ^{d}Innin-Gate District of Uruk, for the price of 20 shekels of silver. Cited in Olmstead, <u>Classical Philology</u> 32 (1937), p. 10 as a latest date for Antiochus IV. Since the text clearly mentions "Antiochus and Antiochus, his son, kings," Olmstead's observation would appear to be inaccurate. Cp. Parker & Dubberstein, <u>Babylonian Chronology</u>, p. 23).
14.	A 2526	Uruk	Šab	20	36	Antiochus I Soter & Seleucus	275	Deed of sale of an empty plot in the ^{d}Innin-Gate District of Uruk for 10 shekels of silver in addition an atru-payment of ¼ shekel of silver. Note the uncharacteristic long-axis of this tablet.
15.	A 3477	X	X	X	X			Deed of sale of [kišub]bû (see line 3': [KI.ŠUB.]BA MU.MEŠ) fragment only; Rev. destroyed.
16.	A 3671	Uruk	X	X	X	[Sele]ucus?		[Deed of sale of] empty plot of land, sold to a man by his mother. Obv. and good part of Rev. destroyed.
17.	A 3496+ 3503+ 3664	Uruk	Abu	X	X			Deed of sale of an empty plot of land, property, and É ki-e-zu. Badly broken text, possibly dating to year 119, Antiochus & Antiochus, his son, if the PN in Rev. 14' is read correctly.

Text	Museum Number	City	Seleucid Era Month	Day	Year	King's Name or Era	B.C.	Description and Comments
18.	A 3675	Uruk	X	X	X			[Deed of Sale or gift of] empty plot of land (see Rev. line 4′ and 7′, amaštum?).
19.	A 2519	Uruk	Sim	24	89	Seleucus III Soter	223	Deed of sale of several built-on house-plots "property of ^{d}Anu" in the ^{d}Innin-Gate District of Uruk, for the price of 1 mina of silver. Latest date for Seleucus III Soter as recorded in Parker & Dubberstein, p. 22. Duplicate BRM 2 28.
20.	A 2520		Ṭeb	20	139	Antiochus IV Epiphanes & Antiochus, his son	172	Deed of sale of built-on house plot in the...Orchard District of Uruk for the price of 12 (13?) shekels of silver. A man sells land "voluntarily and with the consent of his mother."
21.	A 2521	Uruk	X	20	82 or 83	Seleucus II Callinicus	230 or 229	Deed of sale of house and empty plot of land, "property of ^{d}Anu," held in feudal tenure as bīt ritti property, for the price of 2(!) shekels of silver.
22.	A 2522	Uruk	Aya	3	131	Seleucus IV Philopator	181	Deed of sale of a bīt ritti property, part of built-on plot in the ^{d}Innin-Gate District of Uruk, for the price of a mina of silver. What is being sold here is not the "built-on house plot" of line 2, but the "bīt ritti property" attached to that plot. (also line 2)

Text	Museum Number	City	Seleucid Era Month	Day	Year	King's Name or Era	B.C.	Description and Comments
23.	A 2523	Uruk	Add?	16	133	Seleucus IV Philopator	178	Deed of sale of house, "property of [d]Anu, (with) threshold (being) fixed (therein), cross-rafters, the door and the lock being durable, in the [d]Innin-Gate District of Uruk." Duplicate BRM 2 37
24.	A 3683	Uruk	X	X	X			Deed of sale of a built-on house plot in the bīt [d]Adad District of Uruk for the sale price of 27½ shekels of silver.
25.	A 3685	Uruk	Taš	6	155	Demetrius I Soter	157	Deed of sale of ⅓ of a man's share in a house and plot in the É DINGIR MEŠ.GAL.MEŠ⌉ District, for the price of 1 mina of silver.
26.	A 3692	Uruk	Ulu	2	82	Seleucus II Callinicus	230	Deed of sale of built-on plot of land in the bīt [d]Adad District of Uruk.
27.	A 32115	Uruk	X	19	148	Antiochus IV Epiphanes	164	Deed of sale of south room and empty plot of land in the bīt [d]Adad District for the price of 1 mina 10 shekels of silver. Compare Text 29, a duplicate.
28.	A 2525	Uruk	X	X	150	Antiochus V Eupator	162	Deed of sale of south room, enclosure and right-of-way located in the District of the Market-Gate, which is (also) called "District of the Ereškigal Temple," for 12 shekels of silver. BRM 2 54:8 (duplicate) is cited in CAD M/2 muşû A, p. 248a and Falkenstein, Topographie, p. 51.

Text	Museum Number	City	Seleucid Era Month	Day	Year	King's Name or Era	B.C.	Description and Comments
29.	A 32114	Uruk	X	19	148	Antiochus IV Epiphanes	164	Deed of sale of south room and empty plot of land in the bīt [d]Adad District for the price of 1 mina 10 shekels of silver. Compare Text 27, a duplicate.
30.	A 3660		Taš	8	X			[Deed of sale of a] house in ruins [for tearing down and rebuilding?] in the...Orchard District of [Uruk...]. Text is mostly broken away.
31.	A 3682	Uruk	X	X	X			Deed of sale of 2/5 of the share owned by two men in "a ruined house for tearing down and rebuilding" located in the bīt [d]LUGAL.GÌR.RA District. Sale price ½ mina of silver. Note line 9: "staters of Antiochus".
32.	A 3679	Uruk	Abu	30	140	Antiochus IV Epiphanes & Antiochus, his son	172	Deed of sale of a reed storage hut in the bīt [d]Adad District of Uruk for 26 shekels of silver.
33.	A 3687	Uruk	X	30	⌈111⌉ or ⌈121⌉	Antiochus III the Great [/& Antiochus]	⌈201⌉ or ⌈191⌉	Deed of sale of reed hut in the Eanna District of Uruk for the price of ⅓ mina of silver.
34.	A 3691	Uruk	Aya	X	96	Antiochus III the Great	216	Deed of sale of reed hut by a woman in the ⌈É DINGIR.MEŠ⌉ District of Uruk to another woman for the price of 54 shekels of silver.
35.	A 2524	X	X	X	X			Deed of sale of a property É MU.MEŠ i-ṣu u ma-a-du...for 16 shekels of silver. Rev. 2f.

Text	Museum Number	City	Seleucid Era Month	Day	Year	King's Name or Era	B.C.	Description and Comments
36.	A 3662	Uruk	Sim	1	20-31	Seleucus I & Antiochus I Soter	292-281	Deed of sale of real estate located in the [bīt ^{d}]LUGAL.GÌR.RA District.
37.	A 3686	Uruk	Abu	30	X	Antiochus & Antiochus, his son		Deed of sale of storehouse for the price of 6 shekels of silver.
38.	A 3694	X	X	X	X			Deed of sale of real estate for 25 shekels of silver.
39.	A 3455+ 3665	Uruk	X	X	20-36		292-275	Deed of sale or gift [of...] (mostly destroyed). Some witnesses' names and that of the scribe are preserved. If the scribe, Itti-^{d}Anu-nuḫšim, is the same as the figure mentioned in Text 14 Rev. 14, then the date is within the bounds suggested.
								Sale of an allotment (isqu), food allowances, real estate, slaves or gift all have ina ḫūd libbīšu (*see* Doty, CAHU, pp. 52ff.).
40.	A 3499	X	X	X	X			Mostly destroyed deed of sale of slave; note phrases... ana muḫḫi PN ittaši/ittadin (?) (Obv. 7');...PN_2 umarraqma ana PN_3 inandin....PN pūt la širkūtu...nāši (witnesses).
41.	A 3697	Uruk	Kis	27	163	Alexander I Balas	149	Deed of sale of... (see R.E.: LÚ na-din-n[a-nu]).
42.	A 3672	X	X	X	X			[Deed of gift of] empty plot of land, damaged. For the gift-formula restricting power of disposition, see Doty, CAHU, p. 84: [item] šuāti ana kaspi... See also Text 47:6 ff.

Text	Museum Number	City	Seleucid Era Month	Day	Year	King's Name or Era	B.C.	Description and Comments
43.	A 3689	Uruk	Nis (ITI.BAR)	X	AE 120= SE 184	Arsak	128	Deed of dedication of 2 children, brothers, ages 6 and 10 years, to the brickwork service of the temples. The phrase ana nudunnû or rīmūt, is sometimes omitted, as it is here.
44.	A 3690	X	Sim (ITI.SIG)	4	AE 115= (SE 179)	Arsak	133	Deed of dedication of 2 children, girls, ages [X] and 5 years, to the brickwork service of the temples. Scribe omitted SE equivalent in R. 13′. See comments to Text 43.
45.	A 3680	Uruk	Duz	3	92	Antiochus III The Great	220	Document containing division of house and plot of land between two parties, located in the É LUGAL GÌR.RA District.
46.	A 3695	Uruk	Šab	10	85	Seleucus II Callinicus	226	Document containing division between two brothers of house and reed hut in the bīt ^{d}Adad District of Uruk; also empty plot of land, a court, outbuilding. See Text 45.
47.	A 3498	X	X	X	X			Relinquishment of claim to the prebend of office of lamentation-priest (LÚ UŠ.KU-ú-tú = kalūtu).
48.	A 3684	Uruk	Taš?	X	97	Antiochus III The Great	215	Relinquishment of a claim to an empty plot of land in the Royal Orchard District, from a man to another person, for the purpose of building a dividing wall (amaštum).

Text	Museum Number	City	Seleucid Era Month	Day	Year	King's Name or Era	B.C.	Description and Comments
49.	A 3422+ 3489+ 3493+ 3655	Uruk	X	X	151-161	Demetrius I Soter	161-151	(Obv. destroyed) possibly adoption (? see Rev. 1f.) by a woman, of a man who will perform the clay (building and plastering) work for the temples.
50.	A 3375							Letter of PN to PN_2 concerning the quppu in your hands... which is written in the document...(?)
51.	A 3673	Uruk	X	X	111	Antiochus III the Great & Antiochus his son	201	A literary text, perhaps a hymn to ^{d}Adad (lines 5, 15, 16) and ^{d}Ninurta (? line 8).
52.	A 1738	X	X	X	20	Seleucus I & Antiochus I Soter	292	Fragment mentioning LÚ.EN.NUN É.
53.	A 3459	Uruk	Taš	X	X			The list of witnesses from a legal document and part of date are all that is preserved. Note name Niqarrasu.
54.	A 3473	Uruk	X	X	X			Largely broken; Uruk officials are mentioned in lines 2′ and 16′: LÚ GAL and LÚ SAG ša UNUG.KI. A šaṭāru is mentioned in line 12′.

Text #	Method of Line Numbering	Text #	Method of Line Numbering
1.	consecutive	28.	consecutive
2.	R. 1′	29.	consecutive
3.	1′	30.	R. 1′
4.	1′; R. 1′	31.	(Rev. destroyed)
5.	R. 1′	32.	R. 1′
6.	R. 1′	33.	R. 1′
7.	1′	34.	consecutive
8.	1′	35.	consecutive
9.	1′; R. 1′	36.	R. 1′
10.	consecutive	37.	R. 1′
11.	R. 1′	38.	1′
12.	R. 1′	39.	R. 1′
13.	consecutive	40.	1′; R. 1′
14.	consecutive	41.	1′; R. 1′
15.	1′	42.	1′; R. 1′
16.	R. 1′	43.	R. 1′
17.	R. 1′	44.	R. 1′
18.	R. 1′	45.	R. 1′
19.	consecutive	46.	consecutive
20.	consecutive	47.	(Rev. destroyed)
21.	consecutive	48.	consecutive
22.	R. 1′	49.	1′; R. 1′
23.	R. 1′	50.	consecutive
24.	(Rev. destroyed)	51.	R. 1′
25.	consecutive	52.	1′
26.	R. 1′	53.	R. 1′
27.	consecutive	54.	1′; R. consecutive prime

CATALOGUE OF SEAL IMPRESSIONS

Text 1

U.E.	1	seated quadruped facing scorpion monster
	2	quadruped
	3	quadruped
Lo.E.	4	winged quadruped, with crescent and small oblong object in field
	5	winged quadruped
	6	winged quadruped
R.E.	7	(winged?) quadruped, with crescent and small oblong object in field
Le.E.	8	quadruped, with small object in field
	9	winged quadruped, with small object beneath it in field
	10	quadruped, with star and triangle in field

Text 2

U.E.	11	goat-fish
	12	figure with flowing vase
	13	quadruped
	14	winged human-headed quadruped
R.E.	15	twins
Le.E.	16	winged quadruped

Text 4

U.E.	17	quadruped
R.E.	18	winged quadruped
	19	quadruped

Text 5

U.E.	20	winged quadruped
	21	quadruped
	22	quadruped

Text 6

U.E.	23	quadruped
	24	quadruped

Text 8

Lo.E.	25	twin miters
	26	winged quadruped
	27	winged quadruped
R.E.	28	human figure

Text 9

Lo.E.	29	winged quadruped
	30	human figure with cap, facing right
	31	winged quadruped
	32	goat-fish
Le.E.	33	winged quadruped

Text 10

U.E.	34	circle?
	35	quadruped, with crescent and star in field
Lo.E.	36	scorpion creature (only lower part preserved)
	37	god standing on quadruped
	38	two human figures facing each other, divided by vertical object, with crescent and star in field
R.E.	39	goat-fish facing quadruped
Le.E.	40	quadruped facing dolphin
	41	winged quadruped, with crescent and star in field

Text 11

U.E.	42	human-headed quadruped, with two stars and another object in field
	43	quadruped
	44	winged human figure holding animal

Text 12

U.E.	45	portrait
	46	human figure
Lo.E.	47	cult stand from which flow two streams
	48	human headed quadruped
	49	quadruped & human?
R.E.	50	quadruped
Le.E.	51	rear part of goat-fish?

Text 13

U.E.	52	seated human-headed creature with uplifted wings
	53	winged quadruped, with crescent and another object in field
	54	winged quadruped, with crescent and star in field
Lo.E.	55	merman facing goat-fish
	56	human-headed winged quadruped
	57	male figure with bucket
R.E.	58	male figure before cult-object
	59	goat-fish facing bull, separated by cult-object
Le.E.	60	bird-man
	61	facing sphinxes, separated by pillar

Text 14

U.E.	62	winged quadruped

	63	slouching walker
Le.E.	64	merman
	65	winged quadruped

Text 16

U.E.	66	two figures
Lo.E.	67	winged quadruped
R.E.	68	goat-fish

Text 17

U.E.	69	quadruped
R.E.	70	goat-fish

Text 19

U.E.	71	quadruped, with small objects in field
	72	quadruped (front destroyed)
Lo.E.	73	palm tree
	74	quadruped, with object in field
	75	winged quadruped
	76	winged quadruped
	77	winged quadruped
R.E.	78	striding bull
Le.E.	79	quadruped
	80	quadruped
	81	quadruped
	82	circle (mostly destroyed)
	83	quadruped

Text 20

U.E.	84	winged quadruped, with crescents and star in field
	85	crab facing ?
Lo.E.	86	quadruped?, with star in field
	87	two sphinxes facing each other
	88	goat-fish facing quadruped
Le.E.	89	merman?

Text 21

U.E.	90	quadruped
	91	quadruped, with crescent in field
	92	winged quadruped
R.E.	93	quadruped

Text 22

U.E.	94	winged quadruped
	95	crab and fish with crescent and star in field
	96	scorpion man
R.E.	97	seated woman holding branch
Le.E.	98	lion, with crescent and star
	99	quadruped

Text 23

U.E.	100	seated lion-bodied sphinx facing quadruped, with star in field
R.E.	101	crab
Le.E.	102	crab and another object
	103	crab and fish, with star in field

Text 24

U.E.	104	crab, with crescent in field
Lo.E.	105	crab and quadruped
	106	quadruped
Le.E.	107	quadruped (seal partially destroyed)

Text 26

U.E.	108	quadruped, with crescent, triangle and another object in field
	109	scorpion-man
	110	winged, human-headed quadruped with crescent and small object in field
	111	winged quadruped
Lo.E.	112	quadruped, with geometric design above, triangle behind and small figure underneath
	113	quadruped, with small figure underneath
	114	winged quadruped, with crescent behind and small figure underneath
R.E.	115	concentric oblong figures
	116	winged quadruped, with triangle and small objects in field
Le.E.	117	twin figures
	118	quadruped
	119	winged quadruped

Text 27 (← Duplicates →) Text 29

U.E.	(destroyed)	U.E. 128	tail of goat-fish
120	portrait		(destroyed)
121	*portrait*	129	*portrait*
Lo.E. 122	crab	Lo.E.	(destroyed)
123	*seated human figure*	130	*seated human figure*
124	pheasant		(destroyed)
R.E.	(destroyed)	R.E.	(destroyed)
125	animal face		(destroyed)
Le.E. 126	*winged quadruped facing crab*	Le.E. 131	*winged quadruped facing crab*
127	sphinx, with crescent in field		(destroyed)

Text 28

U.E. 132 2 sphinxes seated, facing each other, separated by vertical object
133 winged, human-headed quadruped
134 goat-fish facing quadruped
Lo.E. 135 2 animals separated by vertical object
136 quadruped
137 scorpion, fish and crab, with star in field
R.E. 138 quadruped
Le.E. 139 winged bull, with crescent in field
140 square seal, contents destroyed

Text 31

Le.E. 141 winged, human-headed quadruped
142 quadruped

Text 32

Le.E. 143 quadruped
144 quadruped

Text 33

U.E. 145 quadruped
146 quadruped
Le.E. 147 quadruped

Text 34

U.E. 148 man, holding object, facing right

Lo.E.	149	twins, with crescent in field
Le.E.	150	winged quadruped, with object in field
	151	quadruped, with star in field
	152	twin miters

<u>Text 35</u>

Lo.E.	153	winged quadruped, with crescent in field
	154	crab and geometric object
	155	quadruped with crescent in field
Le.E.	156	winged quadruped, with geometric object in field

<u>Text 36</u>

U.E.	157	winged quadruped with animal head
	158	winged quadruped with human head

<u>Text 39</u>

U.E.	159	winged quadruped
	160	reclining sphinx facing left
Le.E.	161	winged quadruped with human head

<u>Text 40</u>

Lo.E.	162	quadruped
	163	winged creature facing left
R.E.	164	winged quadruped

<u>Text 41</u>

Le.E.	165	quadruped

<u>Text 42</u>

Lo.E.	166	bird-man
	167	winged quadruped, with crescent over wing
	168	quadruped, with triangle in field above
	169	goat-fish, with triangle in field
	170	twin figures
R.E.	171	quadruped
Le.E.	172	quadruped
	173	winged quadruped

Text 43		
U.E.	174	winged quadruped
	175	man? before pole?
	176	winged quadruped
Le.E.	177	winged quadruped

Text 44		
U.E.	178	winged quadruped, with object in field underneath
	179	?
	180	merman?
R.E.	181	?
Le.E.	182	crab?

Text 45		
U.E.	183	quadruped
Lo.E.	184	winged quadruped
Le.E.	185	winged quadruped

Text 46		
U.E.	186	winged quadruped, with triangle in field below
	187	winged quadruped
Lo.E.	188	winged quadruped leaping over fox?
	189	winged quadruped
	190	quadruped, with star in field in front
R.E.	191	quadruped
Le.E.	192	quadruped
	193	quadruped, leaping over object

Text 48		
U.E.	194	human-headed quadruped
	195	quadruped
Lo.E.	196	twins, facing right
R.E.	197	bull
Le.E.	198	quadruped
	199	winged quadruped, with star in field in front

Text 49		
Lo.E.	200	crab and second object
	201	?

INDEX OF PERSONAL NAMES

24. a. of Dipattusu, Qeplunu, and ^{d}Anu-balāṭsu-iqbi, 31:6, 11; a. of ^{d}Anu-uballiṭ (whose second name is Qeplunu) and ^{d}Anu-balāṭsu-iqbi, 6 R. 6′.
25. a. of Ina-qibit-Anu, ^{d}Anu-ikṣur, and Niqiarqusu 45 R. 11′.
26. a. of ^{d}Innin-šum-ēreš, ^{d}Anu-aḫḫē-iddin and ^{d}Anu-ikṣur 45 R. 9′.
27. a. of Kidin-^{d}Anu, ^{d}Anu-bēlšunu, and ^{d}Anu-aḫḫē-iddin, 25:26.
28. a. of Kidin-^{d}Anu and ^{d}Anu-zēr-iddin, 6 R. 11′.
29. a. of Kidin-^{d}Anu, 32 R. 8′.
30. a. of [I]llut-^{d}Anu and Ina-qibit-^{d}Anu, 18 R. 11′.
31. a. of Lābāši and ^{d}Anu-ab-utir, 34:31.
32. a. of Lābāši and ^{d}Anu-aḫḫē-iddin, 2 R. 6′.
33. a. of Lābāši, ^{d}Anu-bēlšunu, and Niqarqurasu, 13:23.
34. a. of Lābāši and Tanittum-^{d}Anu. 34:14, R. 8.
35. a. of Lābāši and Tanittum-^{d}Anu, 33:2.
36. a. of Lābāši, 33 R. 4′.
37. a. of Mukīn-apli and ^{d}Anu-bēlšunu, 2 R. 5′.
38. a. of Mušallim-^{d}Anu and ^{d}Anu-ab-uṣur, 34:27.
39. a. of Nidinti-[...] and Ana-rabîka-^{d}Anu, 22 R. 10′.
40. a. of Nidinti-[...] and [...]-šunu, 12 R. 9′.
41. a. of Nidinti-^{d}Anu, and Ana-rabî-^{d}Anu, 1:29.
42. a. of Nidinti-^{d}Anu and ^{d}Anu-aḫ-ittannu, 29:22.
43. a. of Qeplunu, and ^{d}Anu-balāṭsu-iqbi, 33:4.
44. a. of Tanittum-^{d}Anu and Mukīn-apli, 45 R. 12′.
45. a. of Tanittum-^{d}Anu and Nidinti-^{d}Anu, 45 R. 12′.
46. a. of Tanittum-^{d}Anu and Uppulu, 34:29.
47. a. of Timgirate and ^{d}Anu-balāṭsu-iqbi, 23:10, R. 3.
48. a. of Uppulu, ^{d}Anu-balāṭsu-iqbi, and ^{d}Anu-aḫḫē-iddin, 43:1 (Arsacid).
49. a. of ^{d}Anu-[...], 39 R. 5′.
50. a. of [...]-^{d}Anu, 17 R. 10′.
51. a. of [X X]-^{d}Anu and ^{d}Šamaš-ittannu, 16 R. 8′.
52. a. of [...]-^{d}Anu and Lābāši, 11 R. 2′.
53. a. of [...-]apla-iddin and ^{d}Anu-uballiṭ, 11 R. 4′.
54. a. of [...], and ^{d}Anu-[...], 39 R. 4′.
55. a. of [...] and ^{d}Anu-ab-utir, 11 R. 8′ .
56. a. of [...], and Ina-qibit-^{d}Anu, 48:28.
57. a. of [...] and ^{d}Innin-šum-ēreš, 53 R. 4′.
58. a. of [...], 4 R. 3′.
59. a. of [...], 39 R. 6′.

14. (172 B.C.) 20:14, R. 16.
15. (171 B.C.) 10:9 R. 14.
16. (164 B.C.) f. of Diumukrade, 27:4, f. of Ki'ukrane, 29:3.
17. (164 B.C.) 27:9, R. 14.
18. (164 B.C.) 29:10.
19. (164 B.C.) 29:31.
20. (162 B.C.) 28:12.
21. (162 B.C.) 28:32.
22. (year destroyed) 7:3′.
23. (year destroyed) 8:5′.
24. (year destroyed) 31:9.
25. (year destroyed) 24:11.
26. (year destroyed) 37:9, R. 13′ (twice).
27. (year destroyed) 45:3, R. 7′, 18′.
28. (year destroyed) 17 R. 4′.

Antipatrusu (^{1}an-ti-pad$_{3}$-di-ru-su) (128 B.C.) f.'s name broken, wit., 43 R. 3′ (Arsacid).

^{f}Antum-bānat (174? B.C.) m. of Mattannatum-^{d}Anu (SAL An-tum-KAK-at) 27:1, (SAL (An)-tum-KAK-at, note an- omitted) 29:1.

^{f}Antum-ṭābat (SAL An-tum-DUG$_{3}$.GA-at) (161-151 B.C.) 49 R. 1′, 3′.

^{d}Anu-ab-uṣur (1d60.AD.URU$_{3}$)

1. (230 or 229 B.C.) s. of ^{d}Nanā-iddin, desc. of Kurî, 21:26, Lo.E.
2. (230 B.C.) s. of Sumuttum-^{d}Anu, 26 R. 11′, U.E.
3. (223 B.C.) s. of ^{d}Anu-iššû, desc. of Ḫunzû, 19:33.
4. (223 B.C.) s. of ^{d}Nanā-iddin, desc. of ^{d}Nanā-iddin and Kurî, 19:35.
5. (223 B.C.) br. of ^{d}Anu-ikṣur, s's. of Iddina, desc. of Aḫūtu, 19:32.
6. (223 B.C.) br. of Lābāši, s's. of Mannu-iqapu, desc. of Kurî, 19:30.
7. (223 B.C.) 19 U.E.
8. (223 B.C.) 19 Lo.E. (twice), Le.E.
9. (216 B.C.) s. of ^{d}Innin-šum-ēreš, desc. of Aḫūtu, wit., 34:29.
10. (191 B.C.) s. of ^{d}Anu-aḫḫē-iddin, gs. of ^{d}Anu-aḫ-ittannu, desc. of Aḫūtu, 6 R. 7′.
11. (178 B.C.) s. of Arad-bīt-rēš, desc. of Dumqi-^{d}Anu, atu, 23:1, 5.
12. (164 B.C.) s. of ^{d}Anu-balāṭsu-iqbi, gs. of [...], desc. of Kurî, 29:24.
13. (164 B.C.) desc. of [...] and Kurî, 27:24.
14. (164 B.C.) 27 Le.E.
15. (149 B.C.) s. of Nidinti-^{d}Anu, gs. of Ubar, desc. of Kurî, 41 R. 16′, Le.E.
16. (year destroyed) 42 Lo.E.
17. (n.d.), 38:6′.

4. (191 B.C.) scribe, s. of Nidinti-^{d}Anu, desc. of Ekur-zakir, 6 R. 13′.
5. (174 B.C.) s. of ^{d}Nanā-iddin, br. of ^{d}Anu-zēr-iddin, 13:25.
6. (174 B.C.) 13 L.E.
7. (149 B.C.) s. of Nidinti-^{d}Anu, gs. of ^{d}Anu-balāṭsu-iqbi, desc. of Ekur-zakir, 41 R. 13′.
8. (year destroyed) 42:4′, 8′, R. 2′.
9. (year destroyed) 31 Le. E.
10. f. of ^{d}Anu-bēlšunu, desc. of Ekur-zakir, 22 R. 11′.
11. f. of Tattannu, s. of ^{d}Nanā-[...], desc. of Ḫunzû 12:10.
12. gf. of ^{d}Anu-ab-uṣur, f. of Nidinti-^{d}Anu, desc. of Ḫunzû 44 R. 8′ (Arsacid).

^{d}Anu-aḫ-ittannu (^{1d}60.ŠEŠ.MU-nu)

1. (275 B.C.) 14 U.E.
2. (275 B.C.) 14 Le. E. (twice).
3. (275 B.C.) s. of Tattannu, desc. of Ekur-zakir, 14:30.
4. (275 B.C.) s. of Ana-rabî-^{d}Anu, desc. of ^{d}Sîn-lēq-unnini, 14:32.
5. (234 B.C.) s. of Tattannu, desc. of Ekur-zakir, 1:26.
6. (234 B.C.) 1 U.E.
7. (230 B.C.) s. of Kidin-^{d}Anu, desc. of ^{d}Innin-aḫḫē-iddin, br. of Nidinti-^{d}Anu, 26 R. 11′, Le.E.
8. (226 B.C.) s. of Kidin-^{d}Anu, 46:8, 18, R. 3.
9. (226 B.C.) s. of Nidinti-^{d}Anu, 46:16.
10. (216 B.C.) s. of ^{d}Anu-balāṭsu-iqbi, desc. of Aḫūtu, wit., 34:28, Lo.E.
11. ([^{1d}X.]ŠEŠ.?MU?-nu) (216 B.C.) 34 Le. E.
12. (204 B.C.) wit., 2 U.E.
13. (191 B.C.) s. of [Illū]ṭ-^{d}Anu, desc. of Ḫunzû, 6 R. 9′.
14. (181 B.C.) s. of Illūt-^{d}Anu, 22:9.
15. (174 B.C.) s. of ^{d}Anu-mār-ittannu, br. of ^{d}Anu-bēlšunu, 13:19.
16. (174 B.C.) whose second name is Dumqi-^{d}Anu, s. of Dumqi-^{d}Anu, desc. of Luštammar-^{d}Adad, 13:1.
17. (174 B.C.) 13:16.
18. (174 B.C.) 13 R.E. 1.
19. (172 B.C.) s. of Balāṭu, gs. Tanittum-^{d}Anu, desc. of Luštammar-^{d}Adad, 32 R. 11′.
20. (172 B.C.) s. of Illūt-^{d}Anu, desc. of Ḫunzû, 20:3.
21. (172 B.C.) 32 U.E.
22. (172 B.C.) 32:12.
23. (171 B.C.) s. of Kidin-^{d}Anu, gs. of ^{d}Anu-mukīn-apli, desc. Ekur-zakir, 10:23.
24. (171 B.C.) 10 l.E.
25. (162 B.C.) s. of ^{d}Anu-bēlšunu, gs. of Nidinti-^{d}Anu, desc. of ^{d}Sîn-lēq-unnini, 28:25.

26. (162 B.C.) br. of Arad-AMA-ARḪUŠ (28 R. 1), s. of Idat-^{d}Anu, gs. of Sumuttum-^{d}Anu, ggs. of Rabî-^{d}Anu, desc. of Ḫunzû, 28:1.
27. (162 B.C.) 28:15.
28. (162 B.C.) 28:19.
29. (162 B.C.) 28 U.E.
30. (157 B.C.) s. of ^{d}Anu-iššû, gs. of Nidinti-^{d}Anu, desc. of Ḫunzû, 25:28.
31. (157 B.C.) 25 R.E.
32. (128 B.C.) s. of Mannu-iqapu, gs. of Nidinti-^{d}Anu, a.'s name broken, wit., 43 R. 5′ (Arsacid).
33. (128 B.C.) 43 Le. E. (Arsacid).
34. (year destroyed) desc. of Kidin-^{d}Anu, 24:7.
35. (year destroyed) s. of Nidinti-^{d}Anu, 42:9′.
36. (year destroyed) desc. of Nidinti-^{d}Anu, 24:3.
37. (year destroyed) 37:10, 15.
38. (year destroyed) 31 Le. E.
39. (year destroyed) 9 Le. E.
40. (year destroyed) wit., 47 Le.E.
41. f. of ^{d}Anu-aḫ-tuqqin, desc. of ^{d}Anu-aḫ-tuqqin, 44 R. 10′ (Arsacid).
42. f. of ^{d}Anu-aḫḫē-iddin s. of ^{d}Anu-aḫḫē-iddin, 48:12
43. f. of ^{d}Anu-šum-līšir, desc. of Balāṭu, 32 R. 9′.
44. f. of Balāṭu, desc. of Luštammar-^{d}Adad, 1:28.
45. f. of Nidinti-^{d}Anu, desc. of Illūt-^{d}Anu, 22 R. 12′.
46. f. of Nidinti-^{d}Anu, desc. of ^{d}Bēl-ēreš, 29:21.
47. f. of Nidinti-^{d}Anu, desc. of ^{d}Bēl-ēreš, 27:10, R. 4.
48. f. of Riḫat-^{d}Anu (leather worker) 13:6, 11.
49. f. of Riḫat-^{d}Anu, 19:3.
50. gf. of ^{d}Anu-ab-uṣur, f. of ^{d}Anu-aḫḫē-iddin, desc. of Aḫūtu, 6 R. 7′.
51. gf. of ^{d}Anu-mār-ittannu, f. of Tanittum-^{d}Anu, desc. of Aḫūtu, 10:25.
52. gf. of ^{d}Anu-uballiṭ, f. of ^{d}Anu-bēlšunu, desc. Aḫ[ūtu], 43 R. 6′ (Arsacid).
53. a. of ^{d}Anu-aḫḫē-iddin, 48:9.
54. a. of ^{d}Anu-balāṭsu-iqbi, 25:14, 15.

^{d}Anu-aḫ-tuqqin (^{1d}60.ŠEŠ.LA$_2$)

1. (133 B.C.) s. of ^{d}Anu-aḫ-ittannu, gs. of ^{d}Anu-aḫ-tuqqin, 44 R. 10′.
2. gf. of ^{d}Anu-aḫ-tuqqin, f. of ^{d}Anu-aḫ-ittannu, 44 R. 10′.

^{d}Anu-aḫ-ušabši (^{1d}60.ŠEŠ.GAL$_2$-ši)

1. (291-281 B.C. possible) f.'s name broken, 36:2.
2. (172 B.C.) s. of ^{d}Anu-balāṭsu-iqbi, gs. of Xxxx, desc. of Ekur-zakir, 20:27.

3. (172 B.C.) 20 U.E.
4. (year destroyed) s. of ^{d}Anu-uballiṭsu, desc. of ^{d}Anu-[...], 49 R. 6′.
5. (year destroyed) s. of Kidin-Anu, 42:5′.
6. f. of ^{d}Anu-ab-utir, s. of ^{d}Anu-aḫḫē-iddin, desc. of Aḫūtu, 43 R. 7′ (Arsacid).
7. f. of Lābāši, s. of Ina-qibit-^{d}Anu, desc. of Ekur-zakir, 41 R. 14′.
8. a. of Kidin-^{d}Anu, 17 R. 11′.

^{d}Anu-aḫ-[x.x] (^{1d}60.ŠEŠ.[x.x]) f. of ^{d}Anu-bēlšunu, s. of ^{d}Anu-bēlšunu, desc. of Aḫūtu, 27:22; 29:22.

^{d}Anu-aḫ-x (^{1d}60.⌈ŠEŠ.X⌉) (year destroyed) s. of ^{d}Anu-mār-ittannu, br. of ^{d}Anu-uballiṭsu, 42:7′.

^{d}Anu-aḫḫē-iddin (^{1d}60.ŠEŠ.MEŠ.MU).

1. (230 B.C.) s. of Ubar, desc. of Šumāti, 26 R. 10′.
2. (230 B.C.) 26 Lo.E.
3. (230 or 229 B.C.) wit., br. of Lābāši-^{d}Anu, s. of Tattannu, desc. of Ekur-zakir, 21:23.
4. (230 or 229 B.C.) 21 U.E.
5. (226 B.C.) s. of ^{d}Innin-šum-ēreš, desc. of Aḫūtu, 46:31, U.E.
6. (226 B.C.) s. of Nidintim-^{d}Anu, a.'s name broken, 46:33, Le.E.
7. (223 B.C.) s. of Rabî-^{d}Anu, desc. of Kurî, 19:34.
8. (223 B.C.) 19 Le. E.
9. (216 B.C.) s. of Kidin-^{d}Anu, desc. of Luštammar-^{d}Adad, wit., 34:31, Lo.E.
10. (215 B.C.) s. of ^{d}Anu-aḫ-ittannu, desc. of ^{d}Anu-aḫḫē-iddin, potter, 48:9, 11, R. 3, 4, 5.[25]
11. (181 B.C.) sepīr makkūr ^{d}Anu, s. of Arad-^{d}Ninurta, desc. of Illūt-^{d}Anu, 22:1.
12. (181 B.C.) 22 R. 2′, 4′.
13. (181 B.C.) 22 R.E.
14. (172 B.C.) s. of ^{d}Anu-[x], gs. of Zēriya, desc. of Gimil-^{d}Anu, 20:30.
15. (172 B.C.) 20 Le. E.
16. (172 B.C.) 32 R. 6′.
17. (161-151 B.C.) 49, R.E.
18. (161-151 B.C.) 49 R. 8′.
19. (157 B.C.) s. of Līšir, gs. of ^{d}Anu-aḫḫē-iddin, desc. of Gimil-^{d}Anu, 25:25.
20. (157 B.C.) 25 Lo.E.
21. (157 B.C.) 25:4.
22. (149 B.C.) s. of Nidinti-^{d}Anu, desc. of ^{d}Anu-bēlšunu and ^{d}Sîn-lēq-unnini, 41 R. 6′.
23. (149 B.C.) s. of Nidinti-^{d}Anu and ^{d}Anu-aḫ-ittannu, sepīr makkūr ^{d}Anu, 41 R. 11′.

---

[25]The designation paḫāru, occurring after the ancestor ^{d}Anu-aḫḫē-iddin, refers to the profession of the grandson of the same name in this prosopography. See McEwan, Priest and Temple (1981), p. 40. Lābāši-Anu, s. of ^{d}Anu-uballiṭ, desc. of ^{d}Anu-aḫḫē-iddin, mentioned in this text passim, is the potter's cousin.

59. desc.'s name broken, 48:19.

^{d}Anu-aḫḫē-ittannu (^{1d}60.ŠEŠ.MEŠ.MU-nu) a. of ^{d}Anu-aḫḫē-iddin and Nidinti-^{d}Anu, 41 R. 11′.

^{d}Anu-balāṭsu-iqbi (^{1d}60.IN-su-E).

1. (242 B.C.) s. of^{d}Anu-zēr-iddin and Aḫūtu, 11 R. 3′, U.E.
2. (234 B.C.) s. of Ina-qibit-^{d}Anu, desc. of Aḫūtu, 1:24.
3. (162 B.C.) s. of Lābāši, gs. of Līšir, desc. of Gimil-^{d}Anu, 28:23, Lo.E.
4. (161-151 B.C.) s. of Tattannu, desc. of ^{d}Anu-aḫḫē-iddin, 49 R. 8′, R.E.
5. (157 B.C.) wit., s. of Dumqi-^{d}Anu, gs. of ^{d}Anu-bēlšunu, desc. of Luštammar-^{d}Adad, 25:31, U.E.
6. (157 B.C.) wit., s. of Kidin-^{d}Anu, gs. of ^{d}Anu-bēlšunu, desc. of Aḫūtu, 25:29.
7. (157 B.C.) desc. of ^{d}Anu-aḫ-ittannu, 25:14, 15, R. 2, R.E.
8. f. of ^{d}Anu-ab-uṣur, s. of [...], desc. of Kurî, 29:24.
9. f. of ^{d}Anu-aḫ-ittannu, desc. of Aḫūtu, 34:28.
10. f. of ^{d}Anu-aḫ-ušabši, s. of [x.x.x], desc. of Ekur-zakir, 20:27.
11. f. of ^{d}Anu-mukīn-apli, s. of ^{d}Anu-mukīn-apli, desc. of Ekur-zakir, 20:26.
12. ([^{d}Anu-balāṭ]su-iqbi), f. of ^{d}Anu-uballiṭ (whose second name is Qeplunu), desc. of Aḫūtu, 6 R. 6′; f. of Qeplunu, desc. of Aḫūtu, 31:6; 33:4.
13. (Anu-bal[āṭsu-iqbi] or ^{d}Anu-ub[alliṭ]) f. of Ina-qibit-Anu, 18 R. 10′.
14. f. of Lābāši, desc. of Lābāši, 49 R. 7′.
15. f. of Uppulu, s. of ^{d}Anu-aḫḫē-iddin, desc. of Aḫūtu, 43:1 (Arsacid).
16. f. of X X-^{d}Anu, Nidinti-^{d}Anu, 42:7′.
17. gf. of ^{d}Anu-aḫ-iddin, f. of Nidinti-^{d}Anu, desc. of Ekur-zakir, 41 R. 13′.
18. gf. of Dipattusu, f. of Qeplunu, desc. of Aḫūtu, 31:11.
19. gf.'s name broken, f. of Timgirate, desc. of Aḫūtu, 23:10, R. 2.

^{d}Anu-bēl-zēr (^{1d}60.EN.NUMUN)

1. (223 B.C.) 19:8, 11, 12, 14, 18.
2. f. of ^{d}Nanā-iddin, desc. of Kurî, 19:20.

^{d}Anu-bēlšunu (^{1d}60.EN-šu$_{2}$-nu)

1. (234 B.C.) s. of ^{d}Anu-aḫḫē-iddin, desc. of Aḫūtu, 1:25.
2. (234 B.C.) 1 U.E.
3. (223 B.C.) br. of ^{d}Anu-mukīn-apli, s. of ^{d}Anu-aḫḫē-iddin, desc. of Aḫūtu, 19:31.
4. (223 B.C.) 19 Lo.E.
5. (216 B.C.) s. of Lābāši, desc. of Aḫūtu, wit., 34:26.
6. (201 or 191 B.C.) desc. of Tanittum-Anu and ^{d}Anu-bēlšunu, 33 R. 3′, U.E.
7. scribe, s. of Nidinti-^{d}Anu, desc. of ^{d}Sîn-lēq-unnini, (178 B.C.) 23 R. 13′; (174 B.C.) 13:29; (172 B.C.) 32 R. 13′.
8. (181 B.C.) s. of ^{d}Anu-aḫ-iddin, desc. of Ekur-zakir, 22 R. 11′.

9. (181 B.C.) 22 U.E.
10. (174 B.C.) s. of ^{d}Anu-mār-ittannu, br. of ^{d}Anu-aḫ-ittannu, 13:20.
11. (174 B.C.) s. of ^{d}Anu-mār-ittannu, gs. of ^{d}Anu-bēlšunu, desc. of Aḫūtu, 13:17.
12. (174 B.C.) 13 R.E.
13. (172 B.C.) 20 Lo.E.
14. (164 B.C.) s. of ^{d}Anu-aḫ?-[x x], gs. of ^{d}Anu-bēlšunu, desc. of Aḫūtu, 27:22, Lo.E.; 29:22.
15. (161-151 B.C.) s. of ^{d}Anu-aḫḫē-iddin, gs. of Nikarqusu, desc. of Aḫūtu, 49 R. 9′.
16. (157 B.C.) s. of ^{d}Anu-aḫḫē-iddin, gs. of Niqiarqusu, desc. of Aḫūtu, 25:2, 11, 13, 18, R. 3, 5.
17. (157 B.C.) s. of Tanittum-^{d}Anu, gs. of Lābāši, desc. of Aḫūtu, 25:27, Le.E.
18. (year destroyed) s. of ^{d}Anu-aḫḫē-iddin, gs. of ^{d}Nanā-iddin, desc. of [...?], 44 R. 6′, U.E. (Arsacid).
19. (year destroyed) s. Nidinti-^{d}Anu, 9:4′.
20. (year destroyed) s. of Nidin[tu-Anu], 3:3′.
21. (year destroyed) br. of ^{d}Anu-uballiṭ, s. of Nidinti-^{d}Anu, 9:7′, R. 4.
22. (n.d.) s. of Nidinti-^{d}Anu, desc. of Ekur-zakir, 50:1.
23. f. of ^{d}Anu-aḫ-ittannu, s. of Nidinti-^{d}Anu, desc. of ^{d}Sîn-lēq-unnini, 28:25.
24. f. of ^{d}Anu-uballiṭ, s. of ^{d}Anu-aḫ-ittannu, desc. of Aḫūtu, 43 R. 6′ (Arsacid).
25. f. of [Ina-qib]it-^{d}Anu-ušuzzu, desc. of Kurî, 26 R. 9′.
26. f. of Itti-^{d}Anu-nuḫšu, desc. of ^{d}Sîn-lēq-unnini, 14:35; 39 R. 9′.
27. f. of Kidin-^{d}Anu, s. of ^{d}Anu-aḫḫē-iddin, desc. of Aḫūtu, 25:26.
28. f. of Lābāši, s. of Niqarqurasu, desc. of Aḫūtu, 13:23.
29. f. of Mukīn-apli, desc. of Aḫūtu, 2 R. 5′ ,
30. f. of Nidinti-^{d}Anu, 51 R. 8′.
31. f. of [Nidinti-^{d}Anu], scribe, desc. of ^{d}Sîn-lēq-unnini, 33 R. 8′.[26]
32. f. of [....], 36 R. 7′.
33. gf. of ^{d}Anu-balāṭsu-iqbi, f. of Dumqi-^{d}Anu, desc. of Luštammar-^{d}Adad, 25:31.
34. gf. of ^{d}Anu-balāṭsu-iqbi, f. of Kidin-^{d}Anu, desc. of Aḫūtu, 25:29.
35. gf. of ^{d}Anu-bēlšunu, f. of ^{d}Anu-aḫ-[x x], desc. of Aḫūtu, 27:23; 29:23.
36. gf. of ^{d}Anu-bēlšunu, f. of ^{d}Anu-mār-ittannu, desc. of Aḫūtu, 13:17.
37. gf. of ^{d}Anu-bēlšunu, f. of Tanittum-Anu, 33 R. 3′.

---

[26]The basis for our reconstruction [Nidinti-^{d}Anu]/^{d}Anu-bēlšunu/^{d}Sin-lēq-unnini in 33 R. 8′ is:

The scribe in VAS 15 14:27 (122 SE), 44:27 (121 SE) 52:34 (124 SE), NCBT 1968 [cp. Doty, p. 42, (12[5+x]), Lewenton, Studien zur keilschriftlichen Rechtspraxis Babyloniens in hellenistischer Zeit (1970), p. 104], Nidinti-^{d}Anu/^{d}Anu-bēlšunu/^{d}Sin-lēq-unnini;

Witnesses ^{d}Anu-bēlšunu/Tanittum-^{d}Anu/^{d}Anu-bēlšunu in 33 R. 3′ = BRM 2 44:33, 121 SE, and ^{d}Anu-ab-utir/^{d}Anu-zēr-idin/Illūt-^{d}Anu in 33 R. 6′ = BRM 2 34:20, 124 SE.

^{d}Anu-dumqi (^{1d}60-dum-qi)

1. f. of Dumqi-^{d}Anu, desc. of ^{d}Sîn-lēq-unnini, 26 R. 13′.
2. gf. of ^{d}Nanā-iddin, f. of [...]-Anu, desc. of Kurî, 22 R. 8′.

^{d}Anu-erība (^{1d}60.SU)

1. f. of Aḫ-iddin, 21:29.
2. f. of Ana-rab-Anu, 14:13.
3. f. of ^{d}Innin-šum-ēreš, desc. of Kurî, 34:34; 45 R. 17′ and 48:33.
4. f. of ^{d}Innin-šum-iddin, 1:32.

^{d}Anu-ikṣur (^{1d}60-ik-ṣur)

1. (223 B.C.) s. Tattannu, desc. of Ekur-zakir, 19:33.
2. (223 B.C.) br. of ^{d}Anu-ab-uṣur, s. of Iddina, desc. of Aḫūtu, 19:32, U.E., Le. E.
3. (219 B.C.) s. of Niqiarqusu desc. of Aḫūtu, br. of Ina-qibit-Anu, 45 R. 10′.
4. (204 B.C.) desc. of Tattannu and Ekur-zakir, 2 R. 7′
5. (178 B.C.) s. of Zēriya, gs. of ^{d}Anu-ikṣur, desc. of Luštammar- ^{d}Adad, 23 R. 6′, Lo.E.
6. (year destroyed) 45 Le.E.
7. f. of ^{d}Innin-šum-ēreš and ^{d}Anu-aḫḫē-iddin, desc. of Aḫūtu 45 R. 9′.
8. f. of ^{d}Nanā-iddin, desc. of Ekur-zakir, 14:33.
9. gf. of ^{d}Anu-aḫḫē-iddin, f. of Nidinti-^{d}Anu, desc. of Kurî, 44 R. 9′ (Arsacid).
10. gf. of ^{d}Anu-ikṣur, f. of Zēriya, desc. of Luštammar-^{d}Adad, 23 R. 6′.
11. a. of ^{d}Anu-ittannu, 28:9.

^{d}Anu-iqīšanni (^{1d}60.BA-ša$_2$-an-ni/nu)

1. (275 B.C.) s. of Ina- qibit-^{d}Anu, desc. of Kurî, 14:27 and Lo.E.
2. (230 B.C.) desc. of ^{d}Sîn-lēq-unnini, 26 R. 8′.
3. (220 B.C.) s. of ^{d}Anu-ittannu, desc. of ^{d}Nanā-[iddin], 45:1, 13, 16, R.E.
4. (year destroyed) 7:10′.
5. f. of ^{d}Anu-uballiṭ, desc. of ^{d}Sîn-lēq-unnini, 1:30.
6. f. of Illūt-^{d}Anu, s. of Laqīp. desc. of Rē'î-alpi, 28:29.
7. f. of Nidinti-^{d}Anu, s. of Nidinti-^{d}Anu, desc. of ^{d}Anu-zēr-ušabši, 26:1.
8. f. of Ubar, s. of Ubar, desc. of [x-x]-⌈x-x⌉, 28:26.

^{d}Anu-ittannu (^{1d}60.MU-nu)

1. (230 or 229 B.C.) br. of Arad-bīt-rēš. s. of Illūt-^{d}Anu, 21:1, 14, R. 1, R.E.
2. (215 B.C.) 48 U.E.
3. (162 B.C.) desc. of ^{d}Anu-ikṣur, 28:9.
4. f. of ^{d}Anu-iqīšanni, desc. of ^{d}Nanā-[iddin], 45:1, 13, 16.
5. f. of ^{d}Anu-uballiṭ, desc. of ^{d}Anu-uballiṭ, probably desc.,of Ana-rabîka-Anu and Aḫūtu, 22 R. 9′.
6. f. of Nidinti-^{d}Anu, s. of Nidinti-^{d}Anu, desc. of Kurî, 41 R. 15′.

[27]PN is broken; possibly to be read otherwise.

10. (year destroyed) 42 R. 6′.
11. f. of Kidin-^{d}Anu, 36 R. 5′.
12. (^{1}[...].GUB.A) f. of Lābāši, desc. of Ekur-zakir, 34:31.
13. f. of ^{d}Nanā-iddin, desc. of Luštammar-^{d}Adad, 22 R. 10′.
14. f. of Zēriya, s. of [...], desc. of Gimil-^{d}Anu, 49 R. 10′.
15. gf. of ^{d}Anu-aḫ-ittannu, f. of Kidin-^{d}Anu, desc. of Ekur-zakir, 10:23.
16. gf. of ^{d}Anu-mukīn-apli, f. of ^{d}Anu-balāṭsu-iqbi, desc. of Ekur-zakir, 20:26.
17. gf. of [...]-ittannu, f. of Kidin-^{d}Anu, desc. of Ḫunzû, 6 R. 10′.

^{d}Anu-šum-iddin (^{1d}60.MU.MU) f. of [...], desc. of [...], 25:3.

^{d}Anu-šum-līšir (^{1d}60.MU.GIŠ)

1. (204 B.C.) s. of [...], 2 R. 3′.
2. (172 B.C.) s. of ^{d}Anu-aḫ-ittannu, desc. of Balāṭu, 32 R. 9′.
3. (150 B.C.) s. of Arad-bīt-rēš, gs. of Uṣuršu-^{d}Anu, desc. of ^{d}Sîn-lēq-unnini, 12:1, R.E.
4. (150 B.C.) 12:12, 14.
5. (year destroyed) 5 U.E.
6. (year destroyed) s. of ^{d}Anu-[...], 37 R. 9′.
7. (n.d.), 53:2′.
8. f. of [...], desc. Ḫunzû, 17 R. 14′.
9. f. of [...], s. of ^{d}Anu-uballiṭ, desc. of Ḫunzû, 6 R. 8′.
10. gf. of Ṭāb-^{d}Anu, f. of Ina-qibit-^{d}Anu, desc. of Kurî, 27:27; 29:27.

^{d}Anu-šum-uk[īn] (^{1d}60.MU.G[UB]) (226 B.C.), 46 Lo.E.[28]

^{d}Anu-tukulti (^{d}60.KU) (year destroyed), 17:3

^{d}Anu-uballiṭsu (^{1d}60.TIN.SU)

1. (242 B.C.), 11 U.E.
2. (year destroyed) s. of Erība, desc. of Iddin-^{d}Amurru, 36 R. 4′.
3. (year destroyed) br. of ^{d}Anu-aḫ-[...] s. of ^{d}Anu-mār-ittannu, 42:8′.
4. (year destroyed) 45:8.
5. f. of ^{d}Anu-aḫ-ušabši, s. of ^{d}Anu-[...], 49 R. 7′.
6. f. of Illūt-^{d}Anu, 45:17.

^{d}Anu-uballiṭ (^{1d}60.IN-iṭ)

1. (292-275 B.C.) s. of Nidinti-^{d}Anu, 39 R. 6′.
2. (234 B.C.) s. of ^{d}Anu-iqīšanni, desc. of ^{d}Sîn-lēq-unnini, 1:30.
3. (234 B.C.) 1 Lo.E.
4. (230 B.C.) s. of Riḫat-^{d}Innin, 26 R. 9′, U.E. and Le.E.
5. (230 or 229 B.C.) s. of Kidin-^{d}Anu, desc. of Luštammar-^{d}Adad, 21:27.

---

[28]This PN, which has been collated, appears to be read correctly, though ^{d}Anu-šum-ukīn is not found elsewhere in LB texts. It is the name of a witness which has been lost in the break of Rev. 46.

38. f. of Riḫat-^{d}Anu, desc. of Luštammar-^{d}Adad. 1:26.
39. f. of Uṣuršu-^{d}Anu, desc. of ^{d}Sîn-lēq-unnini, 45 R. 14′.
40. f. of [^{1d}X-]apla-iddin, desc. of Aḫūtu, 11 R. 4′.
41. f. of [...]-ši-^{d}60, 18:5.
42. f. of [...], desc. of ^{d}Sîn-lēq-unnini, 17:1, R.E.
43. gf. of ^{d}Anu-uballiṭ, f. of ^{d}Anu-ittannu, 22 R. 9′.
44. f. of [...], desc. of Kurî, 22:18.
45. gf. of Kidin-^{d}Anu, f. of Lābāši, desc. of Ḫunzû, 49 R. 11′.
46. a. of ^{d}Anu-uballiṭ, and ^{d}Anu-ittannu, probably desc. of Ana-rabîka-^{d}Anu and Aḫūtu 22 R. 9′.
47. gf. of [...], f. of ^{d}Anu-šum-līšir, desc. of Ḫunzû, 6 R. 8′.
48. a. of ^{d}Anu-mukīn-apli, 8:6′.
49. a. of ^{d}Anu-zēr-iddin, desc. of Ekur-zakir, 50:4.
50. f. of Ina-qibit-^{d}Anu, 48:27.
51. a. of ^{f}Nidinti-^{d}Nanā and ^{d}Anu-ittannu, 33:1.

^{d}Anu-ušallim (^{1d}60.GI)

1. (year destroyed), 42 Le. E.
2. f. of [...], desc. of Luštammar-^{d}Adad, 18 R. 12′.
3. gf. of ^{d}Anu-ab-utir, f. of Zēriya, desc. of Gimil-^{d}Anu, 10:26.
4. gf. of ^{d}Šamaš-ēṭir, f. of ^{d}Anu-ittannu, desc. of Luštammar-^{d}Adad, 20:29 and 25:32.

^{d}Anu-zēr-iddin (^{1d}60.NUMUN.MU)

1. (215 B.C.) 48 Lo.E.
2. (174 B.C.) br. of ^{d}Anu-aḫ-iddin, s. of ^{d}Nanā-iddin, 13:25, U.E.
3. (172 B.C.) s. of Kidin-^{d}Anu, desc. of Ḫunzû, 20:5, 10.
4. (157 B.C.) 25:3, 14, R. 4.
5. (year destroyed) s. of ^{d}Anu-uballiṭ, desc. of Ekur-zakir, 50:3.
6. f. of ^{d}Anu-ab-utir, desc. of Aḫūtu, 33 R. 6′.
7. f. of ^{d}Anu-ab-utir, desc. of Ḫunzû, 1:30.
8. f. of ^{d}Anu-[X X X (X)], desc. of Ekur-zakir, 34:32.
9. f. of Kidin-^{d}Anu, desc. of Aḫūtu, 6 R. 11′.
10. f. of Kidin-^{d}Anu, a.'s name broken, 46:34.
11. f. of ^{d}Nanā-iddin, desc. of ^{d}Anu-ab-[x(-x)], 43 R. 1′ (Arsacid).
12. f. of Nidinti-^{d}Anu, s. of Nidinti-^{d}Anu, a's name broken, 44 R. 7′ (Arsacid).
13. f. of [^{d}Anu-balās]su-iqbi desc. of Aḫūtu, 11 R. 3′.

^{d}Anu-zēr-līšir (^{1d}60.NUMUN.GIŠ)

1. (172 B.C.) br. of Ana-rabî-^{d}Anu, s. of Nidinti-^{d}Anu, 20:4,9,11.
2. f. of ^{d}Anu-ab-utir, desc. of Aḫūtu, 10:24.

6. (year destroyed), 18:6.
7. f. of ^{d}Anu-ab-uṣur, desc. of Dumqi-^{d}Anu, 23:1.
8. f. of ^{d}Anu-šum-līšir, s. of Uṣuršu-^{d}Anu, desc. of ^{d}Sîn-lēq-unnini, 12:1 (Seleucid).
9. f. of Uṣuršu-^{d}Anu, 35:16.
10. a. of Idat-^{d}Anu, and Dumqi-^{d}Anu, 35:23, Lo. E.

Arad-^{d}Nergal (^{1}IR$_{3}$.^{d}U.GUR) (year destroyed) 40:5′, 7′, 12′.

Arad-^{d}Ninurta (^{1}IR$_{3}$.^{d}MAŠ)
1. (181 B.C.) f. of ^{d}Bēl-[...], 22:2.
2. (178 B.C.) s. of ^{d}Anu-mār-ittannu, desc. Nidinti-^{d}Innin, sepīr makkūr ^{d}Anu, 23 R. 9′, U.E.
3. (178 B.C.) s. of Nidinti-^{d}Anu, desc. of Nidinti-^{d}Innin, sepīr makkūr ^{d}Anu, 23 R. 11′, U.E.
4. (171 B.C.) s. of ^{d}Anu-mār-ittannu, a.'s name broken, 10:28. Possibly same as #1 above.
5. (171 B.C.) 10 Lo. E.
6. f. of ^{d}Anu-aḫḫē-iddin, desc. of Illūt-^{d}Anu, 22:1.
7. f. of Illūt-^{d}Anu, 22:15.

Ardarmidur (^{1}ar-dar-mi-du-ur, cp. Artemidur, 29:23, same man, wit.) (164 B.C.) 29 U.E.

Aristugirate (^{1}a-ri-si-tu-ug-gi-ra-te-e) (year destroyed), 47:4, 9.

Aristuglae (^{1}a-ri-is-tu-uk-la-e) (year destroyed) s. of Andarniqusu, 44 R. 11′ (Arsacid).

Arsak′ (^{1}ar-sak-′)
1. (128 B.C.) 43 R. 10′ (Arsacid).
2. (year destroyed), 44:5, R. 13′ (Arsacid).

Artemidur (^{1}ar-te-mi-du-ur, = Ardarmidur, 29 U.E.) (164 B.C.) s. of Bāni/Ibni-[...], gs. ^{d}Nanā-iddin, desc. Luštammar-^{d}Adad, 27:23, U.E.; 29:23.

Balāṭu (^{1}ba-la-ṭu or ^{1}TIN)
1. (234 B.C.) s. of ^{d}Anu-aḫ-ittannu, desc. of Luštammar-^{d}Adad, 1:28, U.E.
2. (172 B.C.) 32 R.E., Le.E.
3. (164 B.C.) 29:12.
4. (year destroyed) 42 Le. E.
5. 38:4′.
6. f. of ^{d}Anu-aḫ-ittanu, s. of Tanittum-^{d}Anu, desc. of Luštammar-^{d}Adad, 32 R. 11′.
7. a. of Nidinti-^{d}Anu, 39:1.
8. a. of ^{d}Anu-šum-līšir, and ^{d}Anu-aḫ-ittannu, 32 R. 9′.
9. a. of Dumqi-^{d}Anu, and Riḫat-^{d}Anu, 32 R. 11′.
10. a. of Nidinti-šarri, and ^{d}Anu-aḫḫē-iddin, 1:12.

Barūtu (^{1}ba-ru-tu) (172 B.C.) 32:13.

Barūtūtu-^{d}Anu (^{1}ba-ru-tu-u$_{2}$-tu$_{2}$-^{d}60) (year destroyed) 37:14.

Bassiya (^{1}ba-as-si-ya) (275 B.C.) s. of ^{d}Innin-šum-ēreš, desc. of Ekur-zakir, 14:34, Le.E.

^{d}Bēl-ēreš (^{1d}EN.P[I]N-iš) a. of Nidinti-^{d}Anu, and ^{d}Anu-aḫ-ittannu, 27:11, R. 4; 29:11, R. 5.

Di'ukrane, 29:4, see Di'mukrade.

Di'upanneussu (^{1}di-'-u$_{2}$-pa-an-ne-us-su) f. of [^{f}An-ti]-'-i-ki-su, 6 R. 4′.

13. f. of Idat-^{d}Anu, desc. of Arad-bīt-rēš, 35:23.
14. f. of Rabî-^{d}Anu, desc. of Ḫunzû, 19:30.
15. f. of Tattannu, desc. of Ḫunzû, 1:27; 21:24.
16. f. of [...-d]an?-nu, br. of [...], desc. of Ekur-zakir, 49 R. 9′.
17. a. of ^{d}Anu-ab-uṣur, and Arad-bīt-rēš, 23:1.
18. a. of Dumqi-^{d}Anu, and Riḫat-^{d}Anu, 32 R. 11′.
19. a. of Idat-^{d}Anu, 35:26.

Ebabbar-šum-ibni (^{1}E$_{2}$.BABBAR.MU.DU$_{3}$)

1. a. of Illūt-^{d}Anu, Ša-^{d}Anu-iššû, and ^{d}Nanā-iddin, 41 R. 12′.
2. a. of ^{d}Nanā-iddin, Ša-^{d}Anu-iššû, and ^{d}Nanā-iddin, 23 R. 7′.
3. a. of Rabî-^{d}Anu, ^{d}Anu-[...], and Mukīn-apli, 53:6′.
4. a. of Uṣuršu-^{d}Anu, Ša-^{d}Anu-iššû, and ^{d}Nanā-[iddin], 28:27.[29]
5. a. of [...], 16 R. 14′.

Ekur-zakir (^{1}E$_{2}$.KUR-za-kir)

1. a. of ^{d}Anu-aḫ-ittannu, Kidin-^{d}Anu and ^{d}Anu-mukīn-apli, 10:23.
2. a. of ^{d}Anu-aḫ-ittannu and Tattannu, 14:30.
3. a. of ^{d}Anu-aḫ-ittannu and Tattannu, 1:27.
4. a. of ^{d}Anu-aḫ-iddin and Nidinti-^{d}Anu, 6 R. 13′.
5. a. of ^{d}Anu-aḫ-iddin, Nidinti-^{d}Anu and ^{d}Anu-balāṭsu-iqbi, 41 R. 13′.
6. a. of ^{d}Anu-aḫ-iddin and Riḫat-^{d}Innin, 21:28.
7. a. of ^{d}Anu-aḫ-ušabši, ^{d}Anu-balāṭsu-iqbi and [...] 20:27.
8. a. of ^{d}Anu-aḫ-ušabši and Kidin-^{d}Anu, 42:5′, R. 3.
9. a. of ^{d}Anu-mukīn-apli, ^{d}Anu-balāṭsu-iqbi and ^{d}Anu-mukīn-apli, 20:26.
10. a. of ^{d}Anu-bēlšunu and ^{d}Anu-aḫ-iddin, 22 R. 11′.
11. a. of ^{d}Anu-bēlšunu and Nidinti-^{d}Anu 50:2.
12. a. of ^{d}Anu-ikṣur and Tattannu, 19:34.
13. a. of ^{d}Anu-ikṣur and Tattannu 2 R. 7′.
14. a. of ^{d}Anu-uballiṭ and Riḫat-^{d}Innin, 2 R. 8′.
15. a. of ^{d}Anu-zēr-iddin and ^{d}Anu-uballiṭ, 50:4.
16. a. of ^{d}Anu-[x x x (x)] and ^{d}Anu-zēr-iddin, 34:33.
17. a. of Bassiya and ^{d}Innin-šum-ēreš, 14:34.
18. a. of Ina-qibit-^{d}Anu, [...] and Ina-qibit-^{d}Anu, 12 R. 14′.
19. a. of Ina-qibit-^{d}Anu and Kidin-^{d}Anu, 39 R. 7′.
20. a. of Kidin-^{d}Anu and Tattannu, 14:26.
21. a. of Lābāši, ^{d}Anu-aḫ-ušabši and Ina-qibit-^{d}Anu, 41 R. 14′.

---

[29]Cp. BRM 2 39:35f. (=Year 149, Antiochus being king).

22. a. of Lābāši and [...]-^{d}Anu, 6 R. 9′.
23. a. of Lābāši and [^{d}Anu?-]mukīn-apli, 34:31.
24. a. of Lābāši-^{d}Anu, ^{d}Anu-aḫḫē-iddin and Tattannu, 21:23.
25. a. of Mukīn-apli and Nidinti-^{d}Anu, 22 R. 15′.
26. a. of Mušēzib-^{d}Anu and [...]-^{d}Anu 14:29.
27. a. of ^{d}Nanā-iddin and ^{d}Anu-ikşur, 14:33.
28. a. of Nidinti-^{d}Anu and ^{d}Anu-bēlšunu 51 R. 8′.
29. a. of Nidinti-^{d}Anu, Uşuršu-^{d}Anu and Nidinti-^{d}Anu, 28:24.
30. a. of ^{d}Papsukkal-bāni and Nidinti-^{d}Anu, 29:30.
31. a. of ^{d}Papsukkal-iqīššunu and Nidinti-^{d}Anu, 27:30.
32. a. of ^{d}Sîn-banunu, f. of Tattannu 28:4, 7.
33. a. of Ša-^{d}Anu-iššû, [...] and Ša-^{d}Anu-iššû, 12 R. 6′.
34. a. of ^{d}Šamaš-ēţir and Ina-qibit-^{d}Anu, 28:31.
35. a. of [...-d]an?-nu and Dumqi-^{d}Anu, 49 R. 9′.
36. a. of [...], 49 R. 12′.
37. a. of [...], 16 R. 12′.
38. a. of [...], 40 R. 1′, 2′.
39. a. of [...], 4 R. 4′.
40. a. of [...], 9 R. 10′.

^{f}Erēštum-^{d}Nanā (SAL KAM$_2$-tum-^{d}na-na-a)
1. (year destroyed), bēltu ša Riḫat-^{d}Bēlet-şēri, 35:11, 14.
2. mother of Nidinti-^{d}Anu, daughter of ^{d}Sîn-bēl-ilāni, desc. of [...], desc. of Kurî, 41 R. 5′

Erība (^{1}SU-a)
1. f. of ^{f}Adiešu-Ţāba$_2$, desc. of [^{d}Anu-bēlšunu],[30] 14:12, 19.
2. f. of ^{d}Anu-uballiţsu, desc. of Iddin-^{d}Amurri 36 R. 4′.

Gimil-^{d}Anu (^{1}ŠU.^{d}60)
1. a. of ^{d}Anu-ab-utir, Zēriya, and ^{d}Anu-ušallim, 10:26.[31]
2. a. of ^{d}Anu-aḫḫē-iddin, ^{d}Anu-[x] and Zēriya, 20:30.[32]
3. a. of ^{d}Anu-aḫḫē-iddin, Līšir, and ^{d}Anu-aḫḫē-iddin, 25:25.[33]
4. a. of ^{d}Anu-balāţsu-iqbi, Lābāši, and Līšir, 28:23.[34]

---

[30]^{d}Anu-bēlšunu is restored from BRM II 14:1, year 51 S.E.

[31]Broken; ^{1}GAL.^{d}60 = Rabî-^{d}Anu is also possible.

[32]See previous note.

[33]See previous note.

[34]See previous note.

5. a. of Ina-qibit-^{d}Anu, Lābāši, and Līšir, 25:33.
6. a. of Līšir, and ^{d}Anu-aḫḫē-iddin, 1:29.
7. a. of [Līš]ir, Zēriya, and Līšir, 6 R. 12′.
8. a. of Riḫat-^{d}Anu, Kidin-^{d}Anu, and Nidinti-^{d}Anu, 13:26, 41 R. 10′.
9. a. of Zēriya, ^{d}Anu-aḫḫē-iddin, and Zēriya, 25:30.
10. a. of Zēriya, ^{d}Anu-mukīn-apli and [...], 49:11.
11. a. of [^{1}...MU] and Nidinti-^{d}Anu, 36 R. 5′.
12. a. of [...], Lābāši and [...], 54:14′.
13. a. of [...] and Zēriya, 11 R. 9′.
14. a. of [...] 17 R. 15′.

Ḫaninna′ (^{1}ḫa-nin-na-′)
1. (181 B.C.) s. of Mannu-ki-^{d}Dilbat, 22:8.
2. (181 B.C.) s. of Riḫat-^{d}Bēlet-Ṣēri, 22:5, 11, 12.

ḪAS.DAN (204 B.C.) the second name of Nidinti-^{d}Anu, son of Lābāši, 2:4.

Ḫunzû (^{1}ḫun-zu-u_2)
1. a. of Ana-rabî-^{d}Anu, and Nidinti-^{d}Anu, 20:7.
2. a. of ^{d}Anu-ab-uṣur, and ^{d}Anu-iššû, 19:33.
3. a. of ^{d}Anu-ab-uṣur, Nidinti-^{d}Anu, and ^{d}Anu-aḫ-iddin, 44 R. 8′.
4. a. of ^{d}Anu-ab-utir, ^{d}Anu-uballiṭ, and Kidin-^{d}Anu, 22 R. 14′.
5. a. of ^{d}Anu-ab-utir, and ^{d}Anu-zēr-iddin, 1:30.
6. a. of ^{d}Anu-aḫ-ittannu, Ša-^{d}Anu-iššû, and Nidinti-^{d}Anu, 25:28.
7. a. of ^{d}Anu-aḫ-ittannu and Arad-AMA.ARḪUŠ, Idat-^{d}Anu, Sumuttum-^{d}Anu, and Rabî-^{d}Anu, 28:1.
8. a. of ^{d}Anu-aḫ-ittannu, and Illūt-^{d}Anu, 20:3.
9. a. of ^{d}Anu-aḫ-ittannu, and x-x-^{d}Anu, 6 R. 9′.
10. a. of ^{d}Anu-aḫ-iddin and ^{d}Anu-zēr-iddin, Nanā-iddin and ^{d}Anu-mār-ittannu, 13:26.
11. a. of ^{d}Anu-mukīn-apli, and ^{d}Anu-uballiṭ, 19:29; 34:27.
12. a. of ^{d}Anu-uballiṭ, Nidinti-^{d}Anu, and Ina-qibit-^{d}Anu, 13:25.
13. a. of ^{d}Anu-zēr-iddin, and Kidin-^{d}Anu, 20:6.
14. a. of Dumqi-^{d}Anu and Sumuttum-[^{d}Anu, sons? of...]-^{d}Anu, 18 R. 10′.
15. a. of Rabî-^{d}Anu, Lābāši, and Rabî-^{d}Anu, 32 R. 9′.
16. a. of Illūt-^{d}Anu, Kidin-^{d}Anu, and ^{d}Anu-aḫḫē-iddin, 10:11, R. 4.
17. a. of Ina-qibit-^{d}Anu, ^{d}Anu-ab-uṣur, and ^{d}Anu-mār-ittannu, 23 R. 5′.
18. a. of Ina-qibit-^{d}Anu, [...] and Ina-qibit-^{d}Anu, 12 R. 8′.
19. a. of Kidin-^{d}Anu, Lābāši, and ^{d}Anu-uballiṭ, 49 R. 11′.
20. a. of Lābāši, ^{d}Anu-uballiṭ, and Kidin-^{d}Anu, 13:27.
21. a. of Nanā-iddin and Lābāši, 36 R. 6′.

4. (204 B.C.) scribe, s. Nidinti-^{d}Anu, desc. of ^{d}Sîn-lēq-unnini, 2 R. 9′.
5. (181 B.C.) s. of Arad-^{d}Ninurta, 22:15.
6. (178 B.C.) s. of ^{d}Anu-uballiṭ, desc. of ^{d}Nanā-iddin, 23 R. 8′.
7. (172 B.C.) desc. of Uṣuršu-^{d}Anu, 32:1.
8. (171 B.C.) s. of Ina-qibit-^{d}Anu, desc. of Nidinti-^{d}Anu and [...], 10:27, possibly same man as scribe[35] (r. 13, Le.E.).
9. (171 B.C.) s. of Kidin-^{d}Anu, gs. of ^{d}Anu-aḫḫē-iddin, desc. of Ḫunzû, 10:8, 10, 13, 15, R. 1, 3, 12.
10. (171 B.C.) scribe, s. of Nidinti-^{d}Anu, 10:30.
11. (171 B.C.) 10:12, 15, Le.E., Lo.E.
12. (162 B.C.) s. of ^{d}Anu-iqīšanni, gs. of Laqīp, desc. of Rē'î-alpi, 28:29, Le.E.
13. (149 B.C.) s. of Ša-^{d}Anu-išu, desc. of ^{d}Nanā-iddin and Ebabbar-šum-ibni, 41 R. 12′.
14. (128 B.C.) br. Abi-immim, s. Mattanit′, 43:3, 10.
15. (year destroyed) s. of Ina-qibit-^{d}Anu, desc. of Aḫūtu, 18 R. 11′.
16. (year destroyed), 35 Lo.E.
17. (year destroyed), f.'s name broken, 36:3
18. (year destroyed), s. of ^{f}Silimua, 16 R.E.
19. f. of ^{d}Anu-aḫ-ittannu, 22:9, 6 R. 9′, 20:3..
20. f. of Arad-bīt-rēš and ^{d}Anu-ittannu, 21:1, R. 1.
21. f. of ^{f}Ina-bāni-^{d}Antum and Kidin-^{d}Anu, 22:17.
22. f. of Kidin-^{d}Anu, 26 R. 10′.
23. f. of Kidin-^{d}Anu, 22 R. 7′.
24. possibly f. of Kidin-^{d}Anu, 45 R. 16′.

---

[35]The Personal Name Illūt-^{d}Anu is listed eleven times in Text 10 and apparently belongs to the following different men:

1. #1, s. of Kidin-^{d}Anu, gs. of ^{d}Anu-aḫḫē-iddin, desc. of Ḫunzû, is the *buyer*. He is listed in 10:8, 10, 13, 15, 18, and 20.

2. #2, s. of Ina-qibīt-^{d}Anu, desc. of Nidinti-^{d}Anu, is the sixth witness in the document and *the first witness named Illūt-^{d}Anu to appear*. He is listed in 10:27. Of the two stamp seals of witnesses named Illūṭ-^{d}Anu, he would appear either on the Left or Lower Edge.

3. #3, s. of Kidin-^{d}Anu, gs. of ⌈X⌉[...], is the eighth witness in the document and *the second witness named Illūt-^{d}Anu to appear*. He is listed in 10:29. Of the two stamp seals of witnesses named Illūt-^{d}Anu, he would appear either on the Left or Lower Edge. Since the trace in 10:29 beginning the name of the grandfather does not appear to be ^{d}60, and since we do not expect the buyer to appear as a witness, this man must be someone other than the man listed as #1 in this footnote.

4. #4, The s. of Nidinti-^{d}A[nu, desc. of...], is *the scribe*. He is listed in 10:30, the same man as the sixth witness (see above [this footnote]), #2. He omitted his father's name from the more complete quadripartite rendering of PN's and continued with the name of his grandfather and ancestor.

[36]For the reading qi_2-bit, see AHw 920b, contra Clay, BRM 2, p. 61 f.

26. f. of BA[.X X], desc. of Luštammar-^{d}Adad, 11 R. 7′.
27. f. of [...], desc. of Aḫūtu, 48:28.
28. f. of [...], 18 R. 13′.
29. gf. of ^{d}Anu-uballiṭ, f. of Nidinti-^{d}Anu, desc. of Ḫunzû, 13:25.
30. gf. of Ina-qibit-^{d}Anu, f. of ^{d}Anu-mār-ittannu, desc. of Kurî, 29:25 (his name is broken in the duplicate, 27:25.).
31. gf. of Ina-qibit-^{d}Anu [and...], desc. of Ḫunzû, 12 R. 8′.
32. f. of Nidinti-^{d}Anu, 39 R. 8′.

Ina-qibit-^{d}Anu-ukīn (^{1}ina-E-^{d}60.GUB) (226 B.C.) 46 U.E.

Ina-qibit-^{d}Anu-ušuzzu (^{1}ina-E-^{d}60-GUB-zu) (230 B.C.) 26 R. 9′, U.E.

^{d}Innin-aḫḫē-iddin (^{1d}INNIN.ŠEŠ.MEŠ.MU) a. of ^{d}Anu-aḫ-ittannu, Nidinti-^{d}Anu, and Kidin-^{d}Anu, 26 R. 12′.

^{d}Innin-ḫīṭūa (^{1d}INNIN-ḫi-ṭu-u$_{2}$-a) f. of Kidin-^{d}Anu and [...], 26 R. 1′.[37]

^{d}Innin-šum-ēreš (^{1d}INNIN.MU.KAM$_{2}$)

1. (234 B.C.) scribe, s. of ^{d}Anu-erība, desc. of Kurî, 1:32; (220 B.C.) 45 R. 17′; (216 B.C.) 34:34.
2. (219 B.C.) br. of ^{d}Anu-aḫḫē-iddin, s. of ^{d}Anu-ikṣur desc. of Aḫūtu 45 R. 9′.
3. f. of ^{d}Anu-ab-uṣur, desc. of Aḫūtu, 34:29.
4. f. of ^{d}Anu-aḫḫē-iddin, desc. of Aḫūtu, 46:31.
5. f. of Bassiya, desc. of Ekur-zakir, 14:34.
6. f. of Ša-^{d}Anu-iššû, des. of Ḫunzû, 34:30.
7. f. of [...], desc. of Aḫūtu, 53 R. 4′.

^{d}Innin-šum-iddin (^{1d}INNIN.MU.MU) f. of Ša-^{d}Anu-iššû, desc. of Ḫunzû, 19:33.[38]

^{d}Innin-zēr-ibni (^{1d}INNIN.NUMUN.DU$_{3}$) f. of Uṣuršu-^{d}Anu, desc. of ŠEŠ.X.X.E?, 45:2, 6, R. 2.

Itti-^{d}Anu-nuḫšim (^{1}KI.^{d}60.ḪE$_{2}$.NUN)

1. (292-275 B.C.) scribe, s. of ^{d}Anu-bēlšunu, 39:10′.
2. (275 B.C.) scribe, s. of ^{d}Anu-bēlšunu, desc. of ^{d}Sîn-lēq-unnini, 14:35.

Kidin-^{d}Anu (^{1}ki-din-^{d}60, or ^{1}BARA$_{2}$.^{d}60)[39]

1. (292-281 B.C.) s. of ^{d}Anu-mukīn-apli 36 r 5′.
2. (292-275 B.C.) wit., 39 U.E.
3. (275 B.C.) s. of Tattannu, desc. of Ekur-zakir, 14:26, U.E.
4. (275 B.C.) s. of ^{1}[...], desc. of Kurî, br. of ^{d}Anu-aḫ-iddin, 14:31, Lo.E.

---

[37]Cp. BRM II P. 63b, top.

[38]This PN resembles ^{d}Innin-šum-ēreš (see above, 34:30). However, collation reveals that the last sign is MU rather than KAM$_{2}$ so the two names are apparently distinct.

[39]According to Joannès, TBER 6, p. 425, the name BARA$_{2}$.^{d}60 should be read Kidin-^{d}Anu (not Parak-^{d}Anu) with variance of BARA$_{2}$ and the normal Bar (for kidinnu).

39. f. of Riḫat-^{d}Anu, s. of Nidinti-^{d}Anu, desc. of Gimil-^{d}Anu, 13:26; 41 R. 10′.
40. f. of Ša-^{d}Anu-iššû, s. of ^{d}Anu-balāṭsu, desc. of ^{d}Anu-aḫ-ušabši, 49 R. 6′.
41. f. of [^{1d}X.(X)]-ittannu, s. of ^{d}Anu-mukīn-apli, desc. of Ḫunzû, 6 R. 10′.
42. f. of [^{1}]a-n[ittum-^{d}Anu], desc. of Kurî, 48:5.
43. f. of [...], 48:25.
44. f. of [...], desc. of [...], 15:8′
45. gf. of ^{d}Anu-ab-utir, f. of ^{d}Anu-uballiṭ, desc. of Ḫunzû, 22 R. 14′.
46. gf. of Lābāši, f. of ^{d}Anu-uballiṭ, desc. of Ḫunzû, 13:27.
47. a. of Kidin-^{d}Anu, and ^{d}Anu-aḫḫē-iddin, 23 R. 10′.
48. a. of Kidin-^{d}Anu, and Ṭāb-^{d}Anu, 28:30.
49. a. of [...] and Kidin-^{d}Anu, 26 R. 1′.

Ki-[...] (^{1}KI-[...]) (150 B.C.) s. or desc. of [...], 12 R. 13′.

Kina (^{1}ki-na-a) a. of Nidinti-^{d}Anu and ^{d}Anu-mār-ittannu, 1:1.

Kiplunu *see* Qeplunu.

Kirib-^{d}Bēlti (^{1}ki-rib-^{d}GAŠAN)
1. (164 B.C.) s. of Lābāši, gs. of Riḫat-^{d}Anu, 27:28, U.E., 29:28, U.E.
2. f. of Kidin-^{d}Anu, s. of ^{d}Šamaš-ittannu, desc. of Luštammar[-^{d}Adad], 43 R. 8′.

Ki′ukrane (^{1}ki-′u-uk-ra-ni-e), f. of Ant[ikusu], 29:4.[40]

Kītu-^{d}Anu (^{1}ki-tu-^{d}60)
1. (215 B.C.) desc. of [...], 48:25.
2. (162 B.C.) s. of ^{d}Anu-uballiṭ, gs. of Nidinti-^{d}Anu, desc. of Kurî, 28:5, 13, 15, R. 2, 4, 5.
3. (150 B.C.) 12 R. 13′, L.E.
4. (year destroyed) 35 Le. E.
5. f. of Lābāši, desc. of Lābāši, 24:15.
6. f. of ^{d}Nanā-iddin, Uṣuršu-^{d}Anu, desc. of Lābāši, 46:1, 2, 14, R. 6, 9.
7. f. of ^{d}Nanā-iddin, desc. of Lābāši, 33:6, 10.
8. f. of Sumut-^{d}Anu, a.′s name broken, 46:35.
9. f. of Sumuttum-^{d}Anu, 9:6′, R. 1′, R.E.
10. f. of Uṣuršu-^{d}Anu and ^{d}Nanā-iddin, desc. of Lābāši, 24:1, 12, 16.
11. gf. of Ana-rabî-^{d}Anu, f. of Sumuttum-^{d}Anu, desc. of Kurî, 13:28.
12. gf. of Idat-^{d}Anu, f. of Uṣuršu-^{d}Anu, desc. of Kurî, 28:28.
13. a. of Sumuttum-^{d}Anu, 5:6, 8.

KUD.DAN, the second name of Nidinti-^{d}Anu, 2:24.[41]

Kudurri (^{1}NIG$_{2}$.DU) a. of ^{d}Nabu-ušallim, 40:8′.

---

[40]Possibly scribal error for Di′mukrade, q.v.

[41]Cp. Kudaia or Kudia, e.g., Joannes, TBER 6, p. 390.

Lābāši (^{1}la-ba-ši, ^{1}la-a-ba-ši or NU.TEŠ$_{2}$)

1. (292-275 B.C.) s. of Riḫat-^{d}Anu, 39 R. 3′.
2. (275 B.C.) s. of Mukīn-apli, 14:6.
3. (223 B.C.) wit., br. of ^{d}Anu-ab-uṣur, s. of Mannu-iqapu, desc. of Kurî, 19:30, Lo.E.; 21:25, Lo.E.
4. (223 B.C.) (clearer of claims), s. of Riḫat-^{d}Anu, 19:25, R.E.
5. (216 B.C.) s. of ^{d}Anu-ab-utir, desc. of Aḫūtu wit., 34:30, Le.E.
6. (216 B.C.) s. of [^{d}Anu]-mukīn-apli, desc. of Ekur-zakir wit., 34:31, Lo.E.
7. (216 B.C.) (^{1}la-ba-ši) s. of Tanittum-^{d}Anu, desc. of Aḫūtu, husband of ^{f}Nidinti-^{d}Nanā, 34:14, 25; (201 or 191 B.C.) (^{1}NU.TEŠ$_{2}$) 33:1, 13.
8. (204 B.C.) s. of ^{d}Anu-aḫḫē-iddin, desc. of Aḫūtu, 2 R. 4′, 6′, U.E.
9. (201 or 191 B.C.) desc. of Aḫūtu, 33 R. 4′.
10. (201 or 191 B.C.) s. of ^{d}Anu-ab-uṣur, 33 R. 4′, R.E.
11. (191 B.C.) s. of [...]-^{d}Anu, desc. of Ekur-zakir, 6 R. 8′.
12. (191 B.C.) 6 R.E.
13. (174 B.C.) s. of ^{d}Anu-bēlšunu, gs. of Niqarqurasu, desc. of Aḫūtu, wit., 13:23, U.E.
14. (174 B.C.) s. of ^{d}Anu-uballiṭ, gs. of Kidin-^{d}Anu, desc. of Ḫunzû, 13:27, Lo.E.
15. (174 B.C.) ^{amēl}qaštu, s. of Riḫat-^{d}Anu, gs. of Lābāši, 13:21.
16. (174 B.C.) s. of Riḫat-^{d}Anu, desc. of Lābāši, buyer, 13:5, 14, 16, R. 2, 4
17. (161-151 B.C.) s. of ^{d}Anu-balāṭsu-iqbi, desc. of Lābāši, 49 R. 7′, Lo.E.
18. (149 B.C.) s. of ^{d}Anu-aḫ-ušabši, gs. of Ina-qibit-^{d}Anu, desc. of Ekur-zakir, 41 R. 14′.
19. (year destroyed) s. of Kītu-^{d}Anu, desc. of Lābāši, 24:15.
20. (year destroyed) s. of Mannu-iqāpu, 9 R. 11′.
21. (year destroyed) s. of [...]-^{d}Anu, 37 R. 8′.
22. (year destroyed) 24 U.E.
23. (year destroyed) wit., 47 U.E.
24. (year destroyed) 9 Lo. E.
25. f. of ^{d}Anu-balāṭsu-iqbi, s. of Līšir, desc. of Gimil-^{d}Anu, 28:23.
26. f. of ^{d}Anu-bēlšunu, desc. of Aḫūtu, 34:26.
27. f. of [Bēlšu]nu, desc. of Aḫūtu, 45 R. 10′.
28. f. of Ina-qibit-^{d}Anu, s. of Līšir, desc. of Gimil-^{d}Anu, 25:33.
29. f. of Kidin-^{d}Anu, s. of ^{d}Anu-uballiṭ, desc. of Ḫunzû, 49 R. 11′.
30. f. of Kirib-^{d}Bēlti, s. of Riḫat-^{d}Anu, 27:28; 29:28.
31. f. of ^{d}Nanā-iddin, desc. of Ḫunzû, 36:11′.
32. f. of Nidinti-^{d}Anu, 2:4.
33. f. of Rabî-^{d}Anu, s. of Rabî-^{d}Anu, desc. of Ḫunzû, 32 R. 8′.
34. f. of Riḫat-^{d}Anu, desc. of ^{d}Anu-mār-ittannu, 1:10, 14.

5. a. of ^{d}Anu-aḫḫē-iddin, and Kidin-^{d}Anu, 34:32.
6. a. of ^{d}Anu-balāṭsu-iqbi, Dumqi-^{d}Anu, and ^{d}Anu-bēlšunu, 25:31.
7. a. of ^{d}Anu-ikṣur, Zēriya, and ^{d}Anu-ikṣur, 23 R. 6′.
8. a. of ^{d}Anu-uballiṭ, and Kidin-^{d}Anu, 21:27.
9. a. of ^{d}Anu-uballiṭ and ^{d}Anu-ab-uṣur, 33 R. 5′.
10. a. of Artemidur, Ibni-[...] and ^{d}Nanā-iddin, 27:24; 29:24.
11. a. of Balāṭu, and ^{d}Anu-aḫ-ittannu, 1:28.
12. a. of Ibna, ^{d}Nanā-iddin, and Ibna, 10:22.
13. a. of Kidin-^{d}Anu, Kirib-^{d}Bēlit, and ^{d}Šamaš-ittannu, 43 R. 8′.
14. a. of Libluṭ, and [X.x.x]-^{d}Bēlit, 20:23.
15. a. of ^{d}Nanā-iddin, and ^{d}Anu-mukīn-apli, 22 R. 11′.
16. a. of ^{d}Nanā-iddin, and Dannat-^{d}Bēlti, 14:10, 14.
17. a. of Nidinti-^{d}Anu, and Tanittum-^{d}Anu, 21:25.
18. a. of Riḫat-^{d}Anu, and ^{d}Anu-uballiṭ, 1:26.
19. a. of ^{d}Šamaš-ēṭir, ^{d}Anu-ittannu, and ^{d}Anu-ušallim, 20:29; 25:32.
20. a. of ^{d}Šamaš-ittannu, and ^{d}Anu-ab-uṣur, 46:32.
21. a. of [^{1d}X]-aḫḫē-iddin, and Kidin-^{d}Anu, 17 R. 12′.
22. a. of [X.X]-^{d}Anu, and ^{d}Anu-ab-uṣur, 45 R. 15′.
23. a. of [X]-BA-[X.X], and Ina-qibit-^{d}Anu, 11 R. 7′.
24. a. of [...-]^{d}Bēlti, 16 R. 13′.
25. a. of [...] and ^{d}Anu-ušallim, 18 R. 12′.
26. a. of [...] and Mušēzib-^{d}Anu, 17 R. 13′.
27. a. of [...], 33 R. 5′.
28. a. of [...], 4 R. 2′, 7′, 8′, 9′, 10′.
29. a. of [...], 48:29, 31.

Mannu-iqāpi (^{1}man-nu-i-qa-pi)
1. (216 B.C.) s. of Zēriya, desc. of [...], wit., 34:33.
2. f. of ^{d}Anu-ab-uṣur, and Lābāši, desc. of Kurî, 19:30.
3. f. of ^{d}Anu-aḫ-ittannu, s. of Nidinti-^{d}Anu, a.'s name broken, 43 R. 5′.
4. f. of Lābāši, desc. of Kurî, 21:26.
5. f. of Lābāši, 9 R. 11′.
6. f. of [^{1}]LA[...], desc. of Kurî, 11 R. 6′.
7. f. of Nidinti-^{d}Anu, desc. of Kurî, 45 R. 13′.

Mannu-kî-^{d}Dilbat (^{1}man-nu-ki-i-^{d}dil-bat)
1. (216 B.C.) s. of Riḫat-^{d}Anu, desc. of ^{d}Anu-ab-uṣur, 34:18, 22, R.E.
2. (181 B.C.) s. of Ana-rabîka-^{d}Anu, 22:4, 9.

Mattanit-′ (^{1}mat-ta-nit-′) f. of Abi-immim, and Illūt-^{d}Anu, 43:4, 10.

17. (year destroyed) s. of Kītu-^{d}Anu, br. of Uṣuršu-^{d}Anu, 24:6, 11, 13, 16.
18. (year destroyed) 24 Le. E.
19. (year destroyed) 5 R. 4′.
20. f. of ^{d}Anu-ab-uṣur, desc. of Kurî, 21:26.
21. f. of ^{d}Anu-ab-uṣur, desc. of ^{d}Nanā-iddin, 19:35.
22. f. of ^{d}Anu-uballiṭ, s. of ^{d}Anu-uballiṭ, gs. of ^{d}Anu-aḫḫē-iddin, desc. of ^{d}Sîn-lēq-unnini, 5:1, 8.
23. f. of ^{d}Anu-aḫ-iddin and ^{d}Anu-zēr-iddin, s. of ^{d}Anu mār-ittannu, desc. of Ḫunzû, 13:25.
24. f. of Aristukgrate, 47:5.
25. f. of Ibna, s. of Ibna, desc. of Luštammar-^{d}Adad, 10:22.
26. f. of Idat-^{d}Anu, 22:7.
27. gf. of ^{d}Anu-bēlšunu, f. of ^{d}Anu-aḫḫē-iddin, a.'s name broken, 44 R. 6′.
28. gf. of ^{d}Nanā-iddin, f. of ^{d}Anu-iššû, desc. of Ebabbar-šum-ibni, 23 R. 7′.
29. gf. of ^{d}Anu-iqīšanni, f. of ^{d}Anu-ittannu, 45:1.
30. gf. of Nidinti-^{d}Anu, f. of ^{d}Anu-mār-ittannu, 43 R. 4′.
31. gf. of Uṣuršu-^{d}Anu, f. of Ša-^{d}Anu-iššû, desc. of Ebabbar-šum-ibni, 28:27.
32. gf. of Illūt-^{d}Anu, f. of Ša-^{d}Anu-iššû, desc. of Ebabbar-šum-ibni, 41 R. 12′.
33. gf. of Artemidur, f. of Ibni-[...], desc. of Luštammar-^{d}Adad, 27:24, Le.E., 29:24, Le.E.
34. a. of Riḫat-^{d}Anu, 14:3.
35. a. of [...]-iddin, 40:9′.
36. a. of ^{d}Anu-ab-uṣur, and ^{d}Nanā-iddin, 19:35.
37. a. of Illūt-^{d}Anu, and ^{d}Anu-uballiṭ, 23 R. 8′.

^{d}Nanā-[...] (^{1d}na-na-a-[...]) gf. of Tattannu, f. of ^{d}Anu-aḫ-iddin, desc. of Ḫunzû, 12:10.

^{d}Nanā-[...] (^{1d}na-na-a-[...]), f. of [...], 53:1′.

^{d}Nanā-[...] (^{1d}na-na-a-[...]), , gf. of ^{d}Anu-iqīšannu, f. of ^{d}Anu-idannu, 45:1.

^{d}Nanā-[...], 45:13.

Nidinti-^{d}Anu (^{1}NIG$_{2}$.SUM.MU.^{d}60 or ^{1}ni-din-tum-^{d}60)

1. (292-281 B.C.) wit., 36 R. 3′, U.E.
2. (242 B.C.) s. of [...], desc. of Ana-rabî-^{d}Anu, 11:9.
3. (234 B.C.) s. of ^{d}Anu-mār-ittannu, desc. of Kīna, 1:1, 13, R.E., ^{amēl}qašti.
4. (234 B.C.) s. of Ana-rab-^{d}Anu, desc. of Aḫūtu, 1:31.
5. (230 B.C.) s. of ^{d}Anu-iqīšannu, gs. of Nidinti-^{d}Anu, desc. of ^{d}Anu-zēr-ušabši, 26:1, R.E.
6. (230 B.C.) s. of ^{d}Anu-[...], 26:5.
7. (230 B.C.) 26 R. 3′, 6′.
8. (230 B.C.) br. of ^{d}Anu-aḫ-ittannu, s. of Kidin-^{d}Anu, desc. of ^{d}Innin-aḫḫē-iddin, 26 R. 11′, R.E.
9. (230 or 229 B.C.) s. of Tanittum-^{d}Anu, desc. of Luštammar-^{d}Adad, 21:24, U.E.

---

[42]For the reconstruction [Nidinti-^{d}Anu]/^{d}Anu-bēlšunu/^{d}Sin-lēq-unnini in 33 R. 8′, see footnote above, under ^{d}Anu-bēlšunu.

43. (year destroyed) 38:6′.
44. (year destroyed) 7:4′.
45. (year destroyed) 5 U.E.
46. (year destroyed) 5:4.
47. (year destroyed) 35 Lo. E.
48. (year destroyed) 17 U.E.
49. f. of Ana-rabî-dAnu, 28:9.
50. f. of Ana-rabî-dAnu, desc. of Ḫunzû, 20:6, 18.
51. f. of dAnu-ab-uṣur, s. of dAnu-aḫ-iddin, desc. of Ḫunzû, 44 R. 8′.
52. f. of dAnu-ab-uṣur, s. of Ubar, desc. of Kurî, 41 R. 16′.
53. f. of dAnu-aḫ-ittannu, 24:3; 42:9′; 46:16.
54. f. of dAnu-aḫ-iddin, s. of dAnu-balāṭsu-iqbi, desc. of Ekur-zakir, 41 R. 13′.
55. f. of dAnu-aḫ-iddin, desc. of Ekur-zakir, 6 R. 13′.
56. f. of dAnu-aḫḫē-iddin, s. of dAnu-ikṣur, desc. of Kurî, 44 R. 9′.
57. f. of dAnu-aḫḫē-iddin, desc. of dAnu-aḫ-xx, 41 R. 11′.
58. f. of dAnu-aḫḫē-iddin, desc. of dAnu-bēlšunu and dSîn-lēq-unnini, 41 R. 6′.
59. f. of dAnu-aḫḫē-iddin, desc. of dSîn-lēq-unnini, 43 R. 9′; 44 R. 12′.
60. f. of dAnu-aḫḫē-iddin, a.'s name broken, 46:33.
61. f. of dAnu-bēlšunu, desc. of Ekur-zakir, 50:2.
62. f. of dAnu-bēlšunu, desc. of dSîn-lēq-unnini, 13:29; 23 R. 13′; 32 R. 13′.
63. f. of dAnu-bēlšunu, 3:3′.
64. f. of dAnu-uballiṭ, s. of Ina-qibit-dAnu, desc. of Ḫunzû, 13:24.
65. f. of dAnu-uballiṭ, and dAnu-bēlšunu, 9:4′, 8′, R. 5′.
66. f. of dAnu-zēr-līšir, and Ana-rabî-dAnu, 20:10,.
67. f. of Arad-dNinurta, desc. of Nidinti-dInnin, 23 R. 11′.
68. f. of Bēletsunu, father-in-law of dAnu-ab-utir, 20:15.
69. f. of Idat[-dAnu], 21:2, R. 2.
70. f. of Illūt-dAnu, 10:30.
71. f. of Illūt-dAnu, desc. of dSîn-lēq-unnini, 2 R. 9′.
72. f. of Mukīn-apli, desc. of Ekur-zakir, 22 R. 15′.
73. f. of dNanā-iddin, desc. of Kurî, 19:31.
74. f. of dNanā-iddin, 26:3.
75. f. of Nidinti-dInnin, desc. of Ina-qibit-dAnu-ušuzzu, 26 R. 8′.
76. f. of dPapsukkal-iqiššunu, desc. of Ekur-zakir, 27:30; 29:30.
77. f. of Riḫat-dAnu, s. of Riḫat-dAnu, desc. of dSîn-lēq-unnini, 47:1, 3.
78. f. of Tattannu, s. of Ana-rabî-dAnu, desc. of Ḫunzû, 20:1.
79. f. of Tanittum-dAnu, desc. of Aḫūtu, 45 R. 12′.

[43]Though these two texts are separated by 25 years, the person involved seems to be the same.

Niqalamussu (^{1}ni-qa-la-mu-us-su) (164 B.C.) (whose second name is Riḫat-^{d}Anu), 27:16, R. 3, R.E.; 29:16, R. 3, R.E.

Niqanur (^{1}ni-qa$_3$-nu-ur$_2$) (133 B.C.) wit., 44 U.E.

Niqarqurasu (^{1}ni-iq-ar-qu-ra-su) gf. of Lābāši, f. of ^{d}Anu-bēlšunu, desc. of Aḫūtu, 13:23.[44]

Niqarqusu (^{1}ni-iq$_2$-ar-qu-su), Niqiarqusu

1. f. of ^{d}Anu-ab-utir, desc. of Aḫūtu, 25:8.
2. (^{1}ni-qi$_2$-ar-qu-su) f. of Ina-qibit-^{d}Anu and ^{d}Anu-ikṣur, desc. of Aḫūtu, 45 R. 11′.
3. gf. of ^{d}Anu-bēlšunu, f. of ^{d}Anu-aḫḫe-iddin, a. of ^{d}Anu-bēlšunu, desc. of Aḫūtu, 25:2, 11, R. 5; 49 R. 10′.

Niqarrasu (^{1}ni-iq-ar-ra-su) a. of Nidinti-^{d}Anu, 53:3′.

Niqiarqusu (^{1}ni-qi$_2$-ar-qu-su) see Niqarqusu.

^{f}Nuptum-^{d}Nanā (^{1}SAL nu-up-tum-^{d}na-na-a) (216 B.C.) s. of Ina-pî-^{d}Anu-libluṭ, seller, 34:4, 6, 16, R. 4, R.E.

Nu-[...] (150 B.C.) , f.'s name broken, desc. of Ḫunzû, 12 R. 11′.

^{f}Panā (SAL pa-na-a) mother of Niqalamusu, whose second name is Riḫat-^{d}Anu, 27:17, 29:17.

^{d}Papsukkal-bāni? (^{d}PAP.SUKKAL.BA.DIM$_2$) (164 B.C.) , scribe, s. of Nidinti-^{d}Anu, desc. of Ekur-zakir, 29:30.[45]

^{d}Papsukkal-iqisšunu (^{1}PAP.SUKKAL.BA-šu$_2$-nu) (164 B.C.) s. of Nidinti-^{d}Anu, desc. of Ekur-zakir, 27:30.

Qeplunu (^{1}qi$_2$-ip-lu-u$_2$-nu)

1. (191 B.C.) , 6 R. 5′.
2. f. of Dipattusu, s. of ^{d}Anu-balāṭsu-iqbi, desc. of Aḫūtu, 31:5, 6, 10, 13, 33:3 (Dipattusu not mentioned in this text).

Rabî-^{d}Anu (^{1}GAL.^{d}60)

1. (223 B.C.) s. of Dumqi-^{d}Anu, desc. of Ḫunzû, 19:30, Le.E.
2. (172 B.C.) s. of Lābāši, gs. of Rabî-^{d}Anu desc. Ḫunzû, 32 R. 8′.
3. (162 B.C.) desc. of Nidinti-^{d}Anu, 28:9.
4. (year destroyed), s. of ^{d}Anu-[...] 53:5′.
5. (year destroyed), 37 R. 8′.
6. f. of ^{d}Anu-aḫ-ittannu, desc. of ^{d}Sîn-lēq-unnini, 14:32.
7. f. of ^{d}Anu-aḫḫē-iddin, desc. of Kurî, 19:34.
8. gf. of Rabî-^{d}Anu, f. of Lābāši, 32 R. 8′.
9. gf. of Tattannu, f. of Nidinti-^{d}Anu, desc. of Ḫunzû, 20:1.
10. ggf. of ^{d}Anu-aḫ-ittannu and Arad-AMA.ARḪUŠ, gf. of Idat-^{d}Anu, f. of Sumuttum-^{d}Anu,

[44] This and the following names are variants of Nikarchos.

[45] Cp. BRM 2 43:28.

^{f}Silimūa (^{f}SILIM-a) (year destroyed) mother of Illūt-^{d}Anu, 16 R. 2′, 5′, R.E.[46]

Siluku (^{1}si-lu-ku)

1. (292 B.C.) and Antikusu, 52:2′.
2. (^{1}si-lu-ku?) (275 B.C.) 14:36.
3. (234 B.C.) 1:9, R. 16.
4. (230 B.C.) 26 R. 14′.
5. (230 or 229 B.C.) 21:11, R. 14.
6. (226 B.C.) 46:37.
7. (226 B.C.) 46:3.
8. (223 B.C.) 19:22, 37.
9. (181 B.C.) 22 R. 16′.
10. (178 B.C.) 23:9, R. 14.
11. (year destroyed) 4 R. 12′.
12. (year destroyed) 5:5, R. 7′.
13. (year destroyed) 16 R. 16′.
14. (year destroyed) 54:1′.
15. (year destroyed) and Attikusu, 36 R. 8′.

^{d}Sîn-banunu (^{1d}30-ba-nu-nu) (162 B.C.) desc. of Tattannu and Ekur-zakir, 28:4, 7.

^{d}Sîn-bēl-ilāni(^{1d}30.EN.DINGIR.MEŠ), gf. of Nidintu-^{d}Anu, f. of Erēštum-^{d}Nanā, desc. of [...], desc. of Kurî, 41 R. 5′.

^{d}Sîn-lēq-unnini (^{1d}30.TI.A.ŠI)[47]

1. a. of Ana-rabî-^{d}Anu, ^{d}Anu-uballiṭ and Nidinti-^{d}Anu, 2:1.
2. a. of ^{d}Anu-ab-utir, and [...], 41:5.
3. a. of ^{d}Anu-aḫ-ittannu, ^{d}Anu-bēlšunu, and Nidinti-^{d}Anu, 28:25.
4. a. of ^{d}Anu-aḫ-ittannu and Ana-rabî-^{d}Anu, 14:32.
5. a. of ^{d}Anu-aḫḫē-iddin and Nidinti-^{d}Anu, 43 R. 9′; 44 R. 12′.
6. a. of ^{d}Anu-aḫḫē-iddin, Nidinti-^{d}Anu and ^{d}Anu-bēlšunu, 41 R. 6′.
7. a. of ^{d}Anu-bēlšunu and Nidinti-^{d}Anu, 13:29; 23 R. 13′; 32 R. 13′.
8. a. of ^{d}Anu-iqīšannu, 26 R. 8′.
9. a. of ^{d}Anu-šum-līšir, Arad-bīt-rēš, and Uṣuršu-^{d}Anu, 12:1.
10. a. of ^{d}Anu-uballiṭ, and ^{d}Anu-iqīšanni, 1:30.
11. a. of ^{d}Anu-uballiṭ, ^{d}Nanā-iddin, ^{d}Anu-uballiṭ, and ^{d}Anu-aḫḫē-iddin, 5:1.
12. a. of Dumqi-^{d}Anu, and ^{d}Anu-uballiṭ, 19:36; 26 R. 13′.

---

[46]Compare [^{f}]si-lim-u$_2$-a AMA ša$_2$ Zumbu, TBER 6 61:7.

[47]^{d}Sîn-lēq-unnini occurs only as a family name, see Lambert JCS 11 (1957). In the following list, names are combined as one entry only when they are written identically in texts. Therefore in some cases there could be additional names that belong together.

6. (year destroyed) 4 R.E.
7. f. of ^{d}Anu-ab-uṣur, desc. of Ḫunzû, 19:33.
8. f. of ^{d}Anu-aḫ-ittannu, s. of Nidinti-^{d}Anu, desc. of Ḫunzû, 25:28.
9. f. of Illūt-^{d}Anu, s. of ^{d}Nanā-iddin, desc. of Ebabbar-šum-ibni, 41 R. 12′.
10. f. of ^{d}Nanā-iddin, s. of ^{d}Nanā-iddin, desc. of Ebabbar-šum-ibni, 23 R. 7′.
11. f. of Ša-^{d}Anu-iššû and [...], desc. of Ekur-zakir, 12 R. 6′.
12. f. Uṣuršu-^{d}Anu, s. of ^{d}Nanā-[iddin], desc. of Ebabbar-šum-ibni, 28:27.
13. gf. of Ša-^{d}Anu-iššû, f. of Kidin-^{d}Anu, desc. of ^{d}Anu-aḫ-ušabši, 49 R. 6′.

^{d}Šamaš-ēṭir (^{1d}UTU.SUR)
1. (172 B.C.) s. of ^{d}Anu-ittannu, gs. of ^{d}Anu-ušallim, desc. of Luštammar-^{d}Adad, 20:29, U.E.
2. (172 B.C.) s. of ^{d}Šamaš-ittannu, desc. of ^{d}Šamaš-ēṭir, 32 R. 10′, Le.E.
3. (162 B.C.) scribe, s. of Ina-qibit-^{d}Anu, desc. of Ekur-zakir, 28:31.
4. (157 B.C.) s. of ^{d}Anu-ittannu, gs. of ^{d}Anu-ušallim, desc. of Luštammar-^{d}Adad, 25:32.
5. a. of ^{d}Šamaš-ēṭir, and ^{d}Šamaš-ittannu, 32 R. 10′.

^{d}Šamaš-ittannu (^{1d}UTU.MU-nu)
1. (226 B.C.) s. of ^{d}Anu-ab-uṣur, desc. of Luštammar-^{d}Adad, 46:32.
2. (172 B.C.) s. of Ubar, gs. of [...]-^{d}Anu, desc. of Ḫunzû, 20:28, Lo.E.
3. (year destroyed) 9 Lo. E.
4. f. of ^{d}Šamaš-ēṭir, desc. of ^{d}Šamaš-ēṭir, 32 R. 10′.
5. f. of Tanittum-^{d}Anu, desc. of Kurî, 19:35.
6. f. of [...]-^{d}Anu, desc. of Aḫūtu, 16 R. 8′.
7. gf. of Kidin-^{d}Anu, f. of Kirib-^{d}Bēlit, desc. of Luštammar, 43 R. 8′.

^{f}Šelatti (SAL še-lat-ti-′) (year destroyed) a.'s name broken, 44:2, 10, R.E.

ŠEŠ.X.X-e gf. of Uṣuršu-^{d}Anu, f. of ^{d}Innin-zēr-ibni, 45:2.

Šibqat-^{d}Anu (^{1}šib-ŠU^{II}-^{d}[60]) (year destroyed) s. of [x-x]-^{d}Anu, 42:6′.

Šumāti (^{1}MU.MEŠ) a. of ^{d}Anu-aḫḫē-iddin and Ubar, 26 R. 10′.

Šūzubu (174 B.C.) (^{1}šu-zu-u_2-bu) f. of [...]-apla-iddin (or: [^{d}na]-na-a-iddin), s. of Murašû, desc. of ^{d}Sîn-lēq-unnini, 27:26; 29:26.

Tattannu (^{1}ta-at-tan-nu/^{1}tat-tan-nu)
1. (234 B.C.) s. of Dumqi-^{d}Anu, desc. of Ḫunzû, 1:27.
2. (234 B.C.) 1 Lo. E.
3. (234 B.C.) 1 Le. E.
4. (230 or 229 B.C.) s. of Dumqi-^{d}Anu, desc. of Ḫunzû, 21:24, Lo.E.
5. (178 B.C.) s. of Uṣuršu-^{d}Anu, desc. of Lābāši, 23 R. 12′, Le.E.
6. (172 B.C.) s. of Nidinti-^{d}Anu, gs. of Ana-rabî-^{d}Anu, desc. of Ḫunzû, 20:1, 17, R. 2, R.E.
7. (150 B.C.) s. of ^{d}Anu-aḫ-iddin, gs. of ^{d}Nanā-[...], desc. of Ḫunzû, 12:10, 12, 15, R. 1, 3.
8. (year destroyed) 16 Lo. E.

[481]Ta-nit-tum-^{d}60 (48:4, end) was visible on an early photo, but according to the author's collation of September 1, 1989, only the ta- sign with some traces is preserved.

Ubar (^{1}u$_2$-bar)

1. (174 B.C.) s. of Mušēzib-^{d}Anu, gs. of Ubar, desc. of Kurî, 13:24, Lo.E.
2. (162 B.C.) s. of ^{d}Anu-iqīšanni, gs. of Ubar, desc. of [...], 28:26, Lo.E.
3. f. of ^{d}Anu-aḫḫē-iddin, desc. of Šumāte, 26 R. 10′.
4. f. of ^{d}Šamaš-ittannu, s. of [...]-^{d}Anu, desc. of Ḫunzû, 20:28.
5. gf. of ^{d}Anu-ab-uṣur, f. of Nidinti-^{d}Anu, desc. of Kurî, 41 R. 16′.
6. gf. of Ubar, f. of ^{d}Anu-iqīšanni, desc. of [...], 28:26.
7. gf. of Ubar, f. of Mušēzib-^{d}Anu, desc. of Kurî, 13:24.

^{f}Ubulna[-x?-x?] (SAL u$_2$-bul-na [-x?-x?]) (128 B.C.) 43 R. 10′.

Uppulu (^{1}up-pu-lu)

1. (128 B.C.) s. of ^{d}Anu-balāṭsu-iqbi, gs. of ^{d}Anu-aḫḫē-iddin, desc. of Aḫūtu, 43:1.
2. f. of Tannittum-^{d}Anu, desc. of Aḫūtu, 34:29.
3. gf. of ^{d}Anu-aḫḫē-iddin, ^{d}Anu-uballiṭ, f. of Tanittum-^{d}Anu, desc. of Aḫūtu, 31:1.

Uṣuršu-^{d}Anu (^{1}u$_2$-ṣur-šu$_2$-^{d}60/^{1}URU$_3$-šu$_2$-^{d}60)

1. (226 B.C.) younger br. of ^{d}Nanā-iddin, s. of Kītu-^{d}Anu, 46:1, 10, R. 6, 9.
2. (220 B.C.) s. of ^{d}Anu-uballiṭ, desc. of ^{d}Sîn-lēq-unnini, 45 R. 14′, U.E.
3. (220 B.C.) s. of ^{d}Innin-zēr-ibni, desc. of ŠEŠ-X.X.e, 45:1, 2, 6, R. 2′, R.E.
4. (162 B.C.) s. Ša-^{d}Anu-iššû, gs. of ^{d}Nanā-[iddin], desc. of Ebabbar-šum-ibni, 28:27, U.E.
5. (year destroyed) s. of Arad-bīt-rēš, LU$_2$GAD.DA.A.[X], 35:16.
6. (year destroyed) s. of Kītu-^{d}Anu, desc. of Lābāši, 24:1, 13, 17.
7. (year destroyed) 24 U.E.
8. f. of Idat-^{d}Anu, s. of Kītu-^{d}Anu, desc. of Kurî, 28:28.
9. f. of Illūt-^{1d}Anu, 32:1, 14, R. 2, 4.
10. f. of Ina-qibit-^{1d}Anu, s. of Ina-qibit-^{d}Anu, 41 R. 9′.
11. f. of Nidinti-^{d}Anu, 22 R. 13.
12. f. of Nidinti-^{d}Anu, s. of Nidinti-^{d}Anu, desc. of Ekur-zakir, 28:24.
13. f. of Tattannu, desc. of Lābāši, 23 R. 12′.
14. f. of [...]-^{d}Anu 37:11, R. 3′.
15. gf. of ^{d}Anu-šum-līšir, f. of Arad-bīt-rēš, desc. of ^{d}Sîn-lēq-unnini, 12:1.

Zaki-^{d}Anu (^{1}za-ki-^{d}60) (161-151 B.C.) 49 R. 1′.

Zēriya (^{1}NUMUN-ya)

1. (161-151 B.C.) s. of ^{d}Anu-mukīn-apli, gs. of [...], desc. of Gimil-^{d}Anu, 49 R. 10′, Lo.E.
2. (157 B.C.) s. of ^{d}Anu-aḫḫē-iddin, gs. of Zēriya, desc. of Gimil-^{d}Anu, 25:30.
3. (year destroyed) 31 U.E.
4. (year destroyed- reign of Siluku and Attikusu) 36 U.E.
5. (year destroyed) 31 U.E.
6. f. of ^{d}Anu-ab-utir, s. of ^{d}Anu-ušallim, desc. of Gimil-^{d}Anu, 10:26.

Partially Broken Names

[...]-^{d}Adad ([...]-^{d}IM) (230 or 229 B.C.) 21:6.

[...]-aḫ-iddin (^{1}dx?.ŠEŠ.MU) (year destroyed) s. of Kidin-^{d}Anu, desc. of Luštammar-^{d}Adad, 17 R. 12′.

[...]-aḫ (191 B.C.) 6 Lo.E.

[...]-aḫ (^{1}...-ŠEŠ) f. of ^{d}Nanā-iddin, desc. of Kurî, , 6 R. 10′.

[...]-^{d}Anu (^{1}[...]-^{d}60) (242 B.C.) 11:1.

[...]-^{d}Anu ([...]-^{d}60) (242 B.C.) 11:7.

[...]-^{d}Anu ([...]-^{d}60) (242 B.C.) s. of Lābāši, desc. of Aḫūtu, 11 R. 2′.

[...]-^{d}Anu ([...]-^{d}60) (230 B.C.) 26 R. 3′.

[X.X]-^{d}Anu ([X.X-]^{d}60) (220 B.C.) s. of ^{d}Anu-ab-uṣur, desc. of Luštammar- ^{d}Adad, 45 R. 15′.

[...]-^{d}Anu ([...]-^{d}60) (172 B.C.) 32:15.

[...]-^{d}Anu ([...]-^{d}60) (128 B.C.) 43 Le. E.

[...]-^{d}Anu ([...]-^{d}60) (year destroyed) desc. of Ḫunzû, 18 R. 10′.

[...]-^{d}Anu ([...]-^{d}60) (year destroyed) desc. of [...], 18 R. 13′.

[X-X]-^{d}Anu ([^{1}X-X]-^{d}60) (year destroyed) s. of ^{d}Anu-balāṭsu-iqbi, br. of Nidinti-^{d}Anu, 42:7′.

[...]-^{d}Anu ([^{1}X-X]-^{d}60) (year destroyed) s. of ^{d}Šamaš-ittannu, desc. of Aḫūtu, 16 R. 8′.

[...]-x-^{d}Anu ([...]-x-^{d}60) (year destroyed) 8, R.E.

[...]-^{d}Anu (X-^{d}60) (220 B.C.) , 45:9.

⌈x.x-^{d}Anu-x⌉ (⌈x.x-^{d}60⌉-x) (year destroyed) desc. of ^{d}Sîn-lēq-unnini, 5:10.

[...]-^{d}Anu, f. of Mušēzib-^{d}Anu, desc. of Ekur-zakir, 14:29.

[...]-^{d}Anu (^{1}X.[X.]^{d}60) f. of ^{d}Nanā-iddin, s. of ^{d}Anu-dumq[i], desc. of Kurî, 22 R. 8.

[...]-^{d}Anu (^{1}[...]-^{d}60) f. of ^{d}Anu-aḫ-ittannu, desc. of Ḫunzû, 6 R. 9′.

[...]-^{d}Anu ([^{1}...]-^{d}60) gf.; all other names broken, 20:31.

[...]-^{d}Anu ([^{1}...]-^{d}60) gf. of ^{d}Šamaš-ittannu, f. of Ubar, desc. of Ḫunzû, 20:28.

[...]-^{d}Anu ([...]-^{d}60) desc. of Ekur-zakir, 6 R. 9′.

[...]-^{d}Anu ([...]-^{d}60), br. of Sumuttum-^{d}Anu, 48:26.

[...]-^{d}Anu, (year destroyed) s. of Uṣuršu-^{d}Anu 37:11.

[...]-a/-apla-iddin (164 B.C.) s. of Šūzubu, gs. of Murašû, desc. of ^{d}Sîn-lēq-unnini, 29:26.

^{d}[X.(X)]-apla-iddin (^{1d}[X.X].A.MU) f. of Nidinti-^{d}Anu, s. of ^{d}Anu-aḫḫē-iddin, desc. of [...], 20:25.

[X.X]-BA-[X] (238 B.C.) s. of Ina-qibit-^{d}Anu, desc. of Luštammar- ^{d}Adad, 11 R. 7′.

[...-]^{d}Bēlti ([...-]^{d}GAŠAN) desc. of Luštammar-^{d}Adad, 16 R. 13′.

[...]-^{d}Bēlti ([^{1}...-^{d}G]AŠAN) f. of Libluṭ, desc. of Luštammar-^{d}Adad, 20:23.

[....-][^{d}a]n?-nu (year destroyed) s. of Dumqi-^{d}Anu, desc. of Ekur-zakir, 49 R. 9′.

[^{d}X.X]-ittannu ([^{1d}X.X].MU-nu) (191 B.C.) s. of Kidin-^{d}Anu, gs. of ^{d}Anu-mukīn-apli, 6 R. 10′.

[...]-iddin ([^{1}...]-MU) (year destroyed) s. of ^{d}Nanā-iddin, 40:9′.
[...]-iddin ([^{1}...]-MU) f. of ^{d}Anu-ab-utir, 32 R. 7′.
[...]-lē'û? ($^{1d?}$X.DA?) (year destroyed) 17:10.[49]
[X]-MU ([^{1}]X-MU) f. of Antipatrusu, 43 R. 3′.
[...].MU (292-280 B.C.) desc. of Nidinti-^{d}Anu and Gimil-^{d}Anu, 36 R. 5′.
[...]-^{d}Sîn ([...^{d}]30) (year destroyed) desc. of [...], 18 R. 14′.
[...]-šunu (^{1}[...]-šu$_{2}$-nu) f. of Nidinti-^{d}[X], desc. of Aḫūtu, 12 R. 9′.
[...]-tu$_{2}$ (year destroyed), 37 R. 8′.
[...]-u ([...]-X-u$_{2}$) (year destroyed) desc. of Ebabbar-šum-ibni, 16 R. 14′.
[...]-uṣur ([^{1}...]-uṣur) (164 B.C.) desc. of Kurî, 27:25.
[...]-zu, ([^{1}...]-zu (year destroyed) s. of Dippatusu, desc. of [...], 44:1, R. 5′ (Arsacid).
[...] f. of Lābāši, desc. of Gimil-^{d}Anu, 54:14′.
[...] (191 B.C.) s. of ^{d}Anu-šum-līšir, gs. of ^{d}Anu-uballiṭ, desc. of Ḫunzû, 6 R. 8′.
[...] a. of ^{d}Anu-aḫ-ittanu, Mannu-iqāpu, and Nidinti-^{d}Anu, 43 R. 5′.
[...] (^{d}X[...]) f. Nidinti-^{d}Anu, desc. of Ana-rabî-^{d}Anu, 11:9.
[...] (161-151 B.C.) s. of Dumqi-^{d}Anu, br. of [...], desc. of Ekur-zakir, 49 R. 9′.
[...] f. of Nidinti-^{d}Anu, s. of Riḫat-^{d}Anu, desc. of [...], 20:32.
[...] (^{1}[...]) f. of [...], s. of [...]-^{d}Anu, desc. of [...], 20:31.
[...] gf. of Zēriya, f. of ^{d}Anu-mukīn-apli, desc. of Gimil-^{d}Anu, 49 R. 11′.
[...] a. of (two names broken), and [...]-^{d}Anu, 20:31.
[...] (215 B.C.) desc. of ^{d}Anu-erība and [...], 48:33.
[...], gf. of ^{d}Anu-ab-uṣur, f. of ^{d}Anu-balāṭsu-iqbi, desc. of Kurî, 29:24.
[...], gf. of ^{d}Anu-aḫ-ušabši, f. of ^{d}Anu-balāṭsu-iqbi, desc. of Ekur-zakir, 20:27.
[...], a. of Nidinti-^{d}Anu, [...], and Riḫat-^{d}Anu, 20:32.
[...] a. of Nidinti-^{d}Anu, [...]-apla-iddin, and ^{d}Anu-aḫḫe-iddin, 20:25.
[...] a. of [...] and ^{d}Anu-erība, 48:33.
[...] (201 or 191 B.C.) s. of ^{d}Anu-zēr-iddin, desc. of Aḫūtu, 33 R. 6′.
[...] (year destroyed) s. of Nidinti-^{d}Anu, desc. of ^{d}Sîn-lēq-unnini, 17:11.
[...] (201 or 191 B.C.) desc. of ^{d}Nanā-iddin, 33:11.
[...] a. of Ubar, ^{d}Anu-iqīšanni, and Ubar, 28:26.
[...] a. of Aristun and Dippatusu, 44:1.
[...] (230 B.C.) s. of Kidin-^{d}Anu, desc. of ^{d}Innin-ḫīṭūa, 26 R. 1′.

[49]DA for lē'û does not occur in this collection so this broken PN is problematic.

DIVINE NAMES

FEMININE PERSONAL NAMES

^{f}Adiešu-ṭāba

^{f}Antikisu

^{f}Antum-bānat

^{f}Antum-ṭābat

^{f}Bēletsunu

^{f}Ereštum-^{d}Nanā

^{f}Ina-bāni-Antum

^{f}Naḫīšat

^{f}Nidinti-^{d}Nanā

^{f}Nuptum-^{d}Nanā

^{f}Panā

^{f}Riḫat-abū[a?]

^{f}Silimūa

^{f}Šelatti

^{f}Ṭābat-^{d}Nanā

^{f}Ubulna[...]

GREEK PERSONAL NAMES[50]

Aliksandar RN[51]	'Αλέξανδρος[52]
Andarniqusu	'Ανδρόνικος[53]
ᶠAntikisu	'Αντιοχίς[54]
Antikusu, Attikusu RN	'Αντίοχος[55]
Antipatrusu	'Αντίπατρος[56]
Ardarmidur *see* Artemidur	
Aristugirate	'Αριστοκράτης[57]
Aristuglae	'Αριστοκλῆς[58]; 'Αρίστοκλος[59]
Artemidur, Ardarmidur	'Αρτεμίδωρος[60]

[50] See L.T. Doty, CAHU (1977), pp. 156-59. A Lexicon of Greek personal Names, Volume I: The Aegean Islands, Cyprus, Cyrenaica, edited by P. M. Fraser and E. Matthews, Oxford, Clarendon Press, 1987, has proven helpful in identifying some of the names, even though it does not cover Mesopotamia.

[51] Kings bearing the same name among the Seleucids: Antiochus (13); Seleucus (6); Demetrius (3); Alexander (2 in Seleucid Era dated texts).

[52] Röllig, "Griechische Eigennamen..." Or 29 (1960) p. 382 9).

[53] Röllig, p. 380.

[54] Röllig, pp. 377f, Bowman, "Anu-Uballiṭ-Kefalon," AJSL 56 (1939), pp. 235-6, 243.

[55] Röllig, p. 377.

[56] Röllig, p. 379.

[57] Röllig, p. 379.

[58] Fick, Die Griechischen Personennamen nach ihrer Bildung erklärt (Göttingen, 1894), p. 68. For the reading Aristuglae (with *g* rather than *k* before *l*) *see* Röllig, p. 381.

[59] Fick, p. 68.

[60] Röllig, p. 384, Clay, BRM 2 p. 17

Attikusu *see* Antikusu	
Bassiya	Πασέας, Πασίας[61]
Demetrisu RN	Δημήτριος[62]
Di'mukrade, Di'ukrane, Ki'ukrane	Δημοκράτης[63]
Di'pattusu	Διπατας?[64]
Di'ukrane *see* Di'mukrade	
Di'upanneussu	Δι-φάνης[65], Διοφάνης[66]
Ki'ukrane *see* Di'mukrade	
Niqalamussu	Νικόλαος[67]
Niqanur	Νικάνωρ[68]
Niqarqurasu	Νίκαρχος[69]
Niqarqusu, Niqiarqusu	Νίκαρχος[70]
Niqarrasu	Νικορρᾶς[71]

---

[61] Röllig, pp. 381f., Fick, p. 231.

[62] Röllig, p. 379.

[63] Röllig p. 379.

[64] Röllig, p. 379.

[65] Fick, p. 98.

[66] Röllig, p. 378, Clay, BRM 2, p. 17.

[67] Röllig, pp. 380, 383. For *mu*, Röllig reads wu_4 (see Borger, Zeichenliste, p. 285b).

[68] Röllig, pp. 380f. (correct p. 381 n. (1) "d) Ni-qá-nu-úr, BRM 2,53,8" to "Ni-qà-nu-úr"); Clay, BRM 2, p. 17.

[69] According to Clay, BRM 2, p. 17, note 9, this name is related to Niqarqusu.

[70] Röllig, p. 378, note (2).

[71] Clay, BRM 2 p. 17, note 10. According to Röllig, p. 386 § 16), o should be represented in Cuneiform spellings only by *u*. If the identification proposed by Clay, citing Prof. Oertel, is correct, the second vowel in Niqarrasu would be a problem.

Niqiarqusu[72]	*see* Niqarqusu	
Qeplunu		Κεφάλων[73]
Siluku	RN	Σέλευκος[74]
Timala'e		Τίμαλλος[75] or Τιμόλεως: Τιμολλῶ, Τιμόλλει, Τιμολείας[76]
Timgirate		Τιμοκράτης[77]

---

[72] Röllig, p. 378, note (2).

[73] Röllig, p. 378, Clay, BRM 2, p. 17. Note the spelling קפלון in the Aramaic inscription from Uruk studied by Bowman and others, JNES 56 (1939) pp. 231ff.

[74] Röllig, p. 380.

[75] Fick, p. 265.

[76] Fick, p. 266.

[77] Röllig, p. 379.

THE DATABLE TEXTS IN CHRONOLOGICAL ORDER[78]

SE (=AE)	BC	Text #
20	292	52
20-31	292-281	36
20-36	292-275	39
36	275	14
70	242	11
77	234	01
82	230	26
82 or 83	230 or 229	21
85	226	46
89	223	19
92	220	45
96	216	34
97	215	48
108	204	02
111	201	51
111 or 121	201 or 191	33
121	191	06
131	181	22
133	178	23
137	174	13
139	172	20
140	172	32
141	171	10
148	164	27
148	164	29
150	162	28
151-161	161-151	49
155	157	25
162	150	12
163	149	41
179 = AE 115	133	44
184 = AE 120	128	43

[78] Oelsner (pp. 158ff.) offers the following additional suggestions:
For text 9: "1. Jh. SÄ."

For text 16, [Si-lu-k]u is identified with Seleucus IV Philopator, since he gives "zwischen 124 und 137 SÄ."

CONCORDANCE OF MUSEUM NUMBERS

Museum No.	No.
A 1738	52
A 2518	13
A 2519	19
A 2520	20
A 2521	21
A 2522	22
A 2523	23
A 2524	35
A 2525	28
A 2526	14
A 2527	1
A 3375	50
A 3422+3489+3493+3655	49
A 3455+3665	39
A 3459	53
A 3473	54
A 3477	15
A 3489	*see* 3422+
A 3493	*see* 3422+
A 3496+3503+3664	17
A 3497	2
A 3498	47
A 3499	40
A 3503	*see* 3496+
A 3509	3
A 3653	4
A 3655	*see* 3422+
A 3660	30
A 3662	36
A 3664	*see* 3496+
A 3665	*see* 3455+
A 3671	16
A 3672	42
A 3673	51
A 3675	18
A 3676	5
A 3678	6
A 3679	32
A 3680	45
A 3681	9
A 3682	31
A 3683	24
A 3684	48
A 3685	25
A 3686	37
A 3687	33
A 3688	10
A 3689	43
A 3690	44
A 3691	34
A 3692	26
A 3693	11
A 3694	38
A 3695	46
A 3697	41
A 3698	12
A 32114	29
A 32115	27
OITC Deposit 2.1	8
OITC Deposit 2.2	7

1

O.

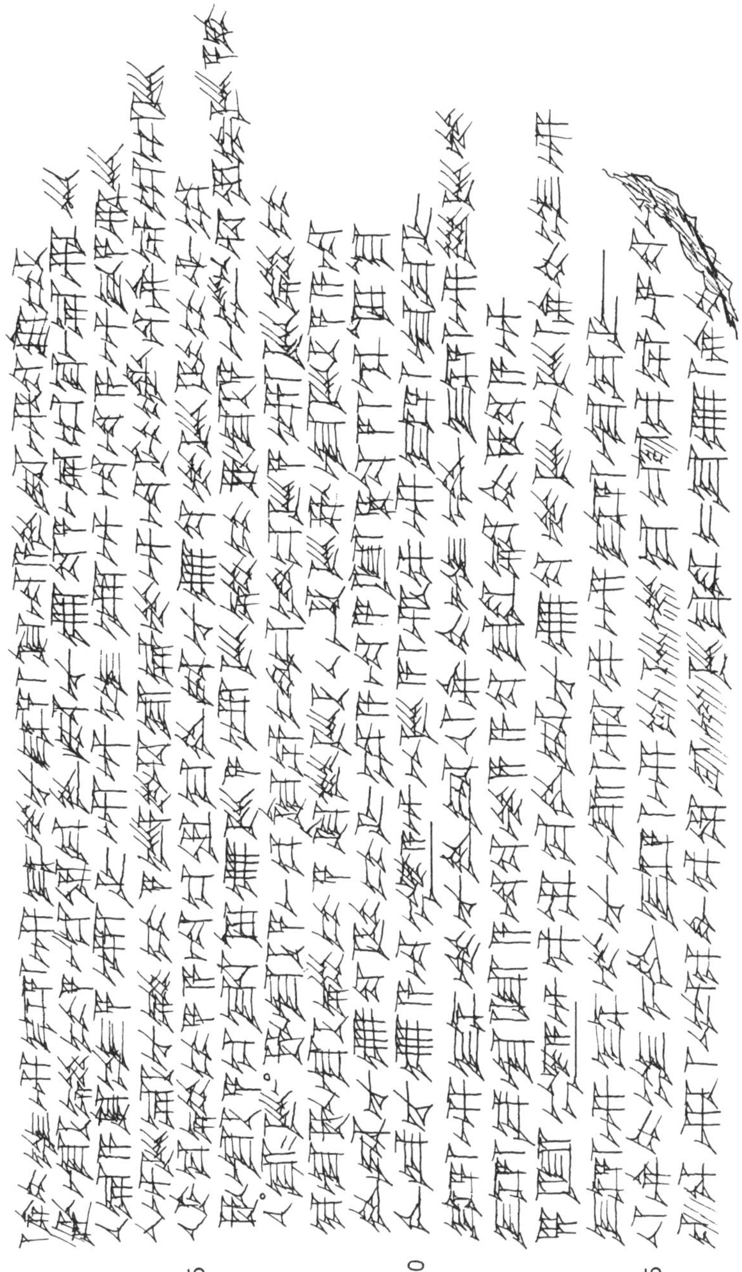

°over erasure°

PLATE 2

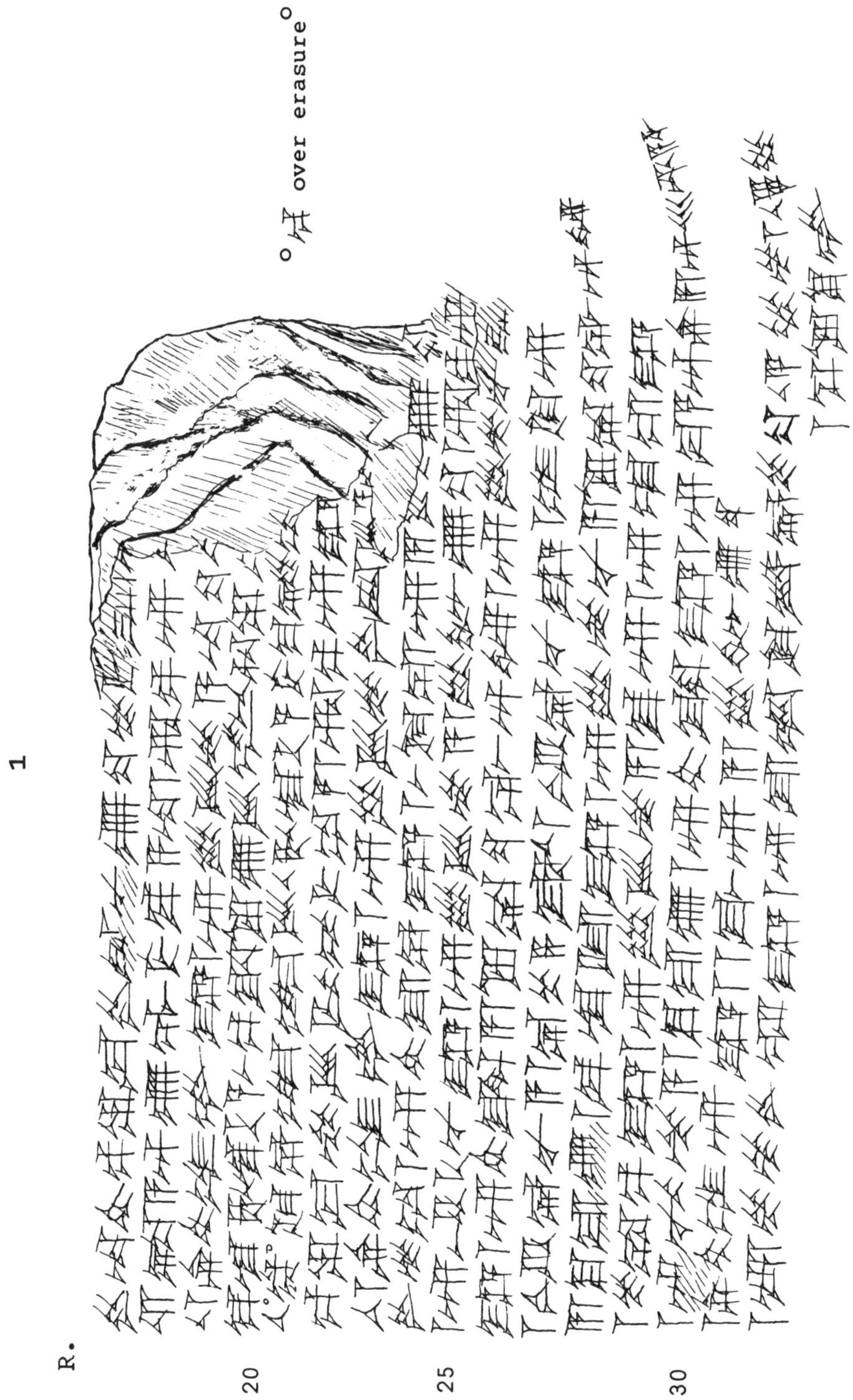

1

U.E.

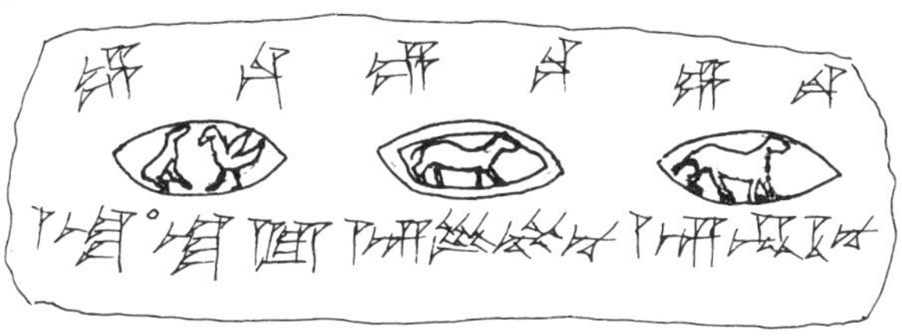

°sic for

R.E.

Le.E.

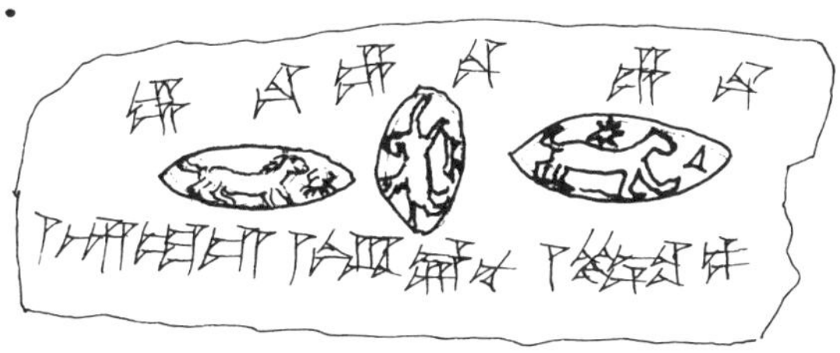

Lo.E.

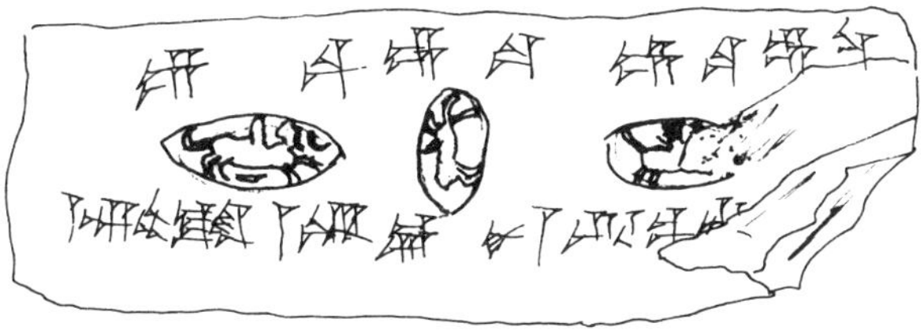

2

O.

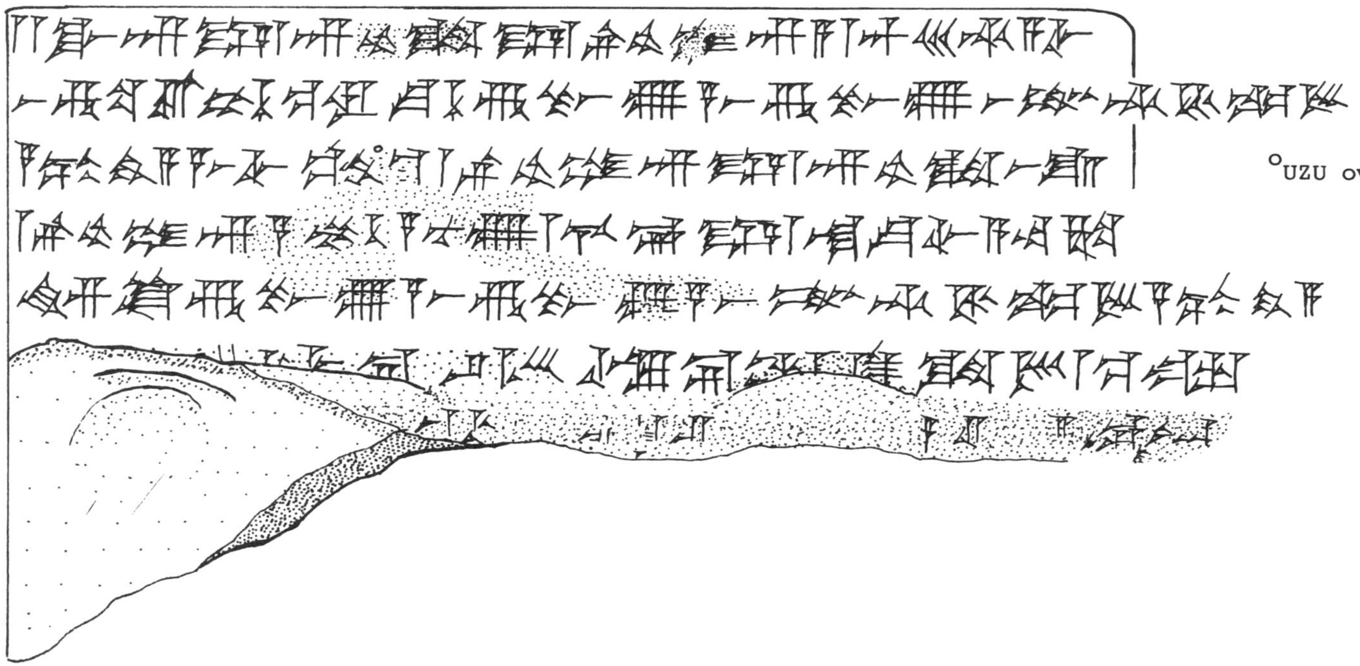

°UZU over erasure?

Le.E.

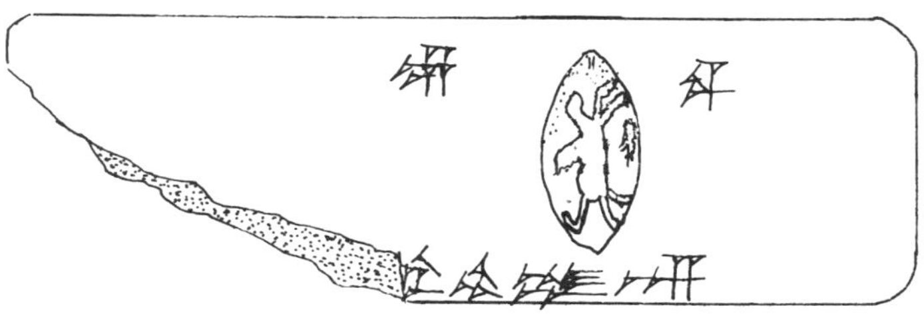

(Lo.E. destroyed)

2

R.E.

R.

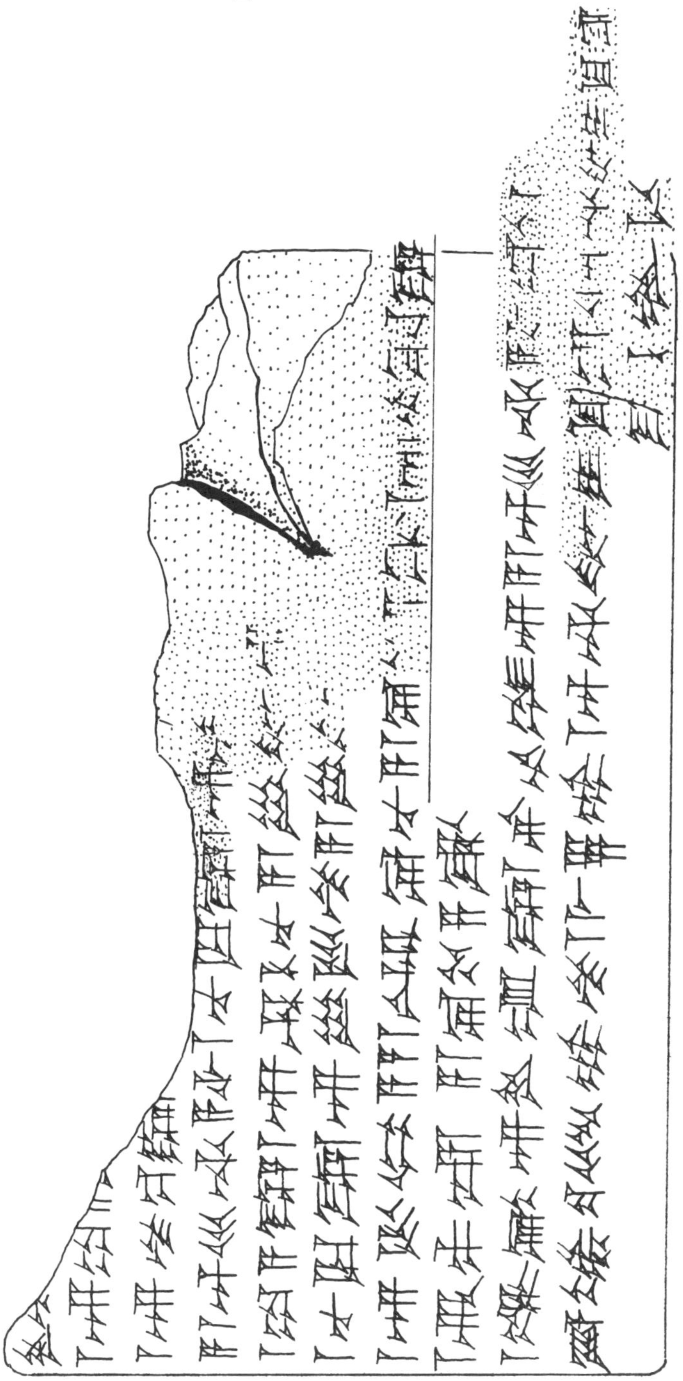

U.E.

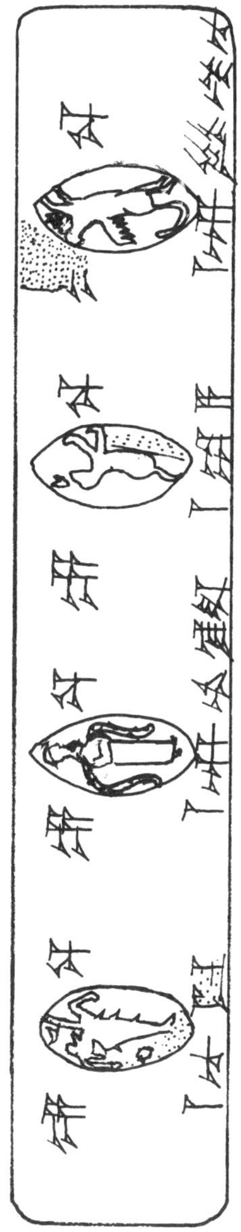

PLATE 6

3

O.

1'

5'

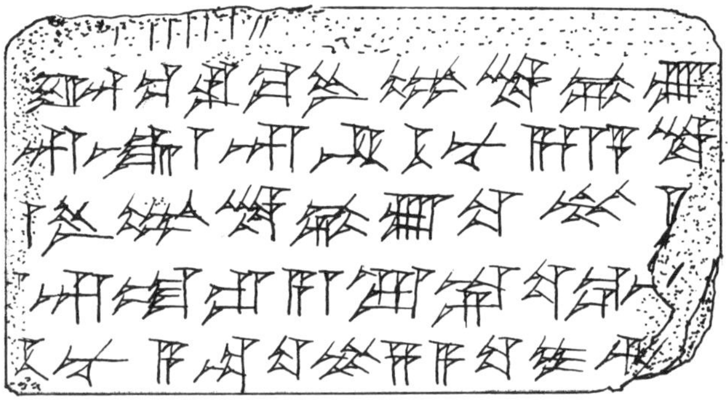

Edges and Reverse have been filed down.

4

O.

11'

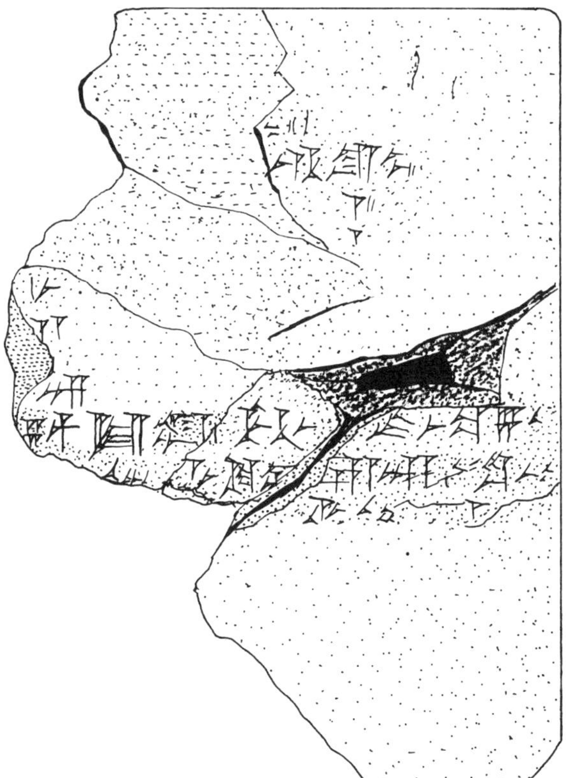

unplaced fragment

4

R.

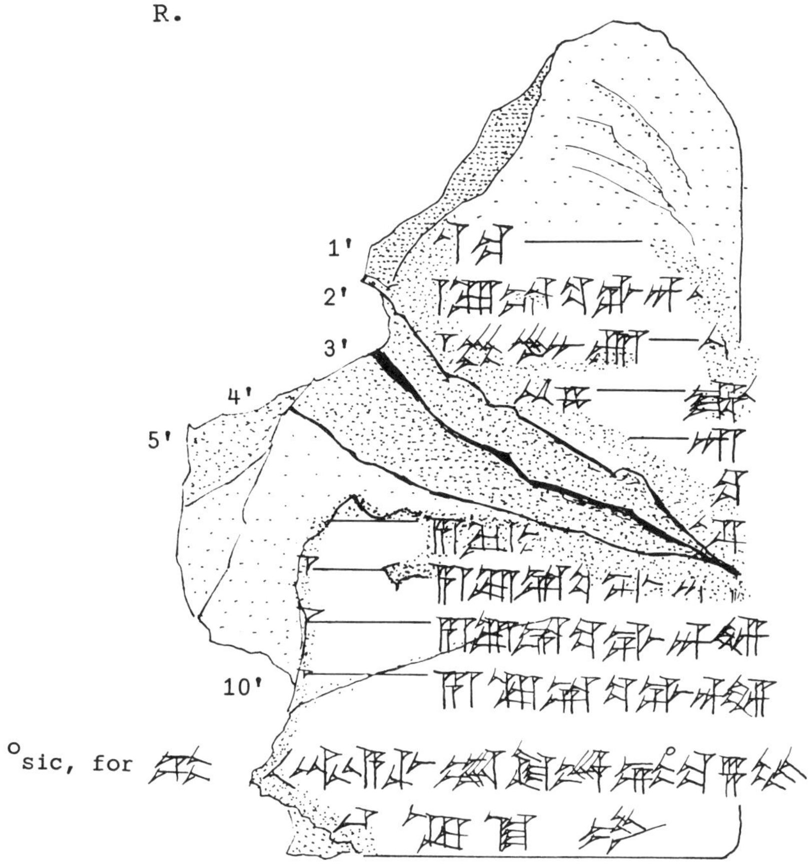

R.E.

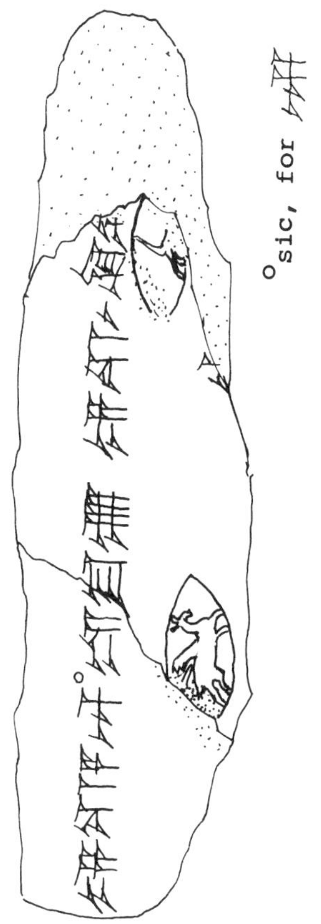

U.E.

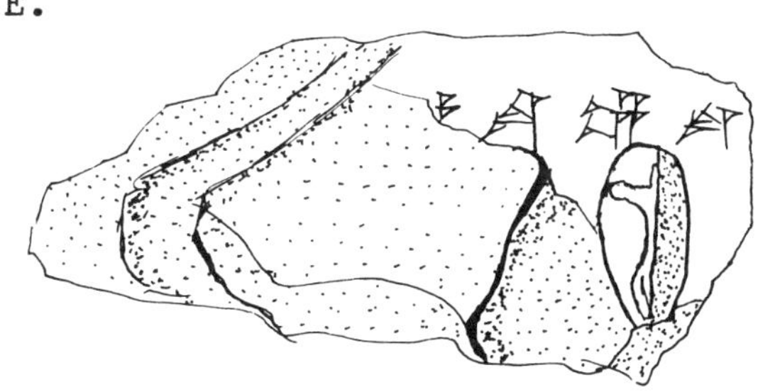

PLATE 8

5

O.

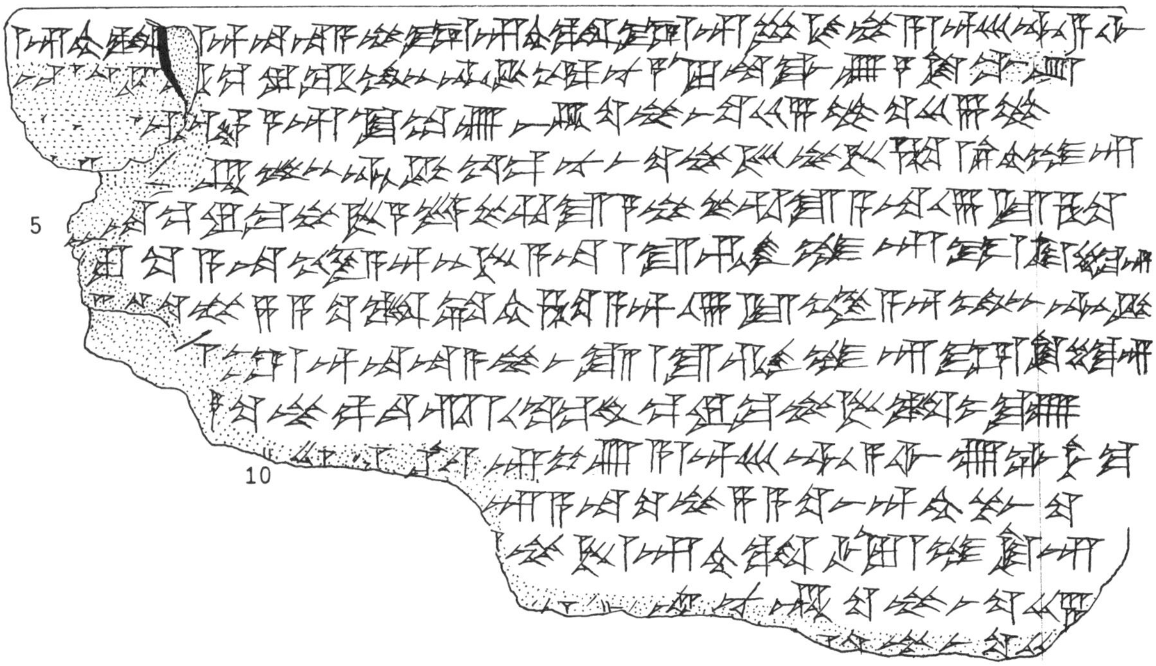

Obverse extending onto R.E.,

continuation of line 4 on R.E. 

continuation of line 5 on R.E. 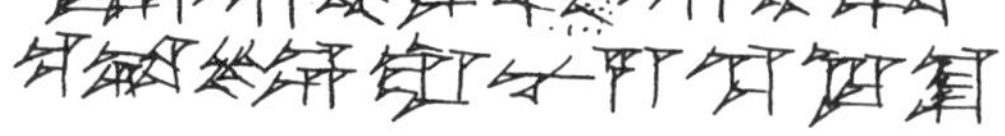

continuation of line 7 on R.E. 

5

R.

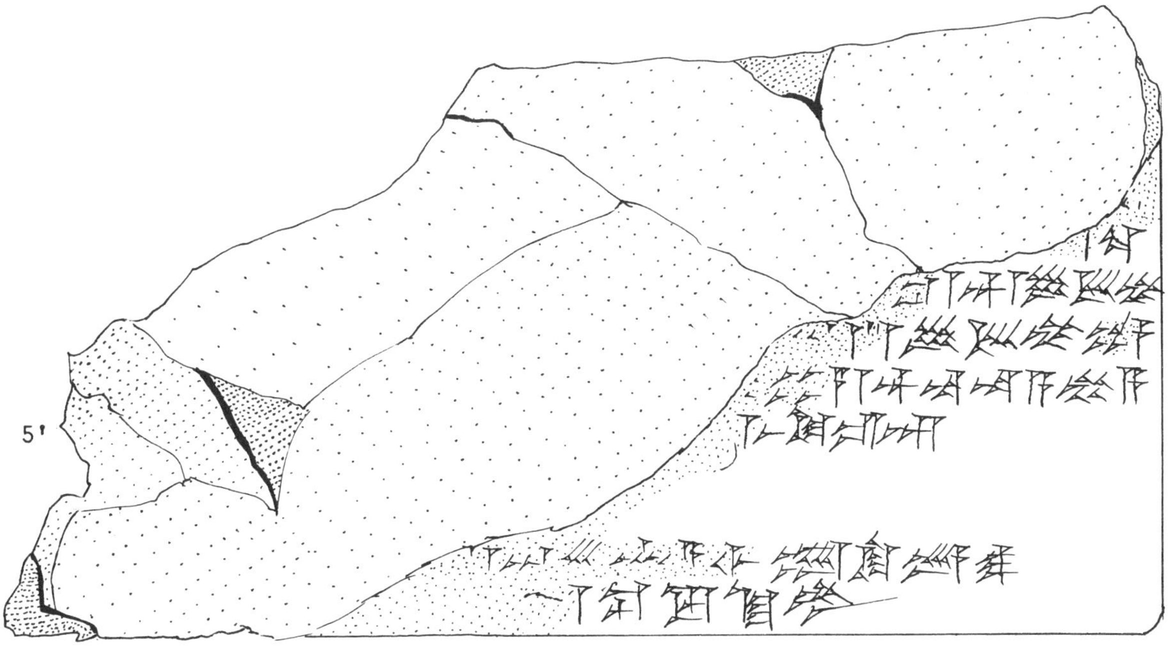

R.E.

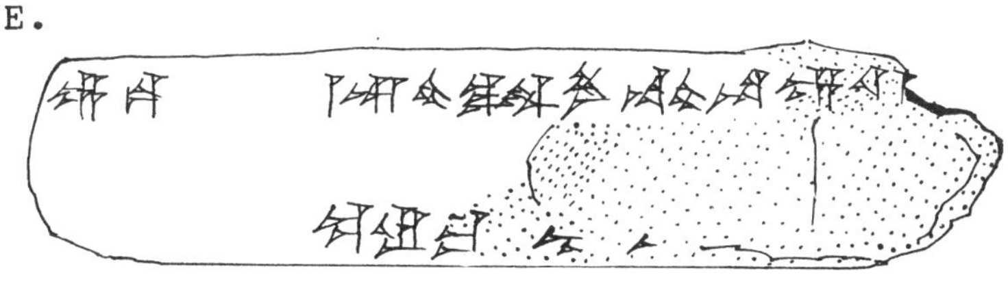

U.E.

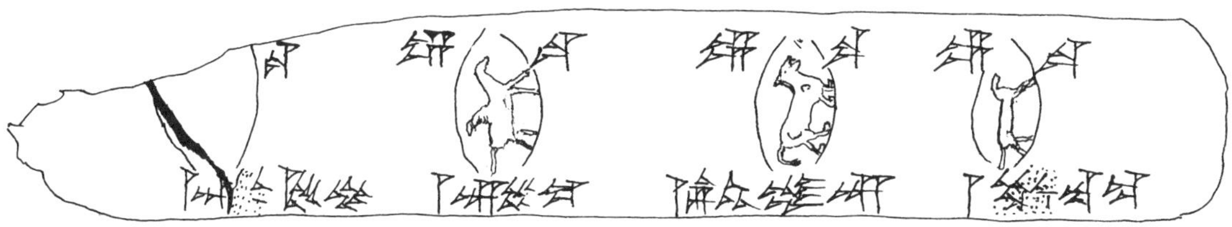

6

O.

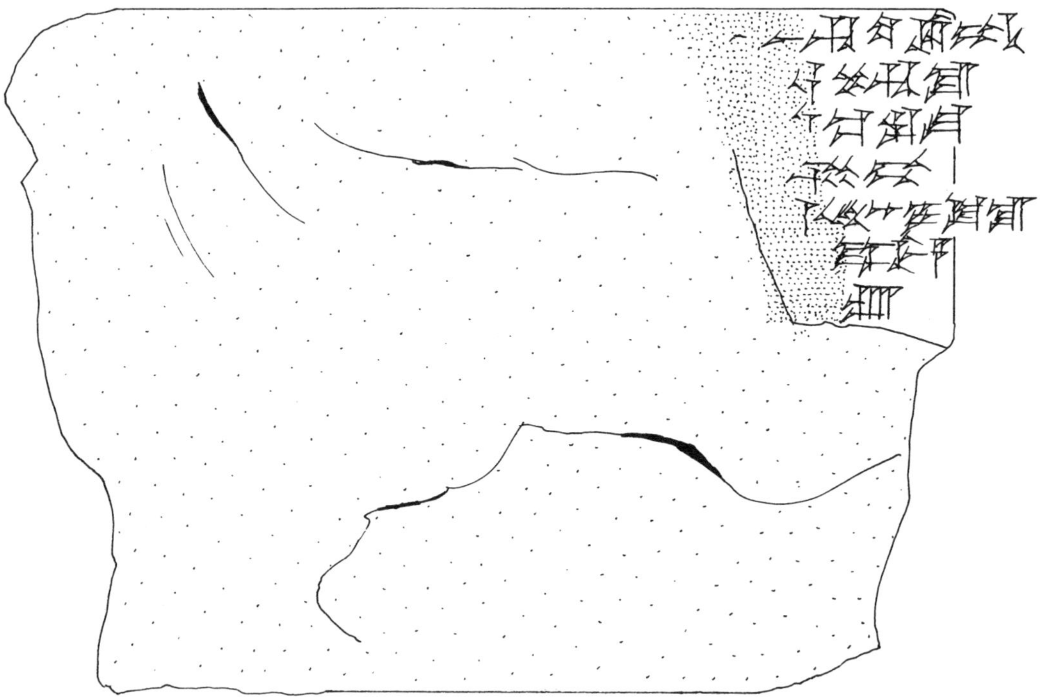

Lo.E.

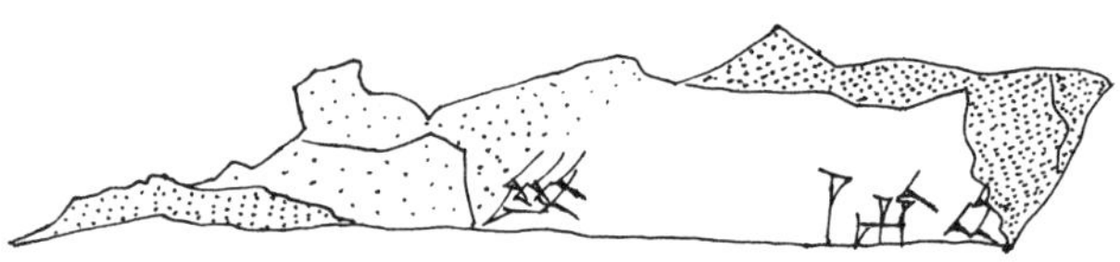

6

R.

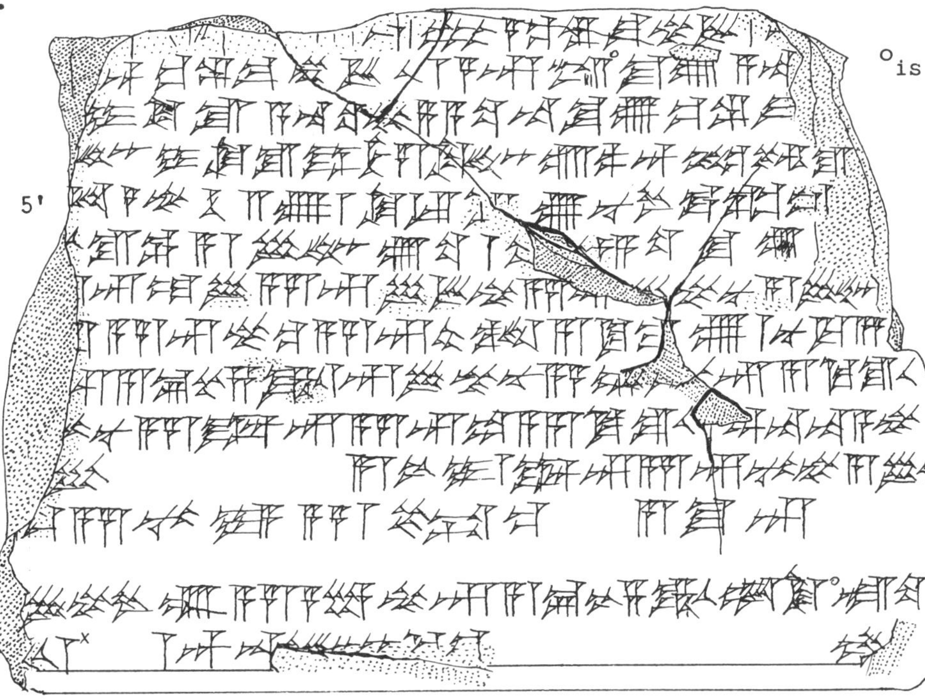

° is over erasure

° ITI omitted

^{x} KAM omitted

^{x} KAM omitted

R.E.

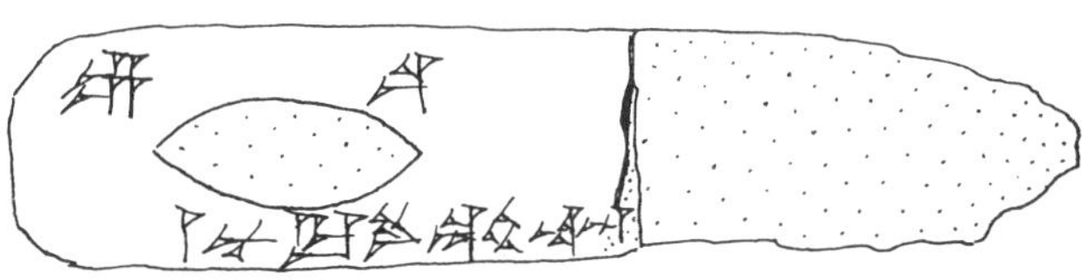

U.E.

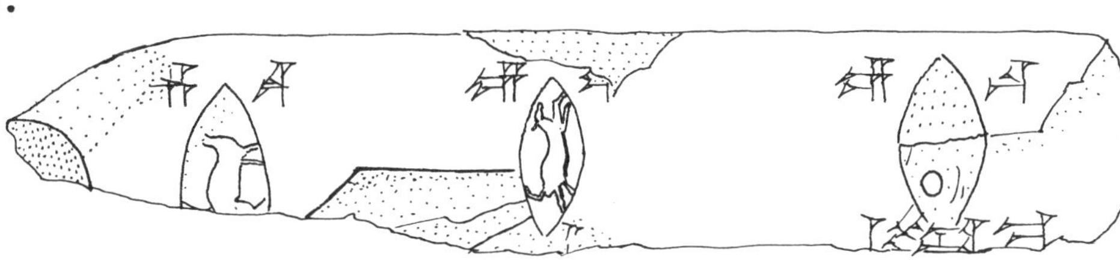

7

O.

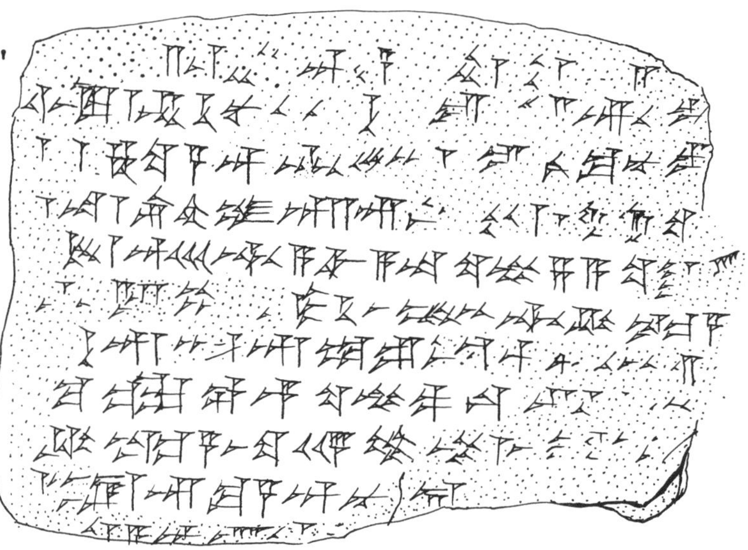

(Reverse destroyed)

8

O.

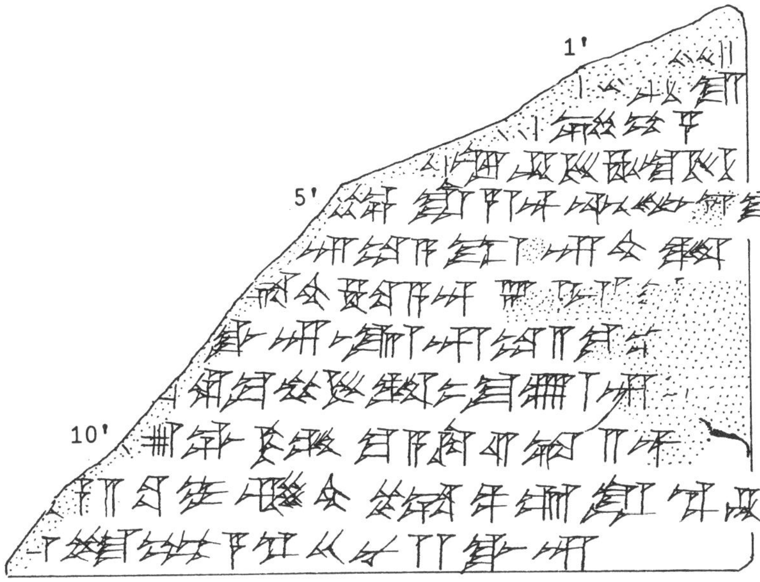

(Reverse destroyed)

Lo.E.

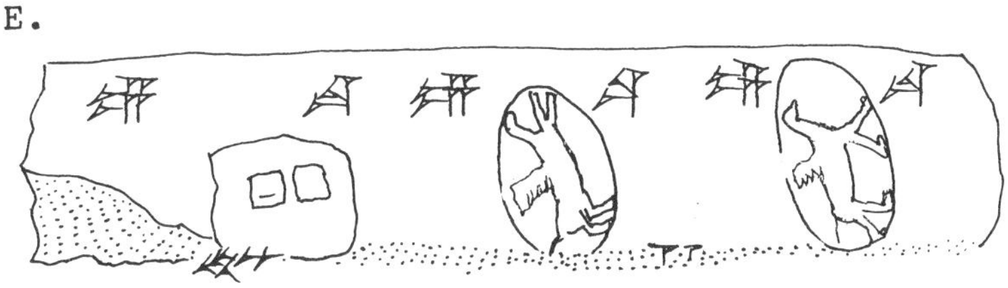

R.E.

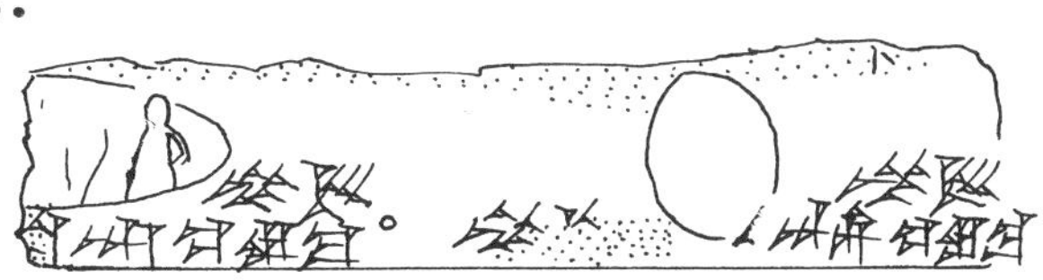

°su-sign obtrudes here from Obverse

9

O.

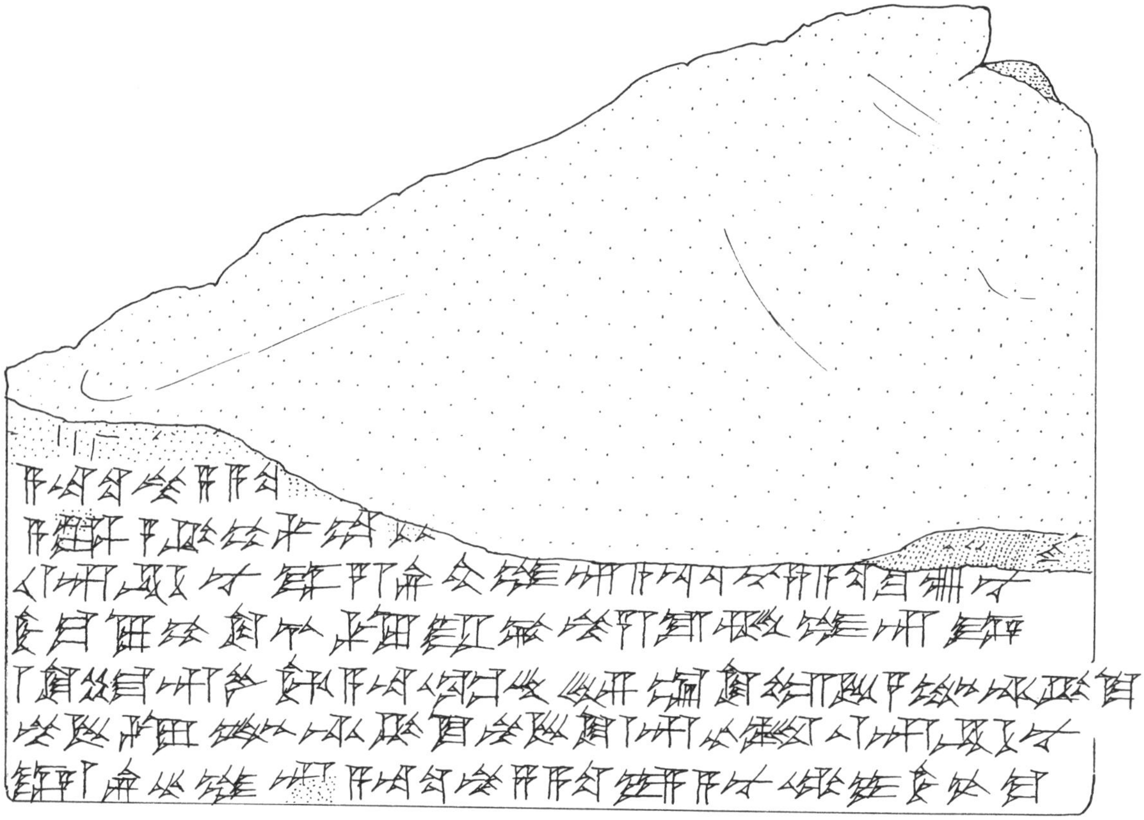

Le.E.

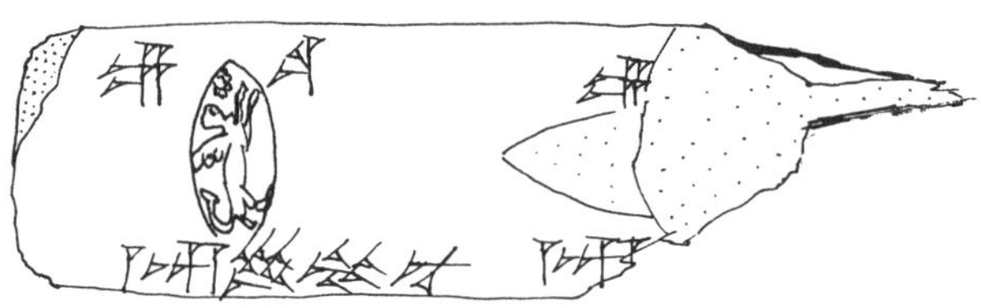

Lo.E.

9

R.

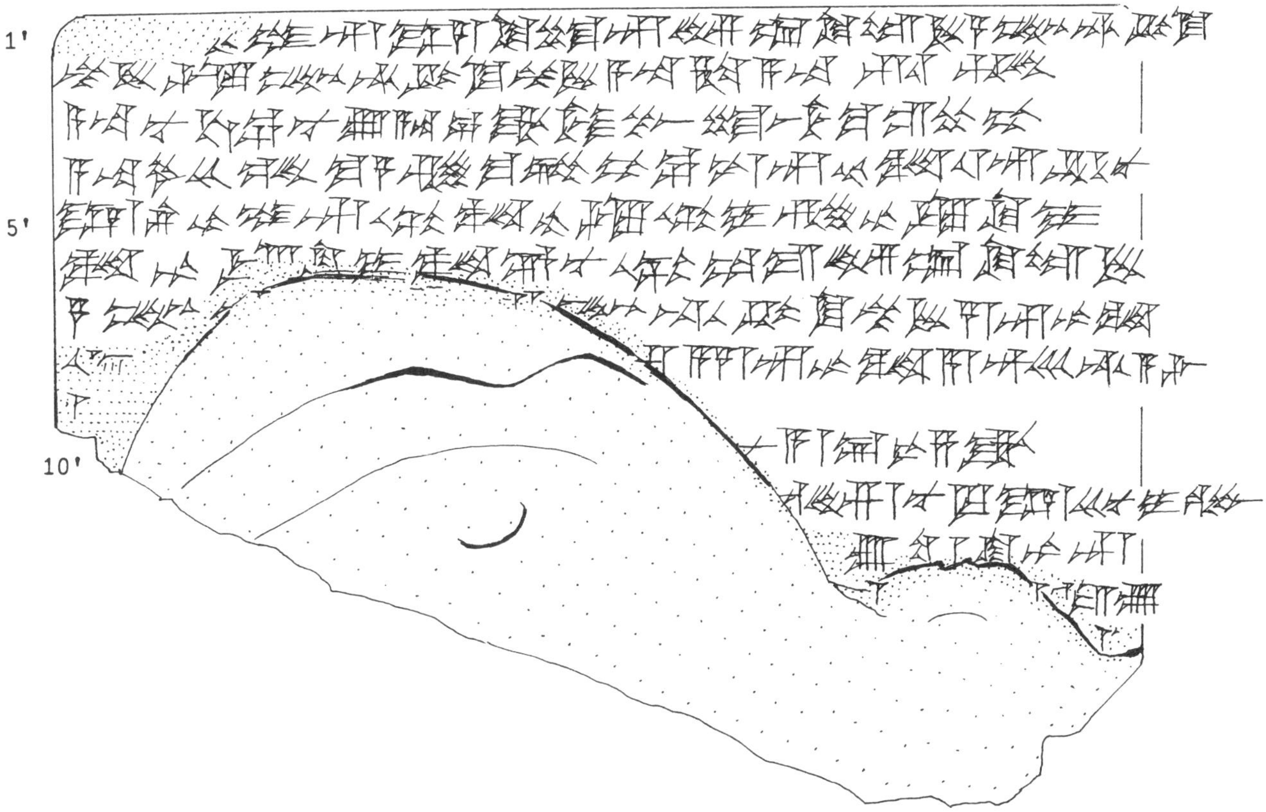

R.E.

(U.E. destroyed)

10

O.

°note extra wedge

°note extra wedge

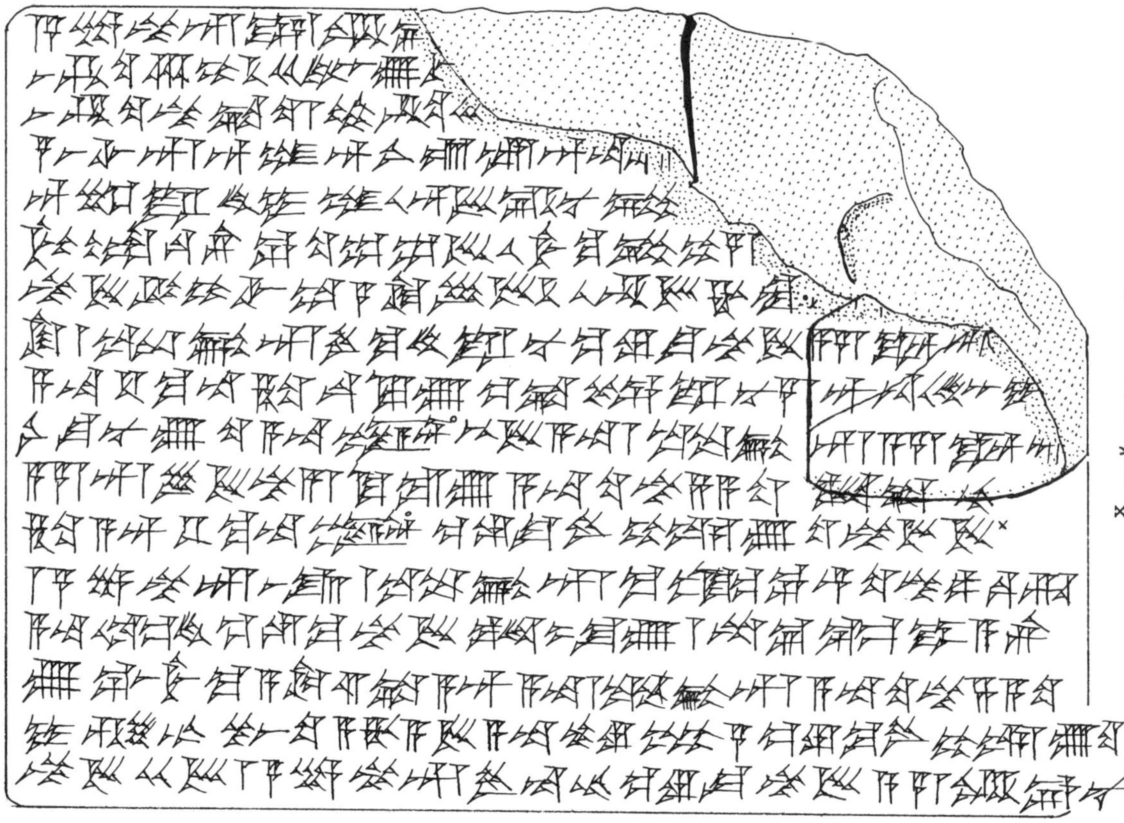

x MEŠ dittography

Le.E.

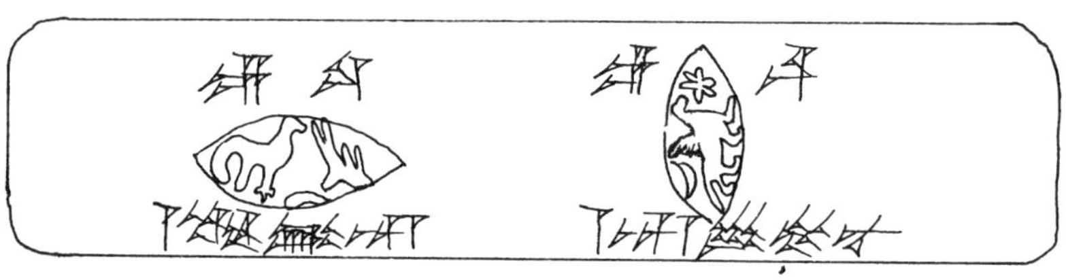

Lo.E.

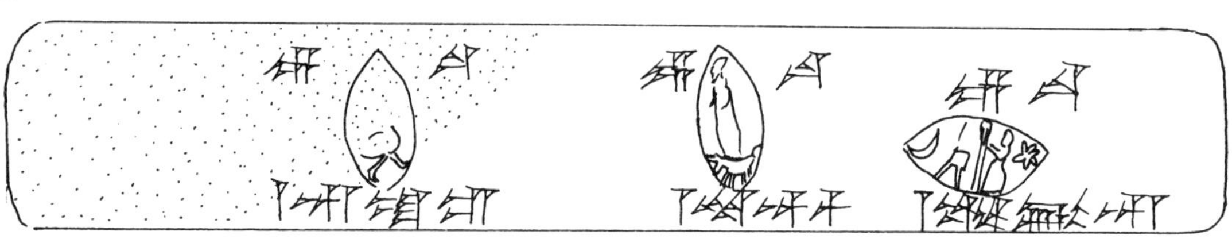

10

R.

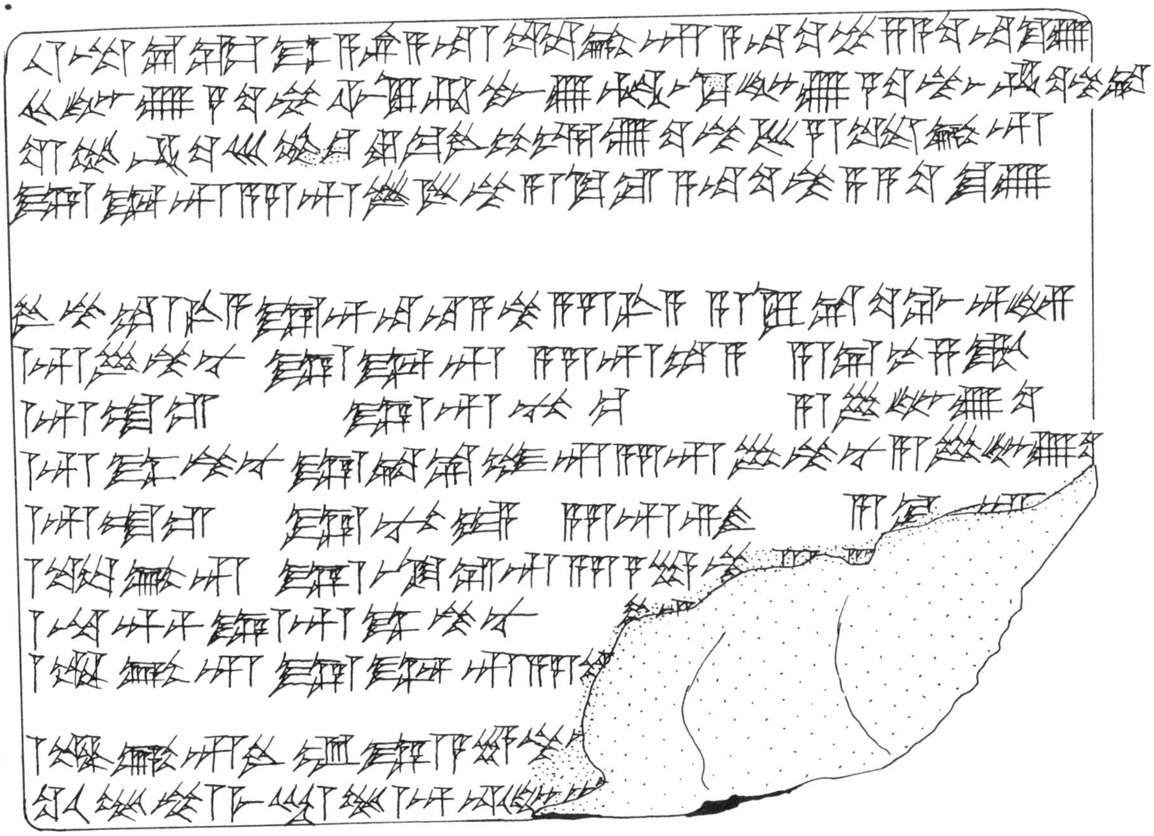

R.E.

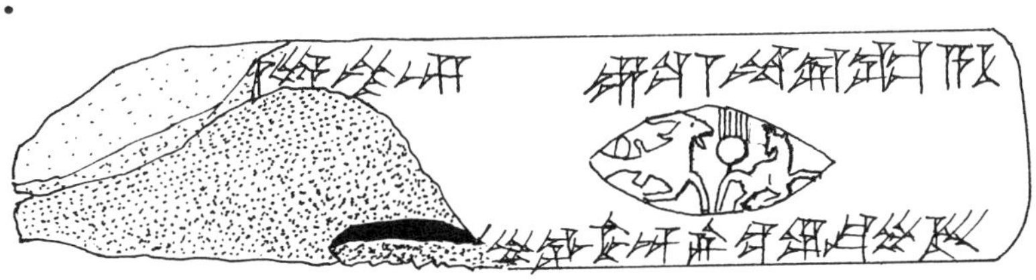

U.E.

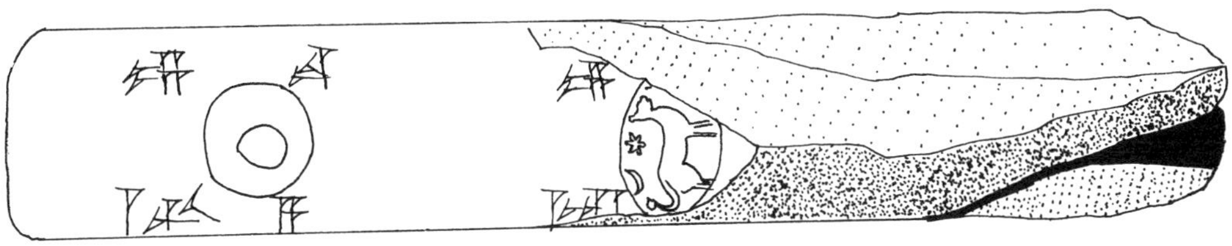

11

O.

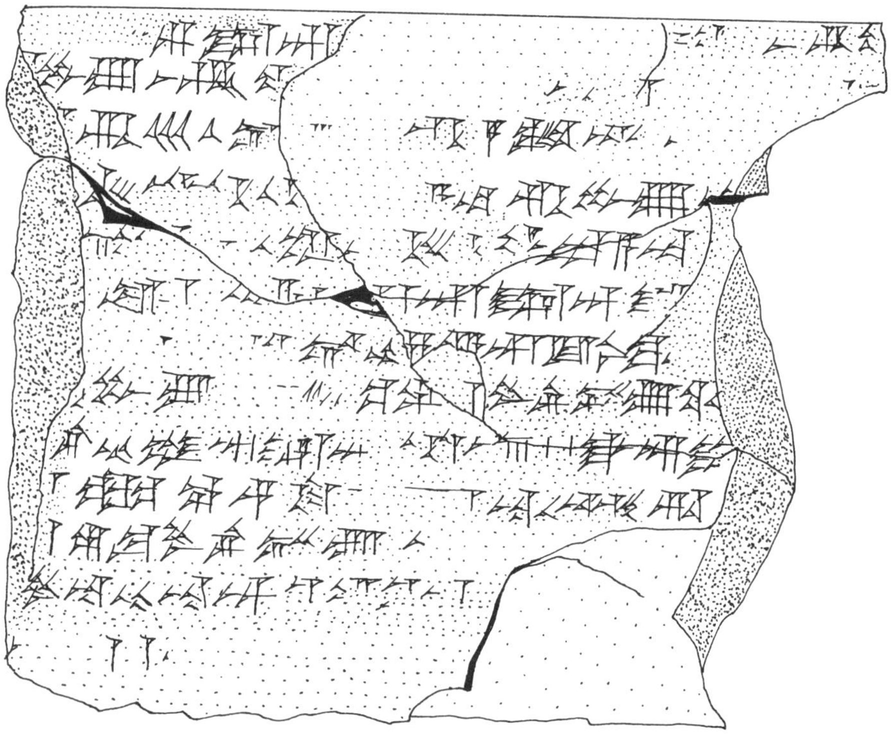

11

R.

Traces at top from Lo.E.

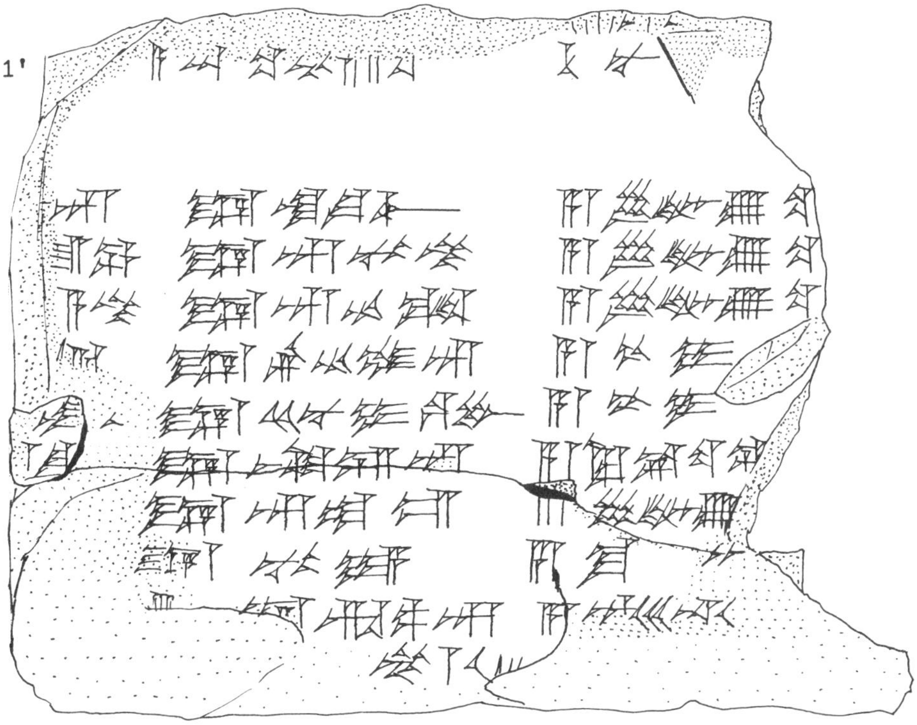

U.E.

PLATE 20

12

O.

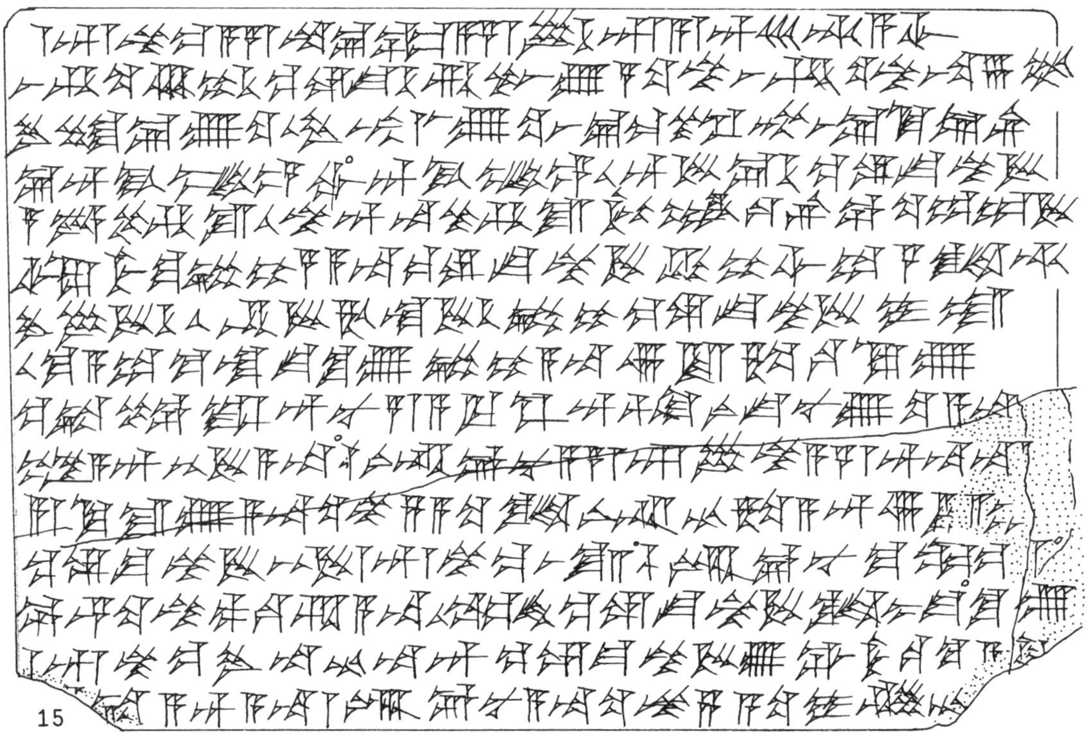

Le.E.

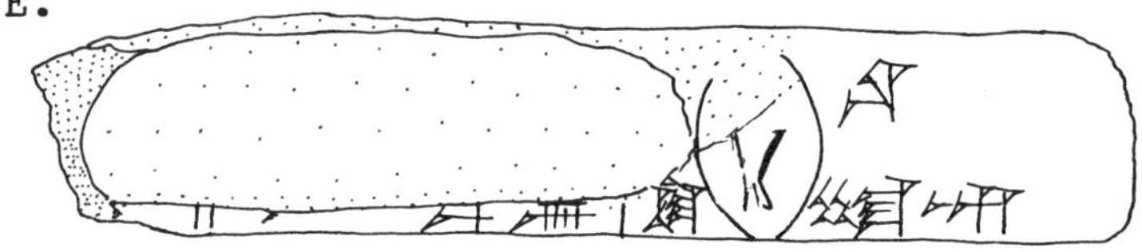

Lo.E.

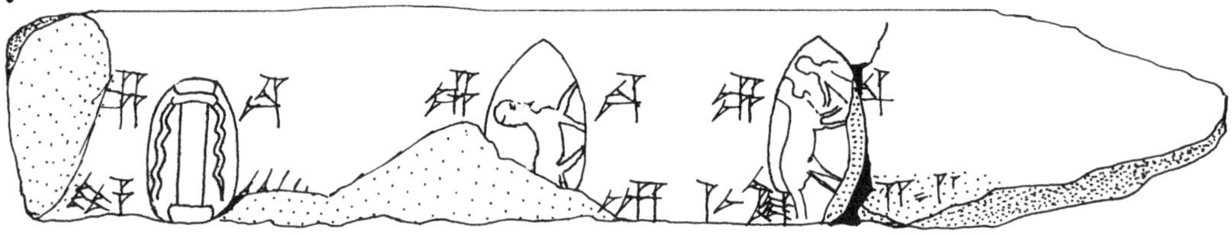

12

R.

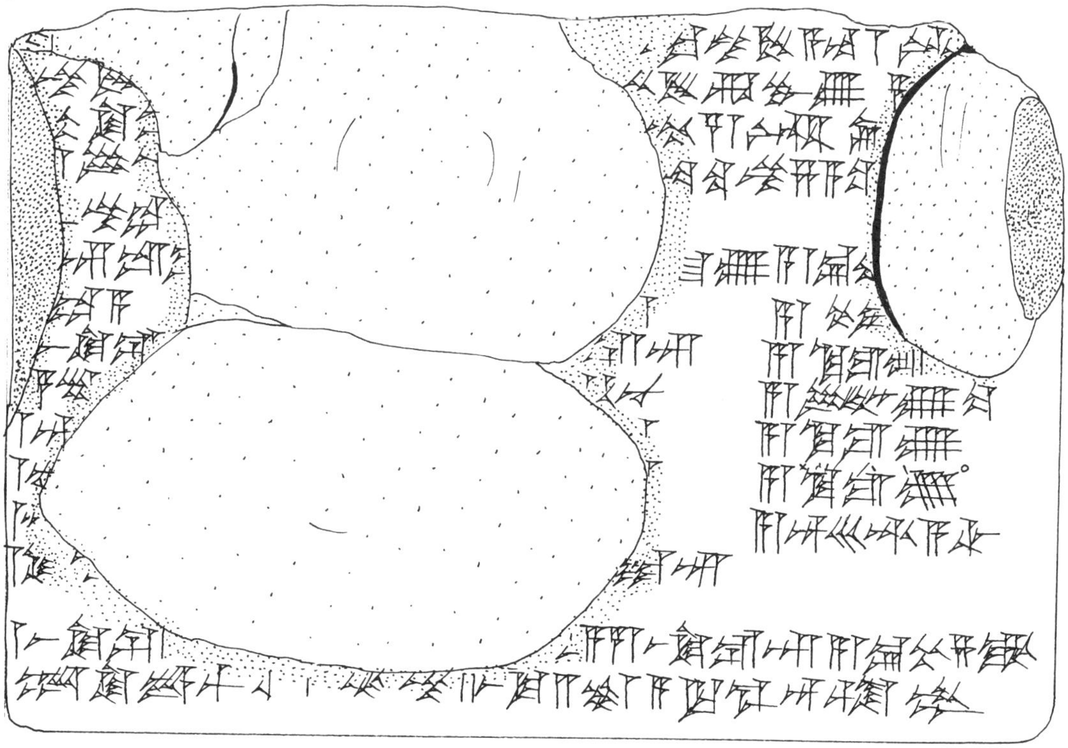

x erasures
o note ú sign

R.E.

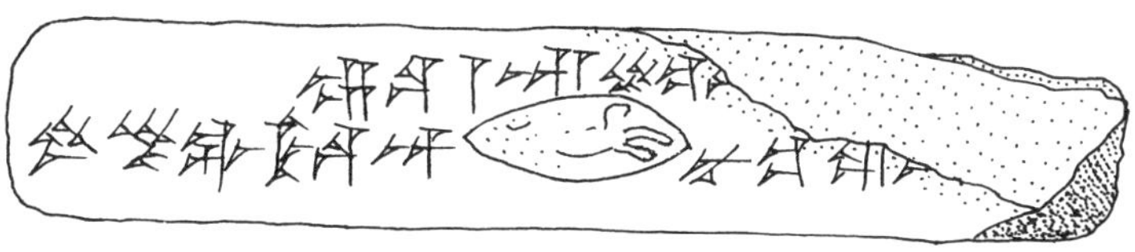

U.E.

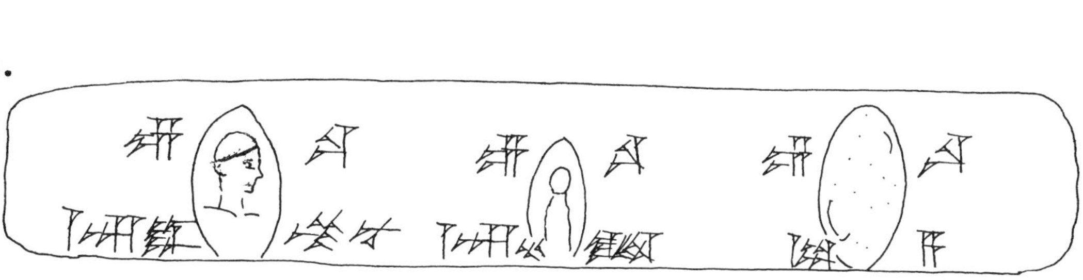

PLATE 22

13

O.

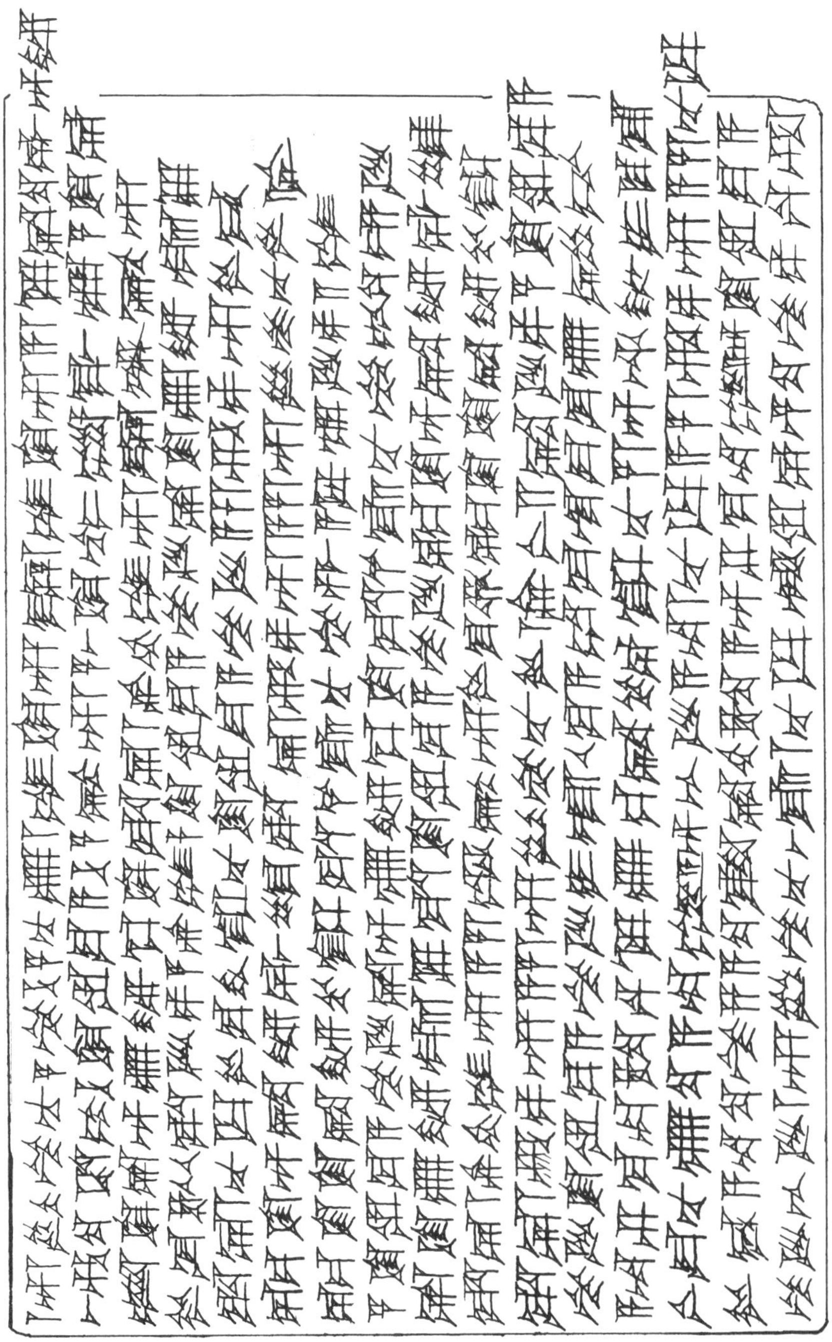

13

R.

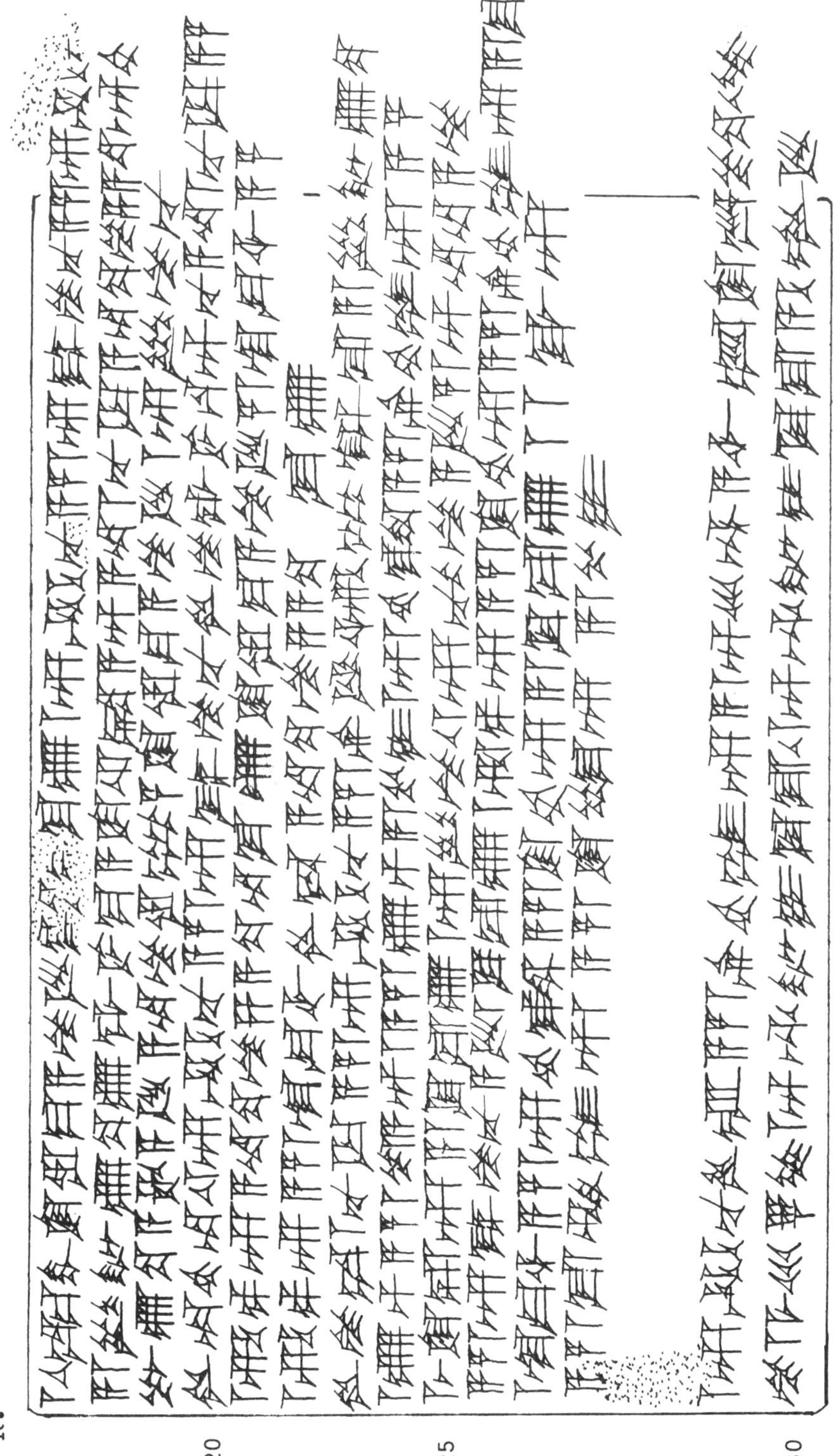

PLATE 24

13

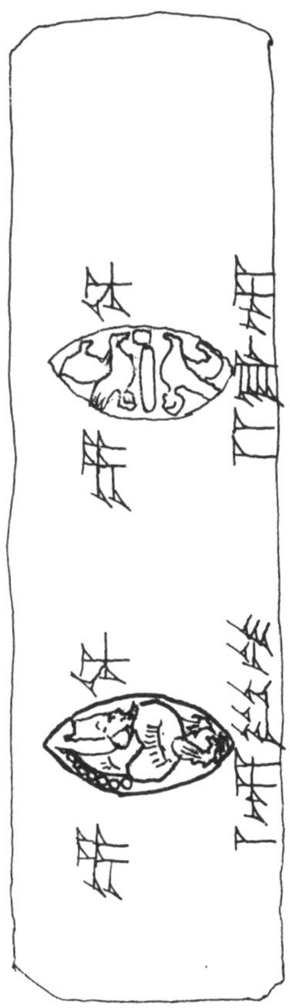

Le.E.

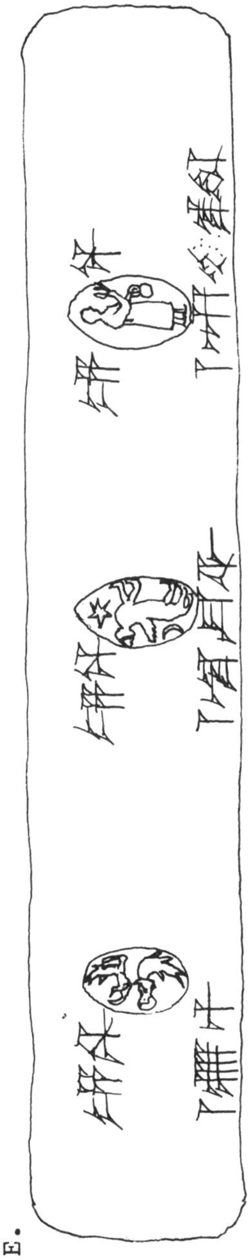

Lo.E.

13

R.E.

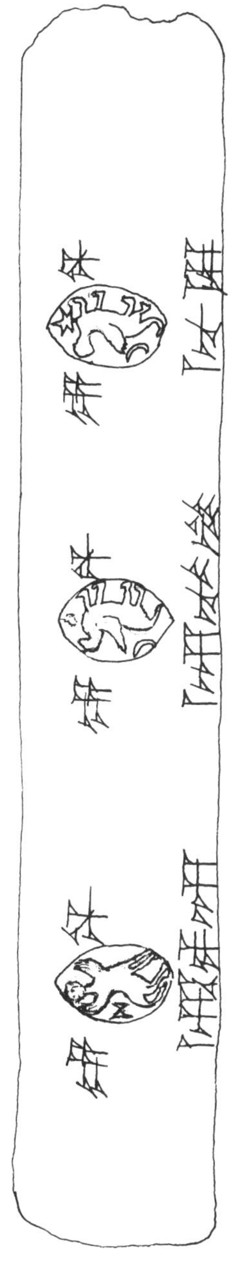

U.E.

14

O.

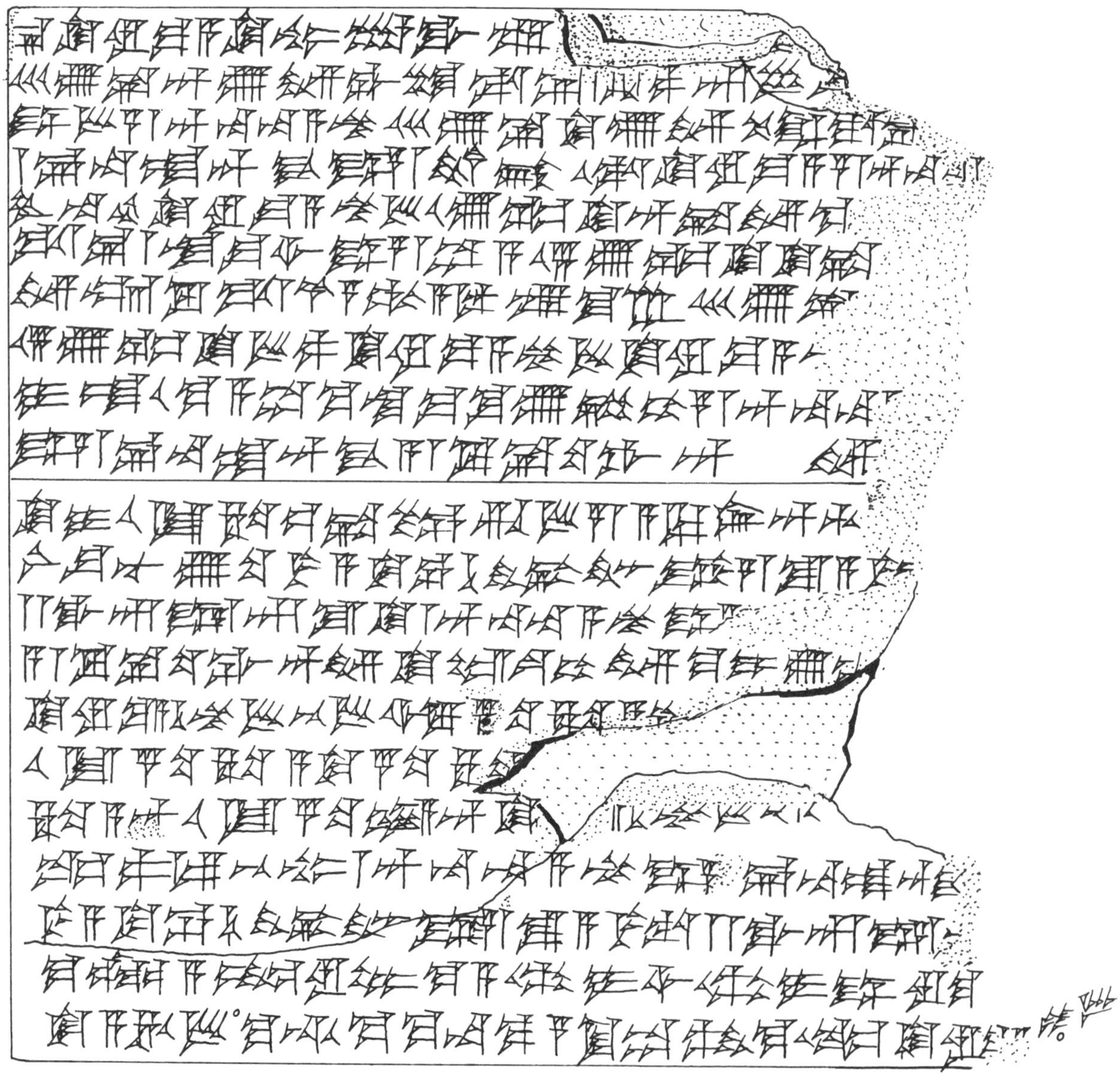

°<ul i-rag-gu-mu>

14

R.

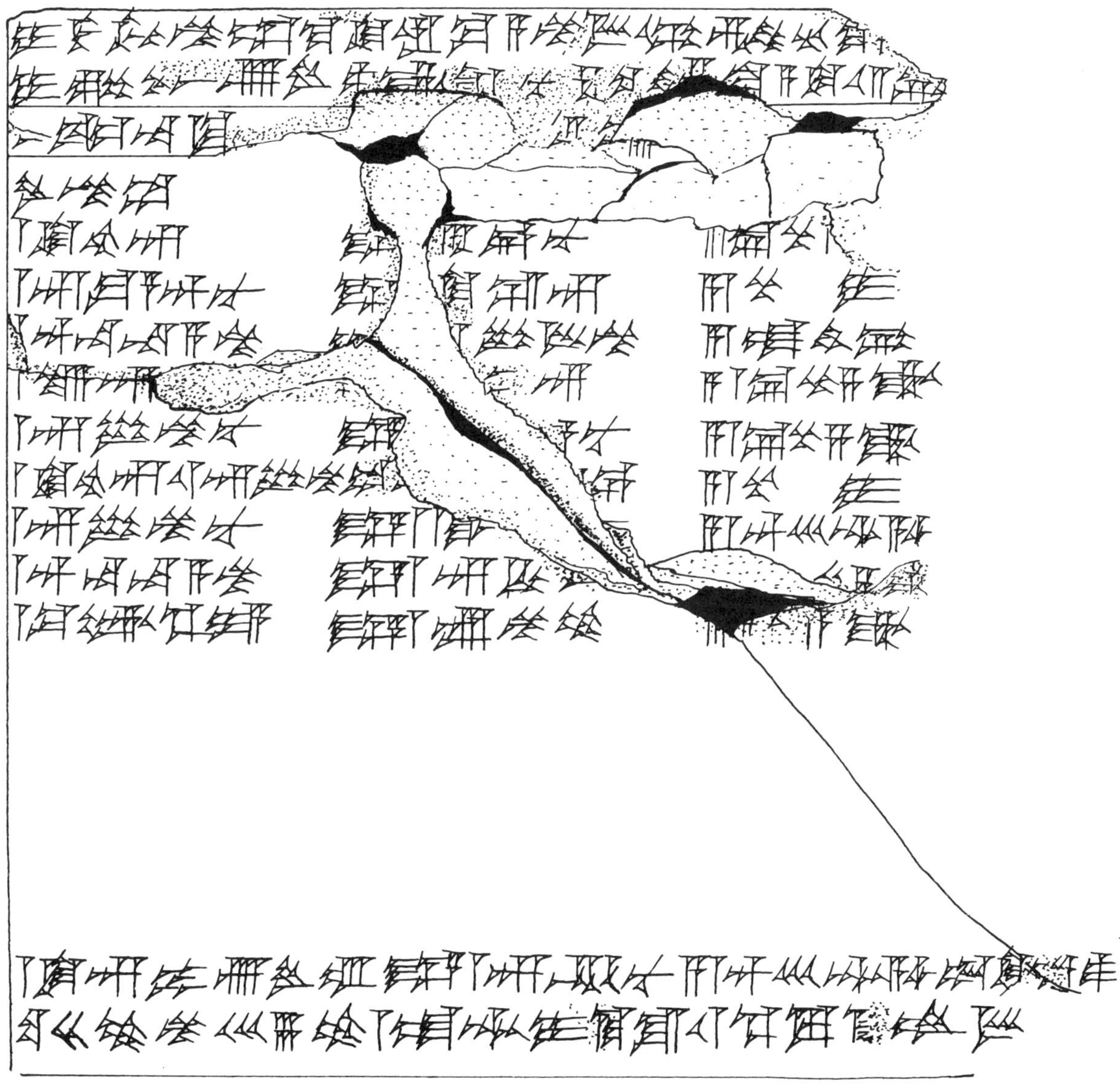

PLATE 28

14

U.E.

R.E.

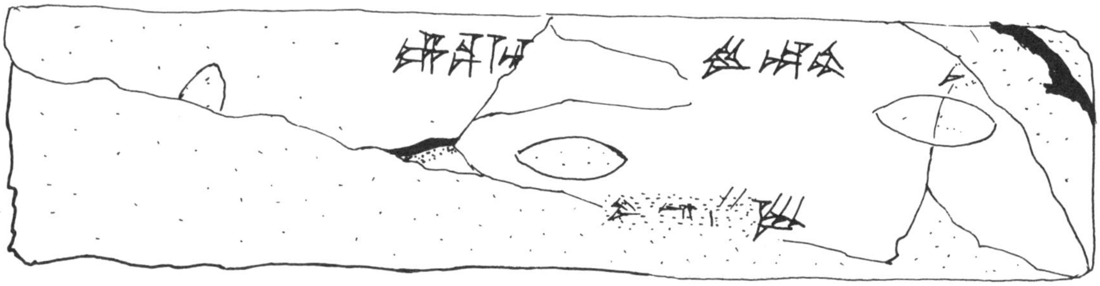

Le.E.

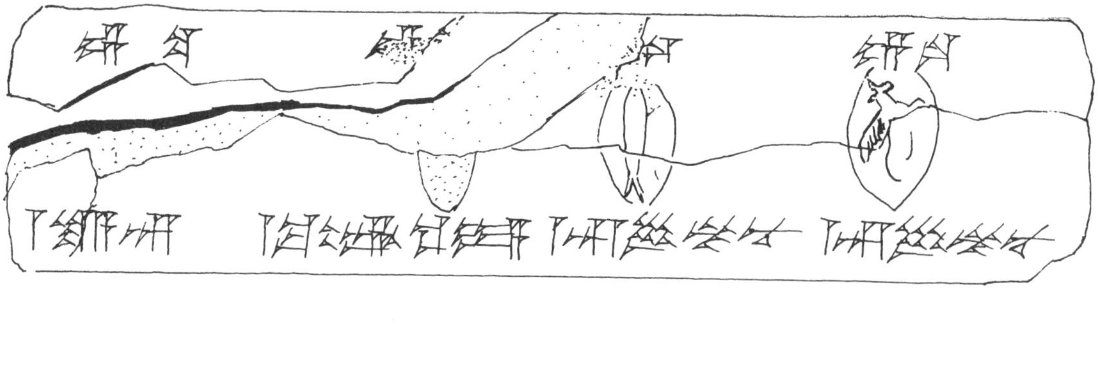

Lo.E.

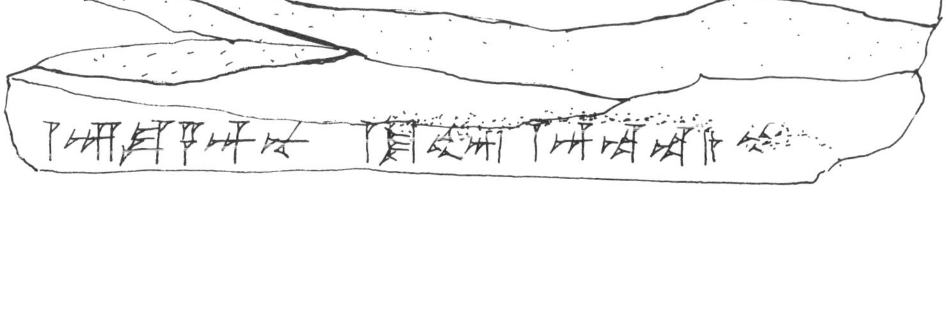

15

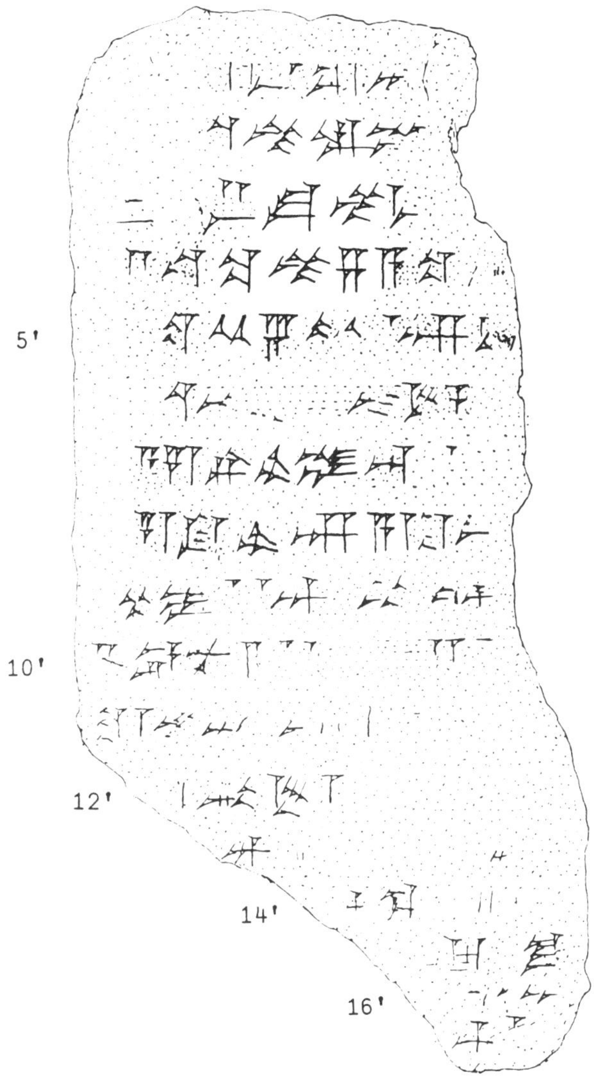

(Rest destroyed)

PLATE 30

16

R.

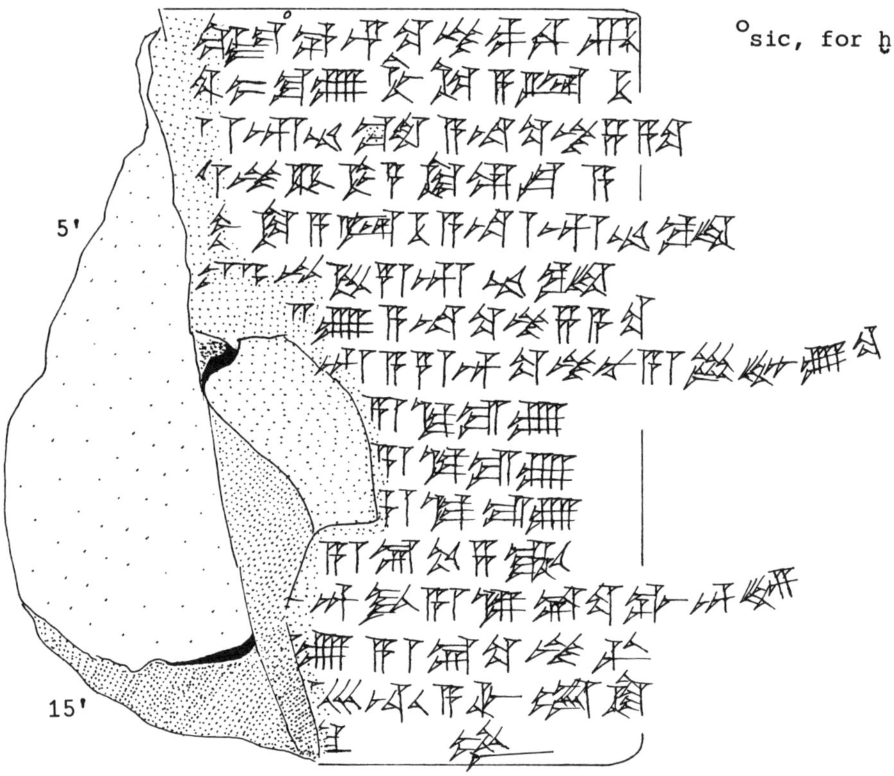

°sic, for ḫir

(Obverse destroyed)

16

U.E.

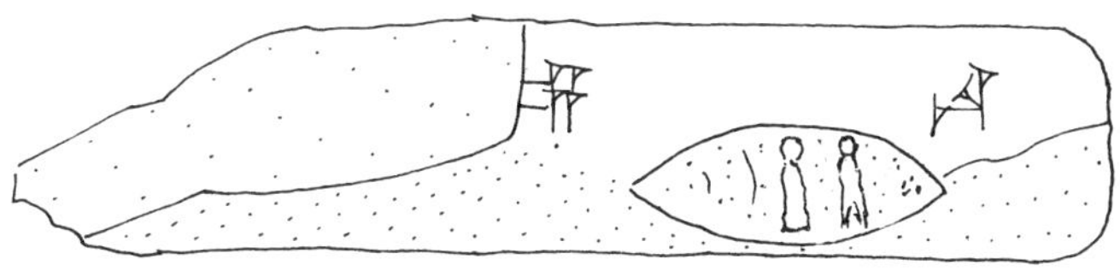

R.E.

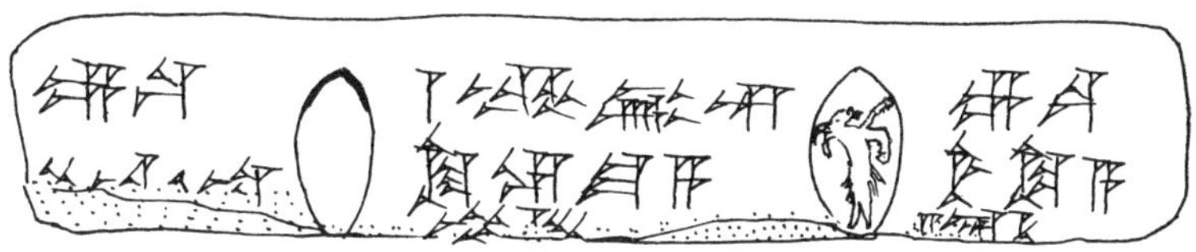

Lo.E.

(Le.E. destroyed)

PLATE 32

17

O.

A 3664 A 3503 A 3496

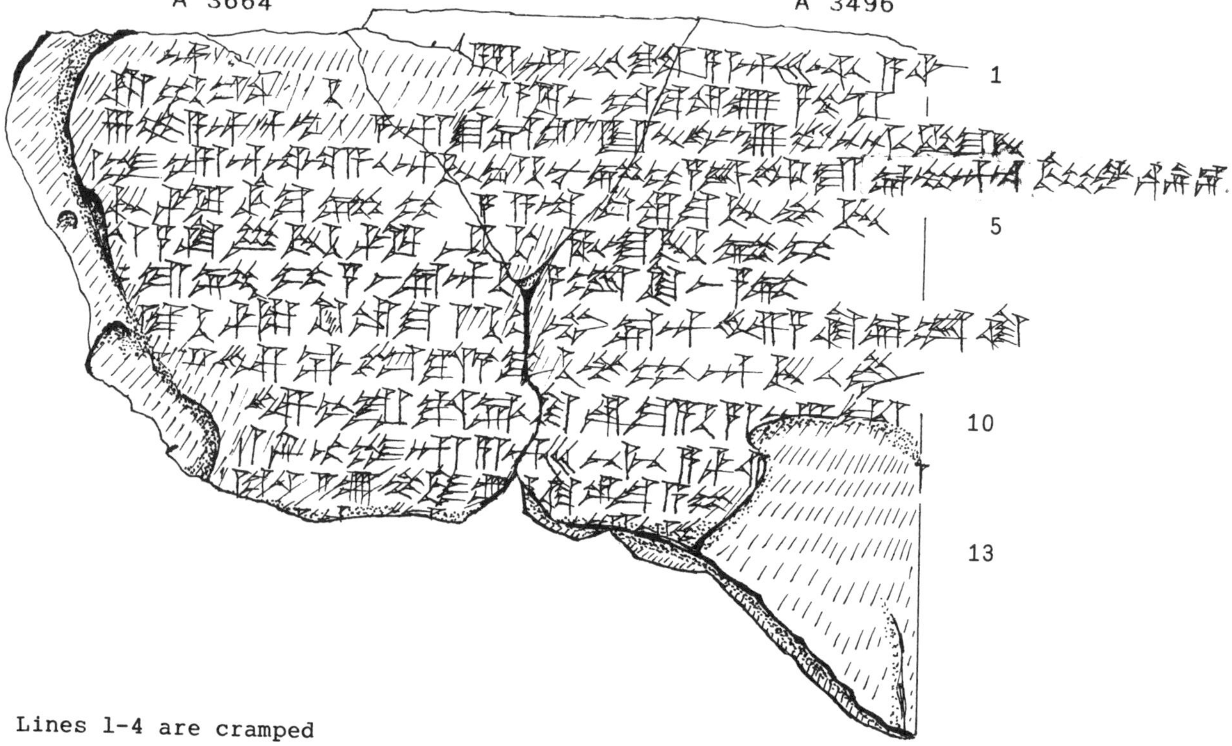

Lines 1-4 are cramped

Le.E. and Lo.E. destroyed)

17

R.

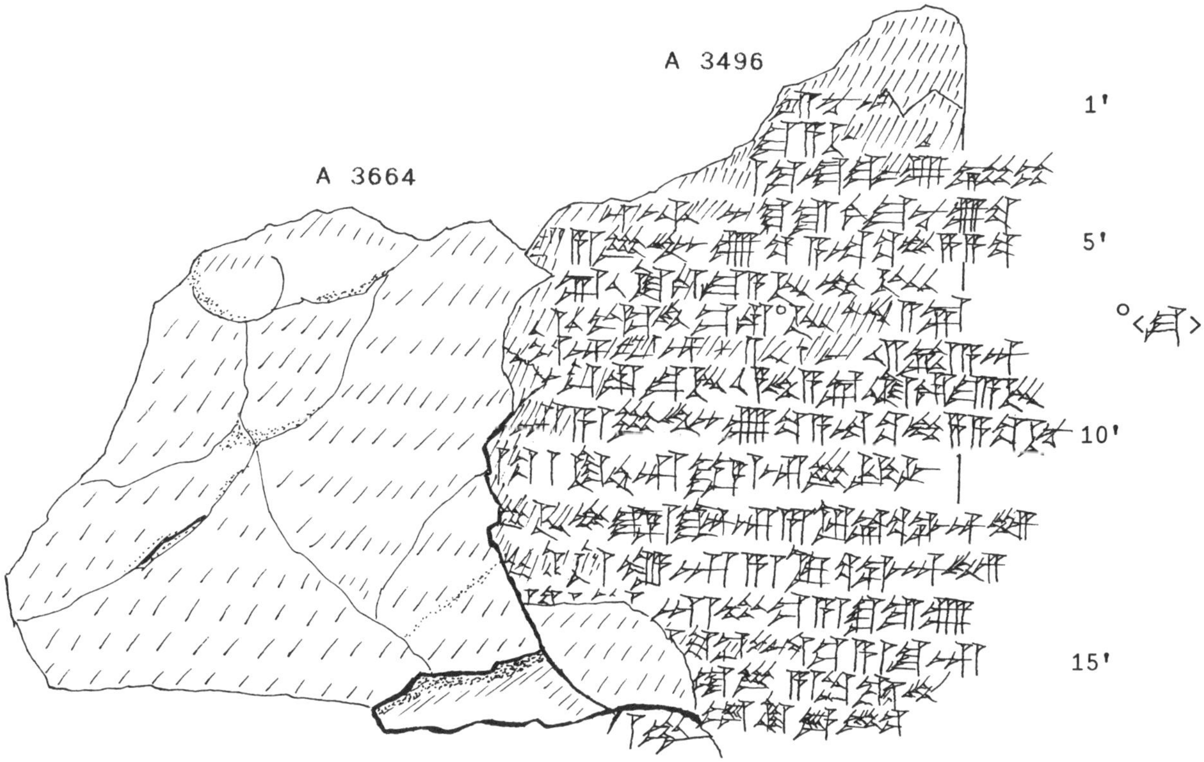

Writing from R. obtrudes onto R.E.

R.E.

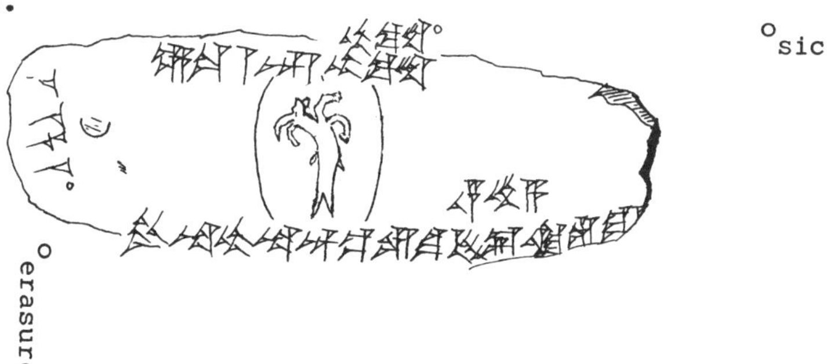

U.E.

18

O.

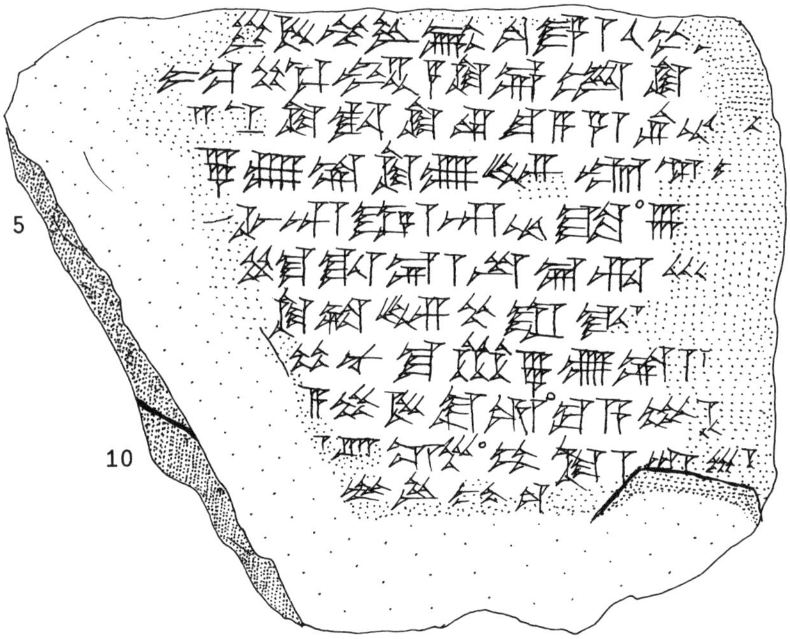

°sic, for iṭ

°sic, for šub

°sic, for gab

18

R.

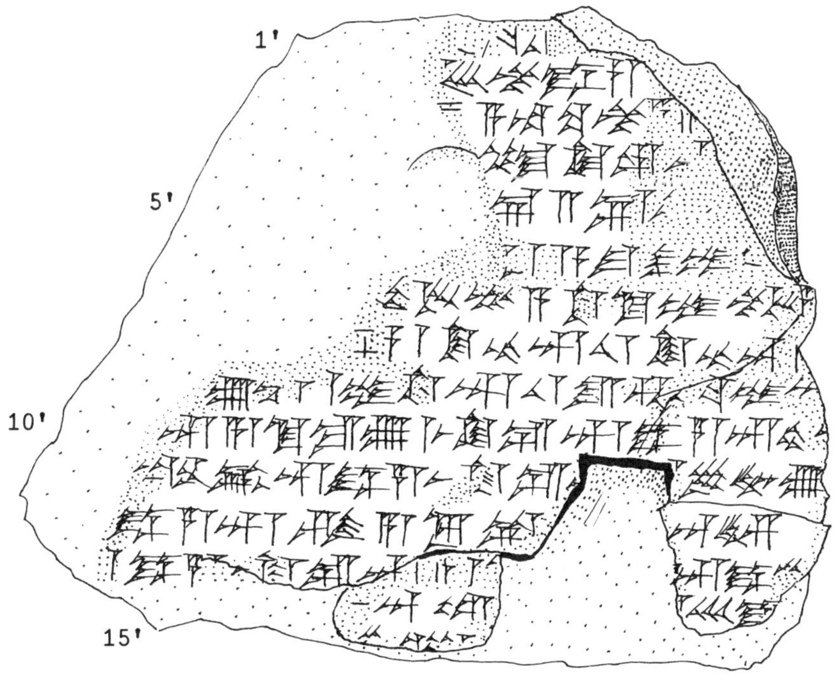

(Edges destroyed)

PLATE 36

19

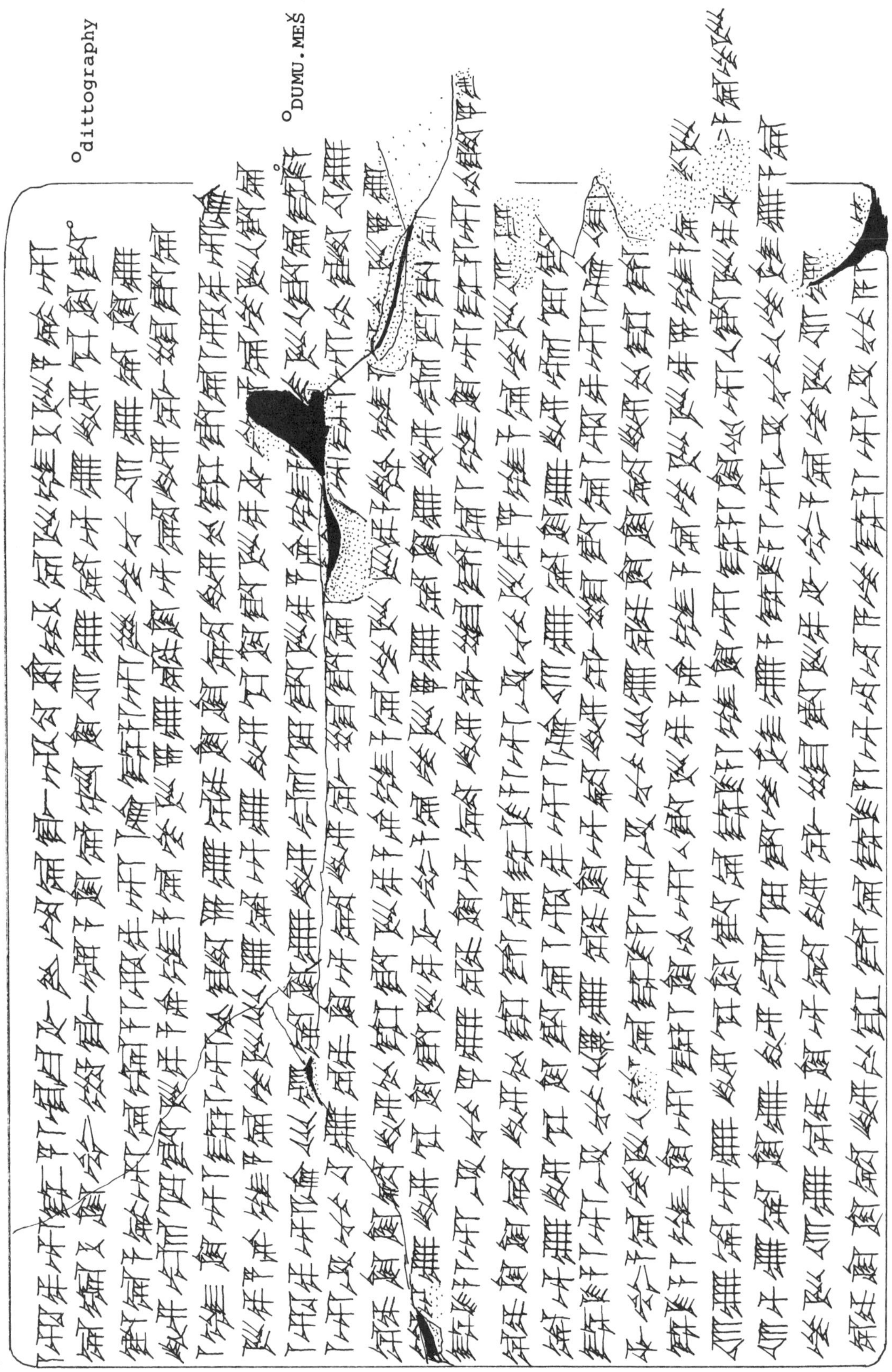

19

R.

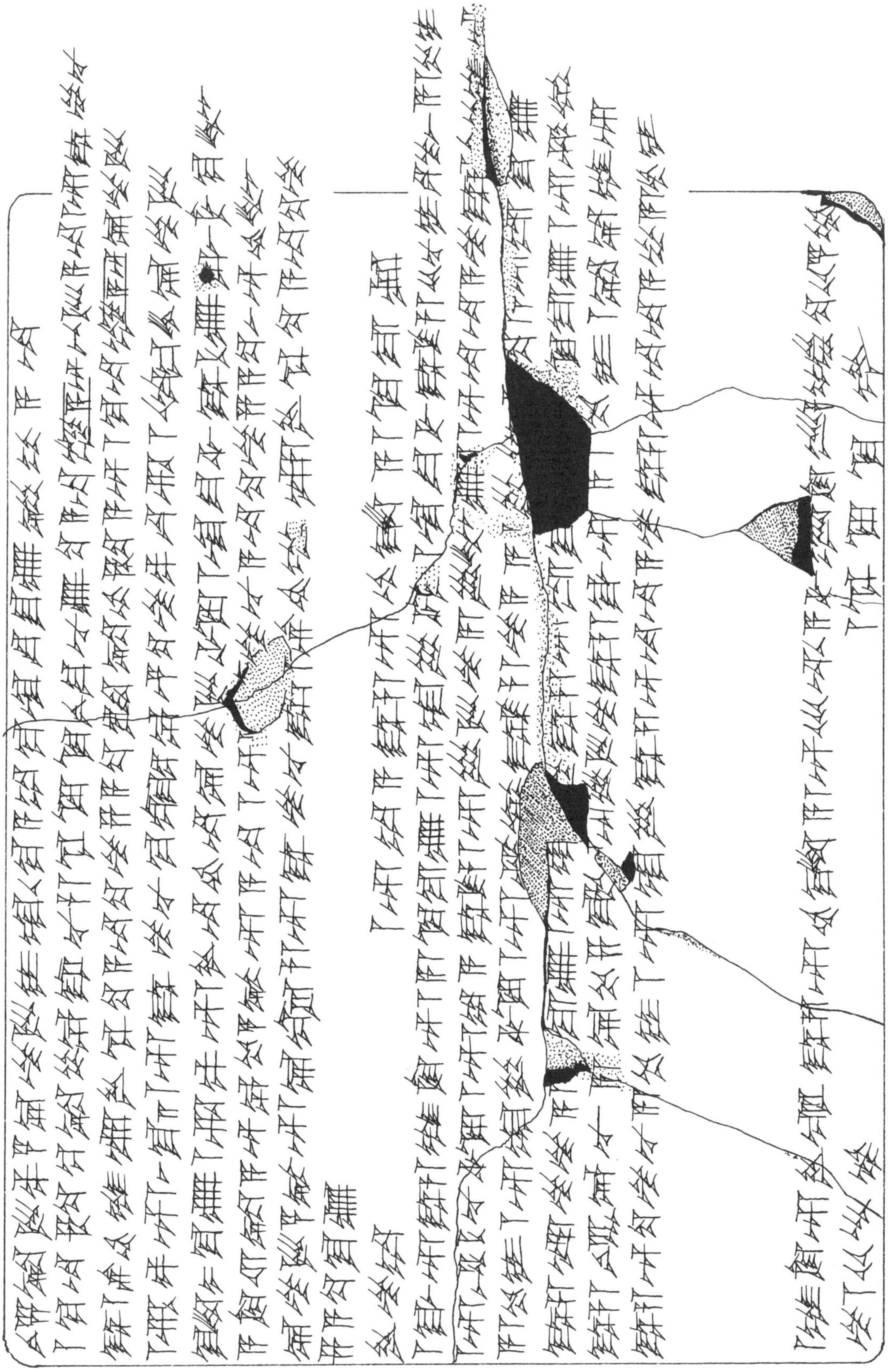

PLATE 38

19

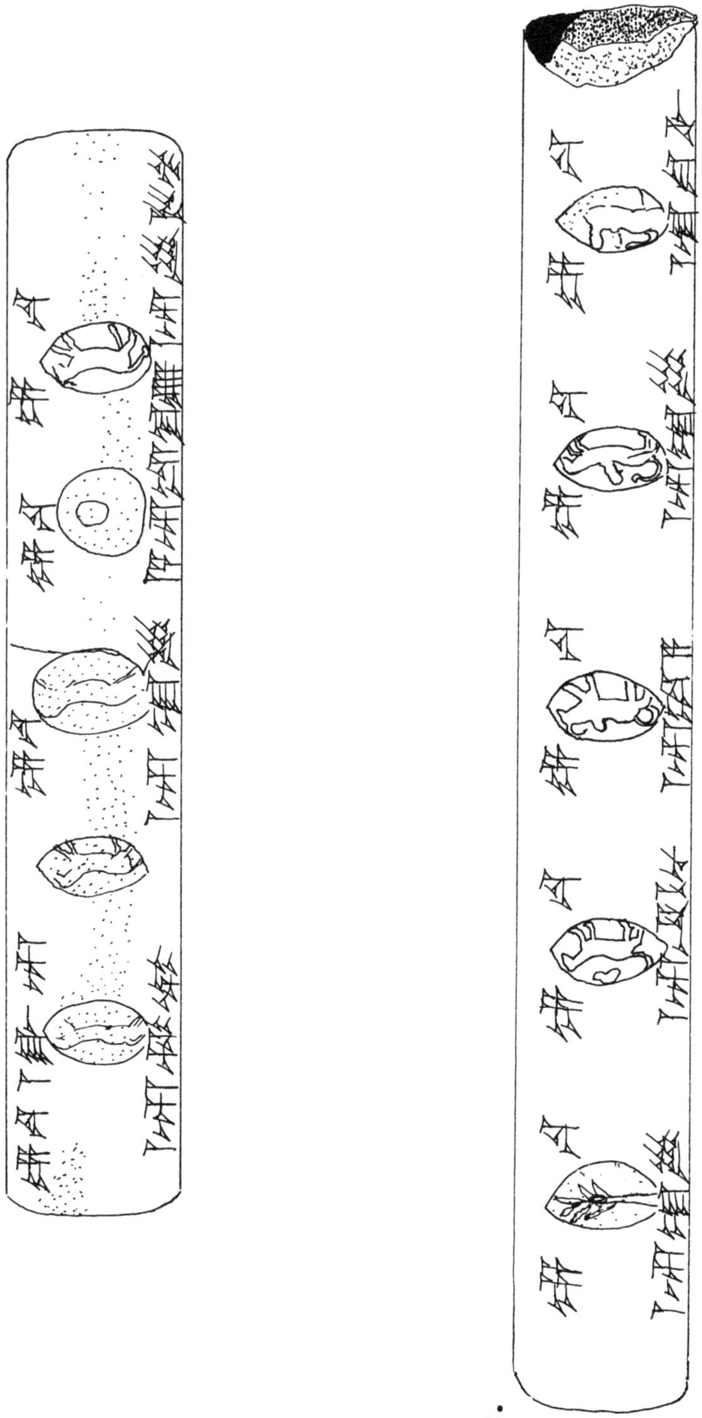

Le.E.

Lo.E.

19

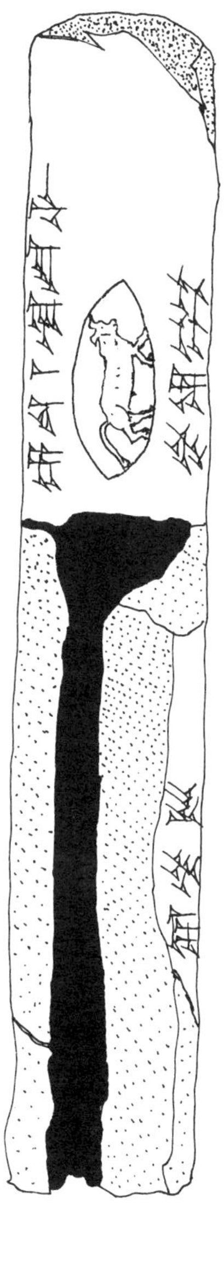

R.E.

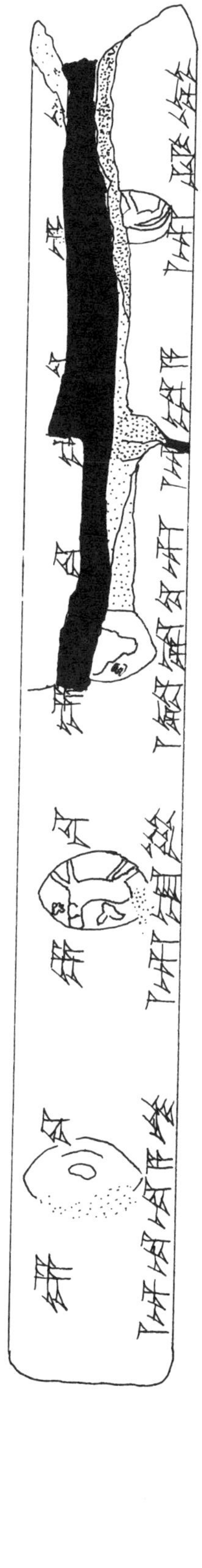

U.E.

PLATE 40

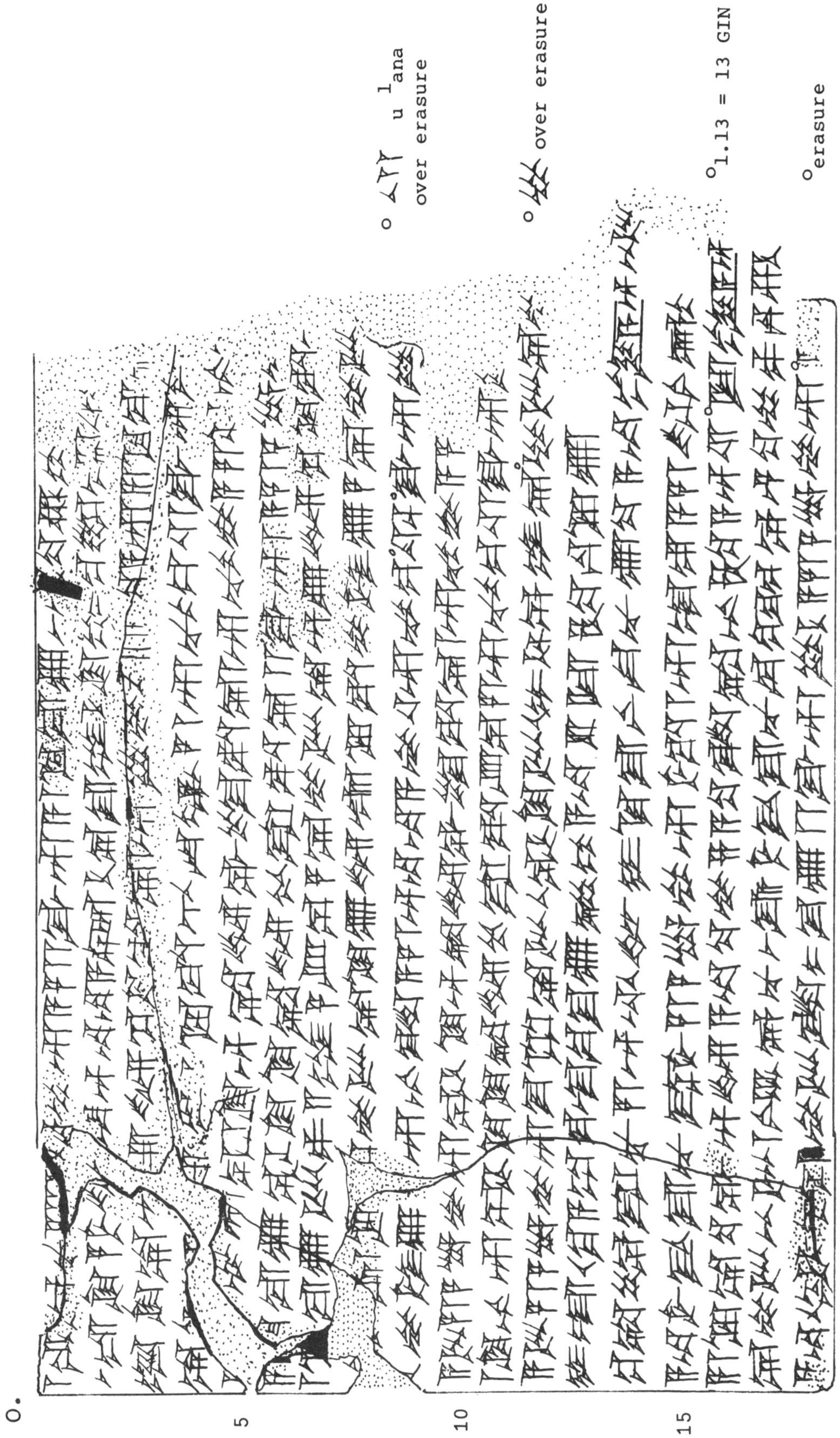

20

R.

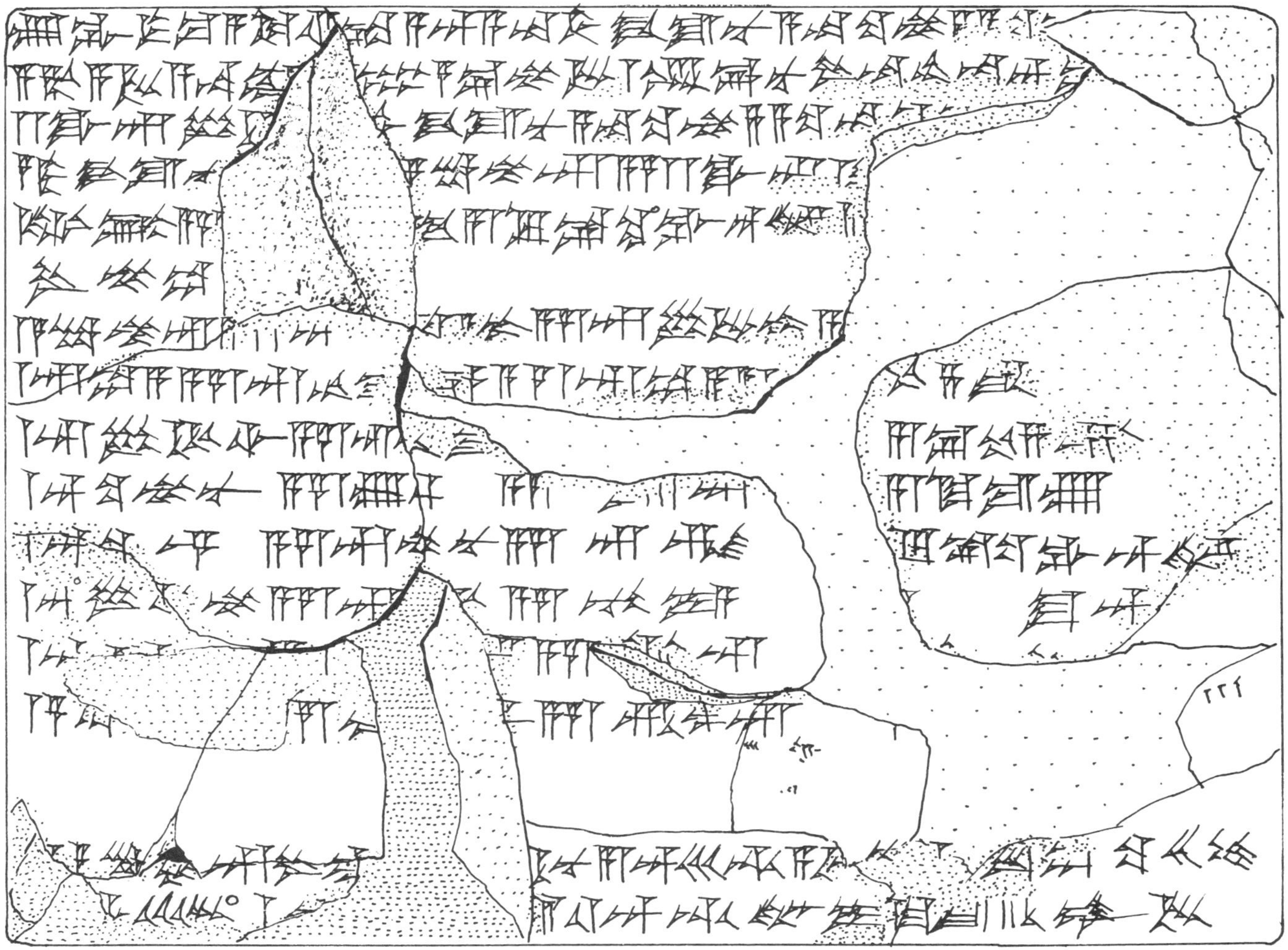

° over erasure

°<Y> (upright omitted)

° (no KÁM)

PLATE 41

PLATE 42

20

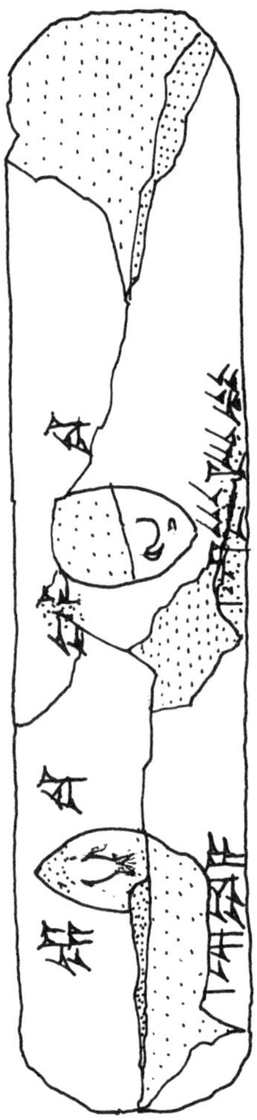

Le.E.

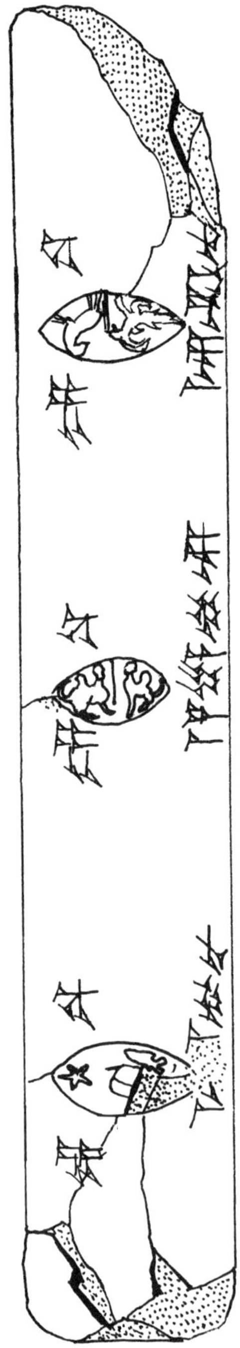

Lo.E.

20

R.E.

(Rest destroyed)

U.E.

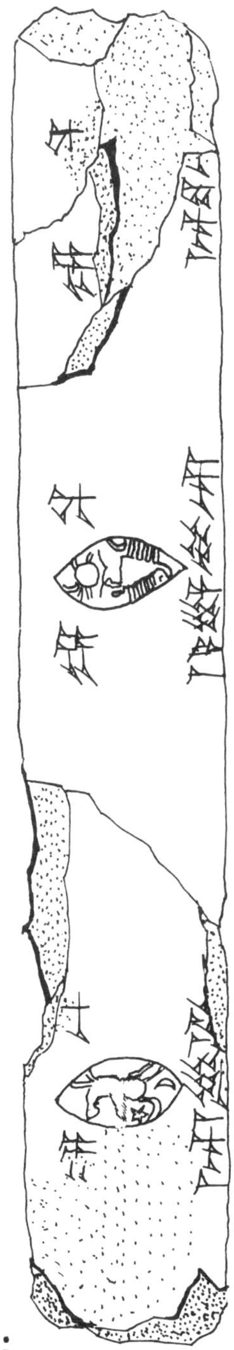

21

O.

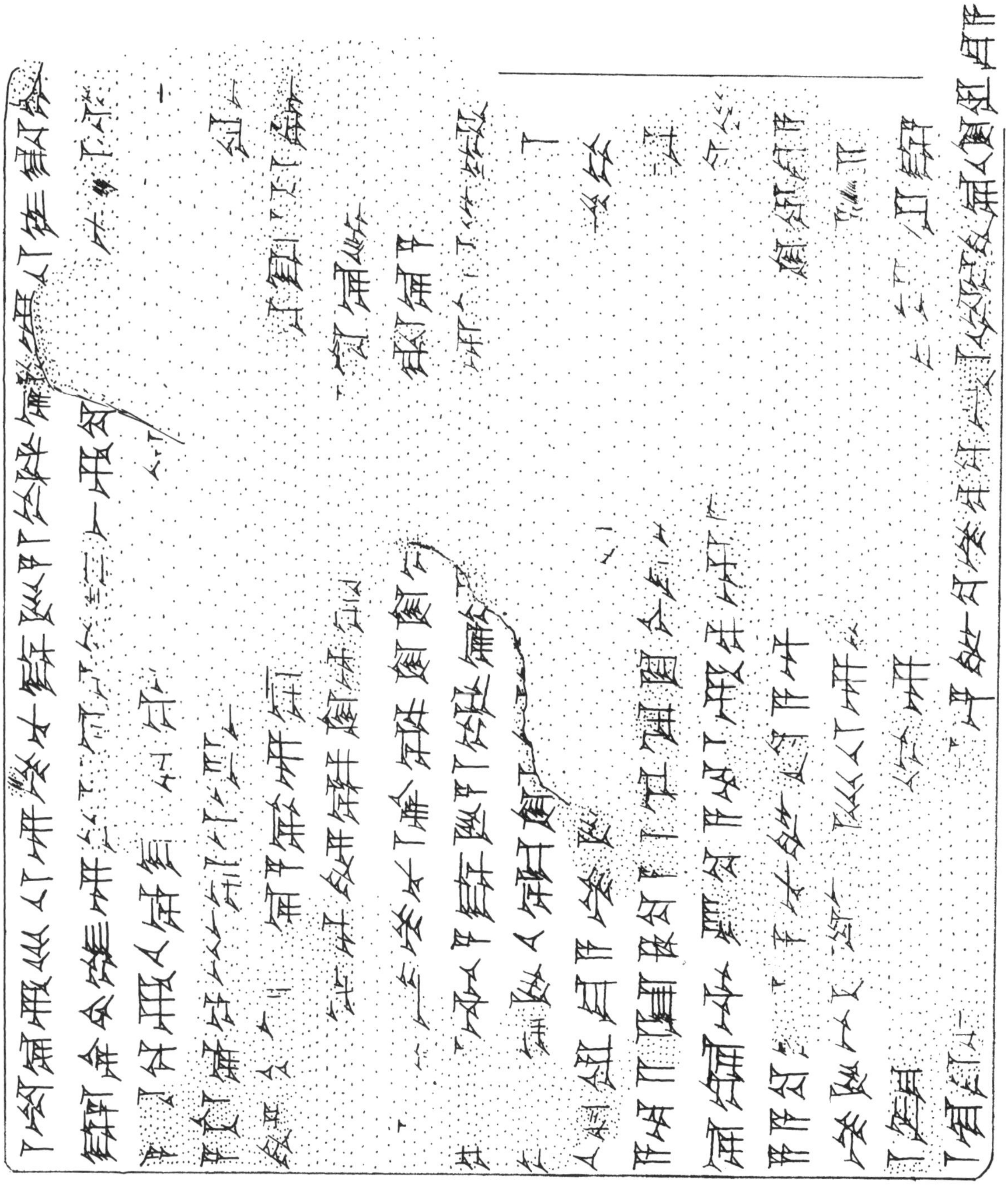

21

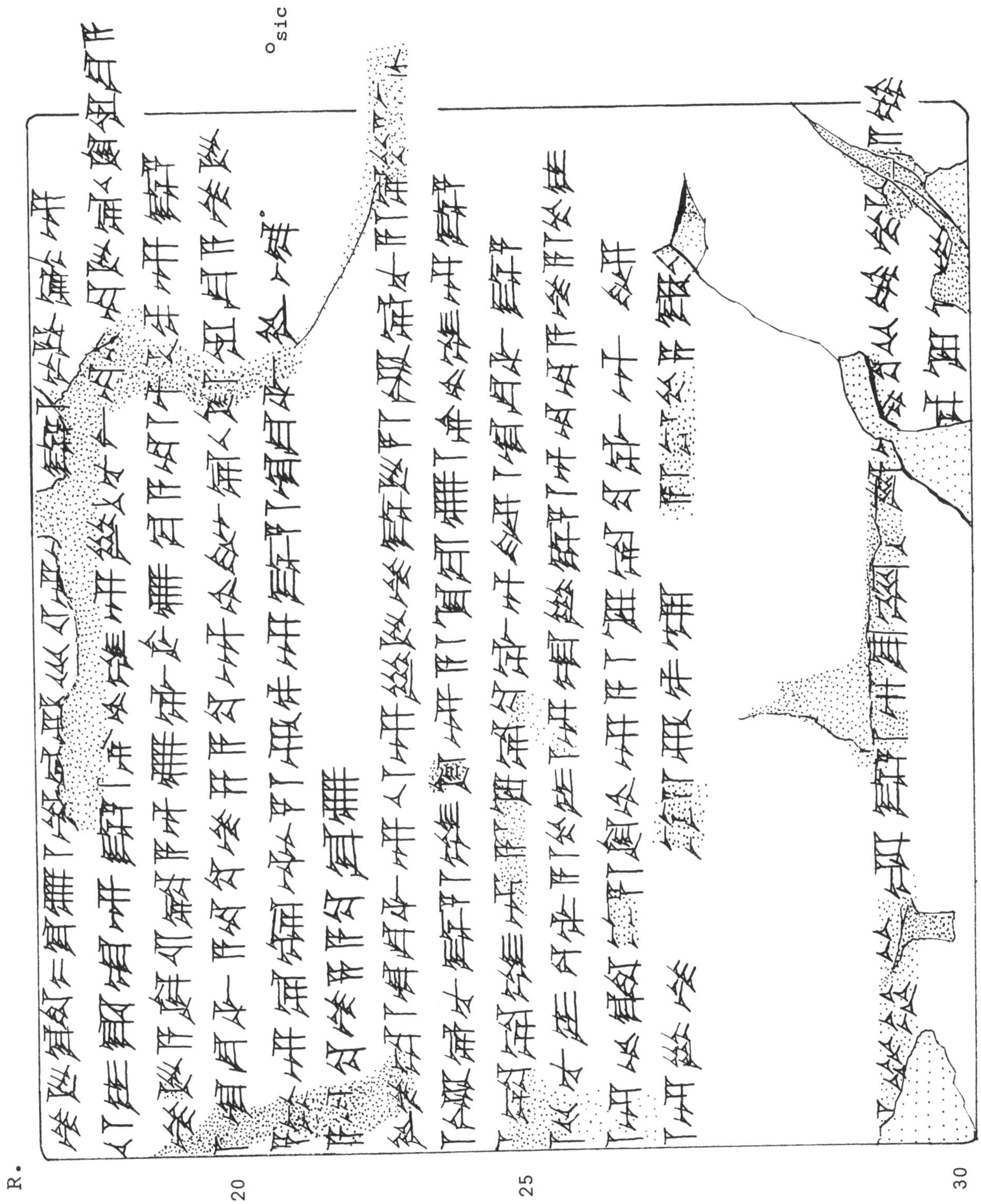

PLATE 46

21

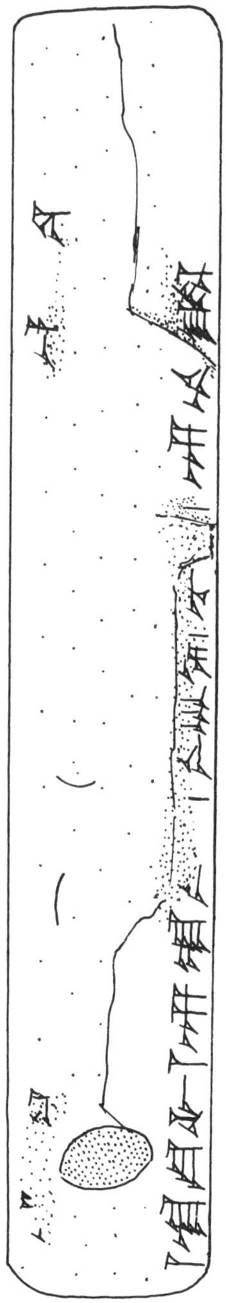

Lo.E.

(Le.E. blank)

PLATE 47

21

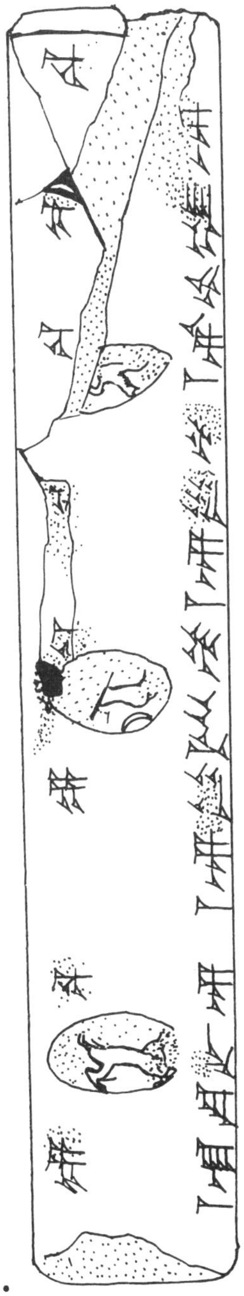

U.E.

R.E.

22

O.

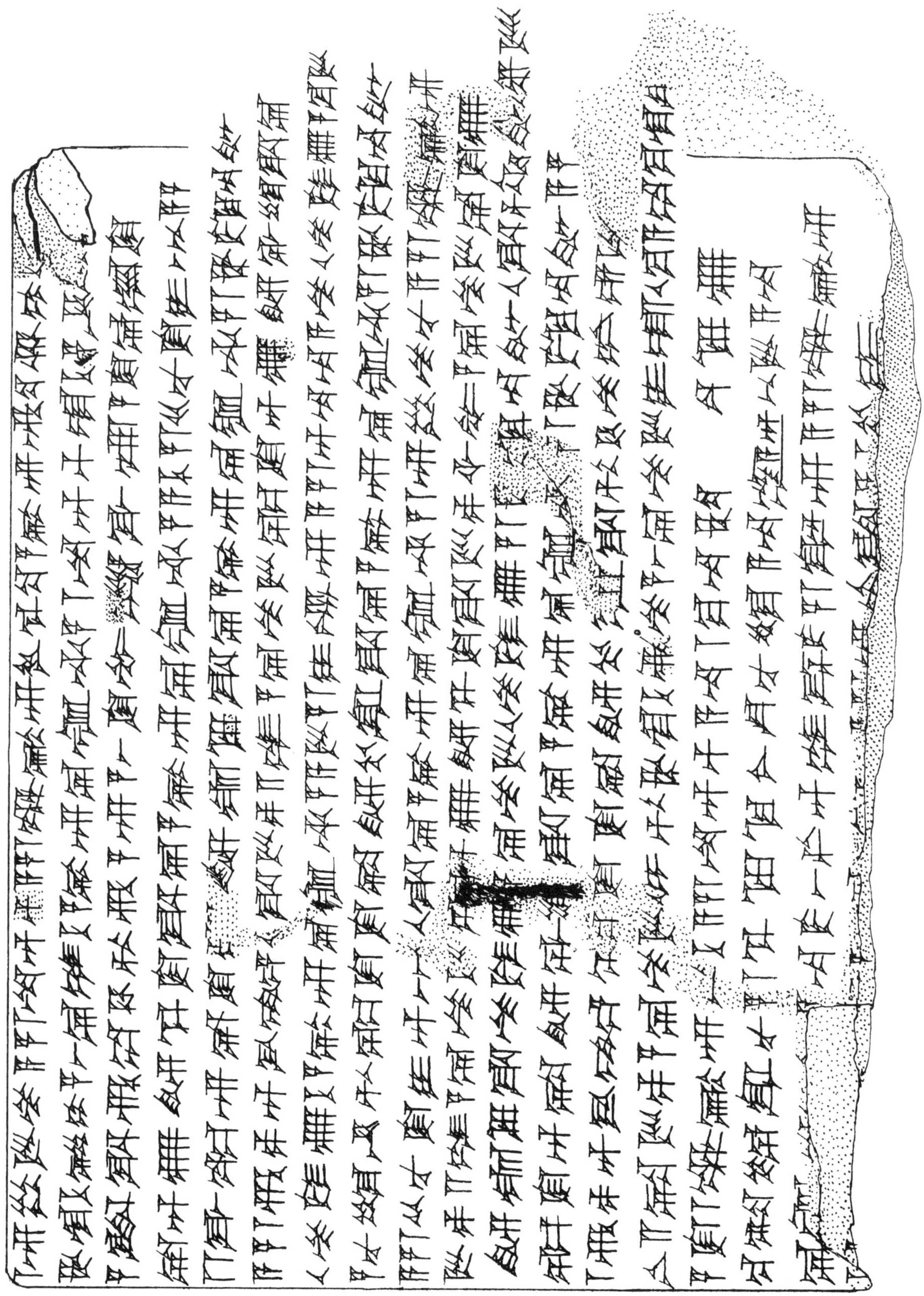

°GI over erasure

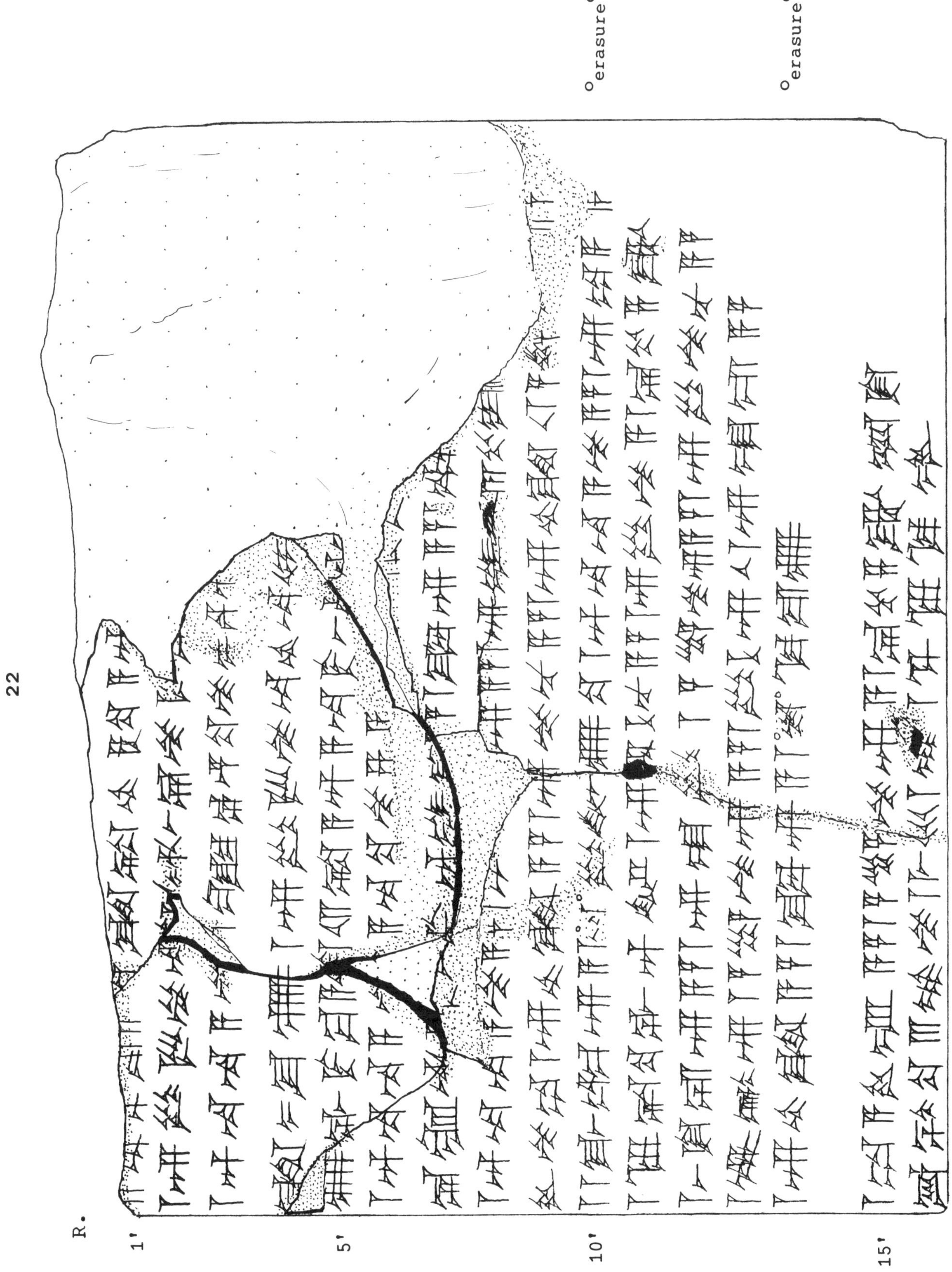
22
R.
1'
5'
10'
15'
°erasure°
°erasure°

22

Le.E.

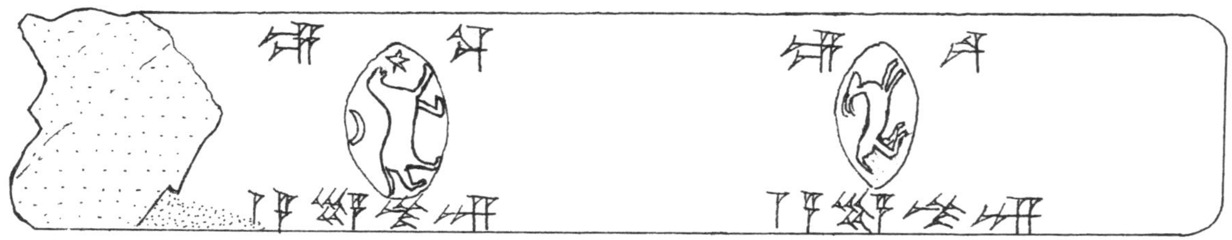

Lo.E.

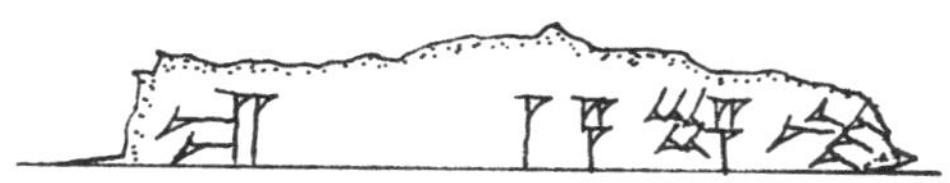

(Rest of Lo. E. destroyed)

PLATE 51

22

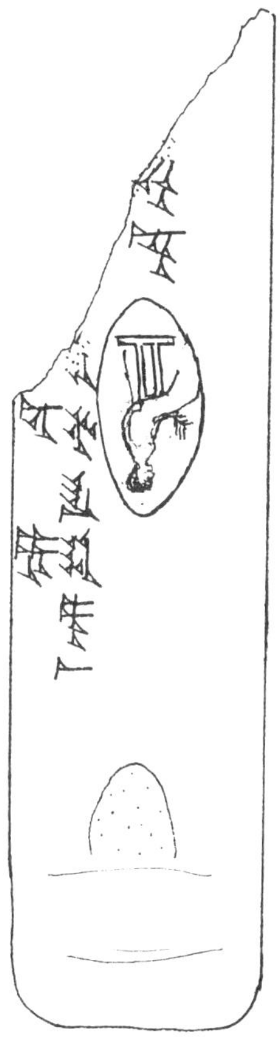

R.E.

U.E.

PLATE 52

23

° [sign] over erasure

O.

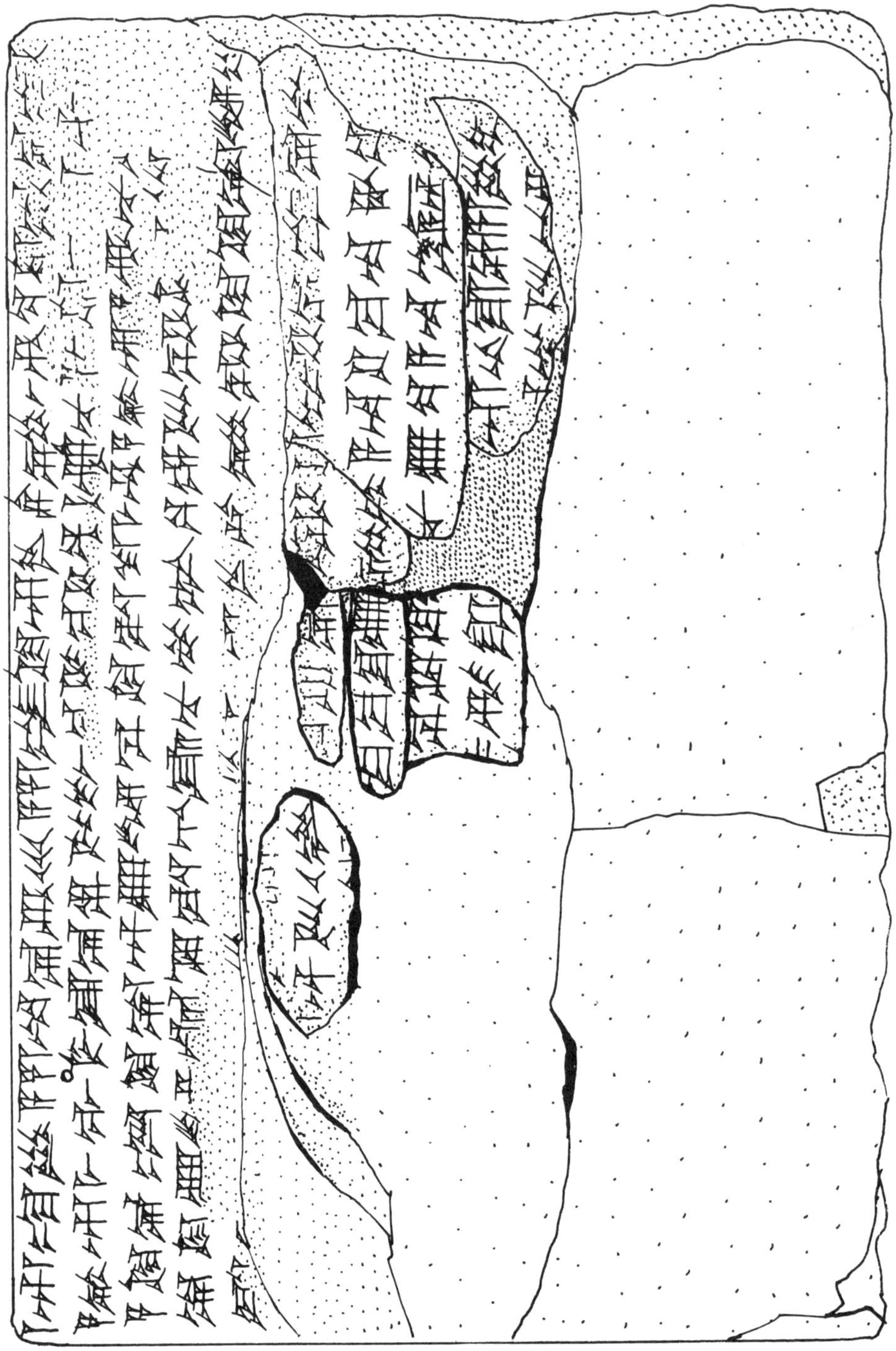

23

°erasure

R.

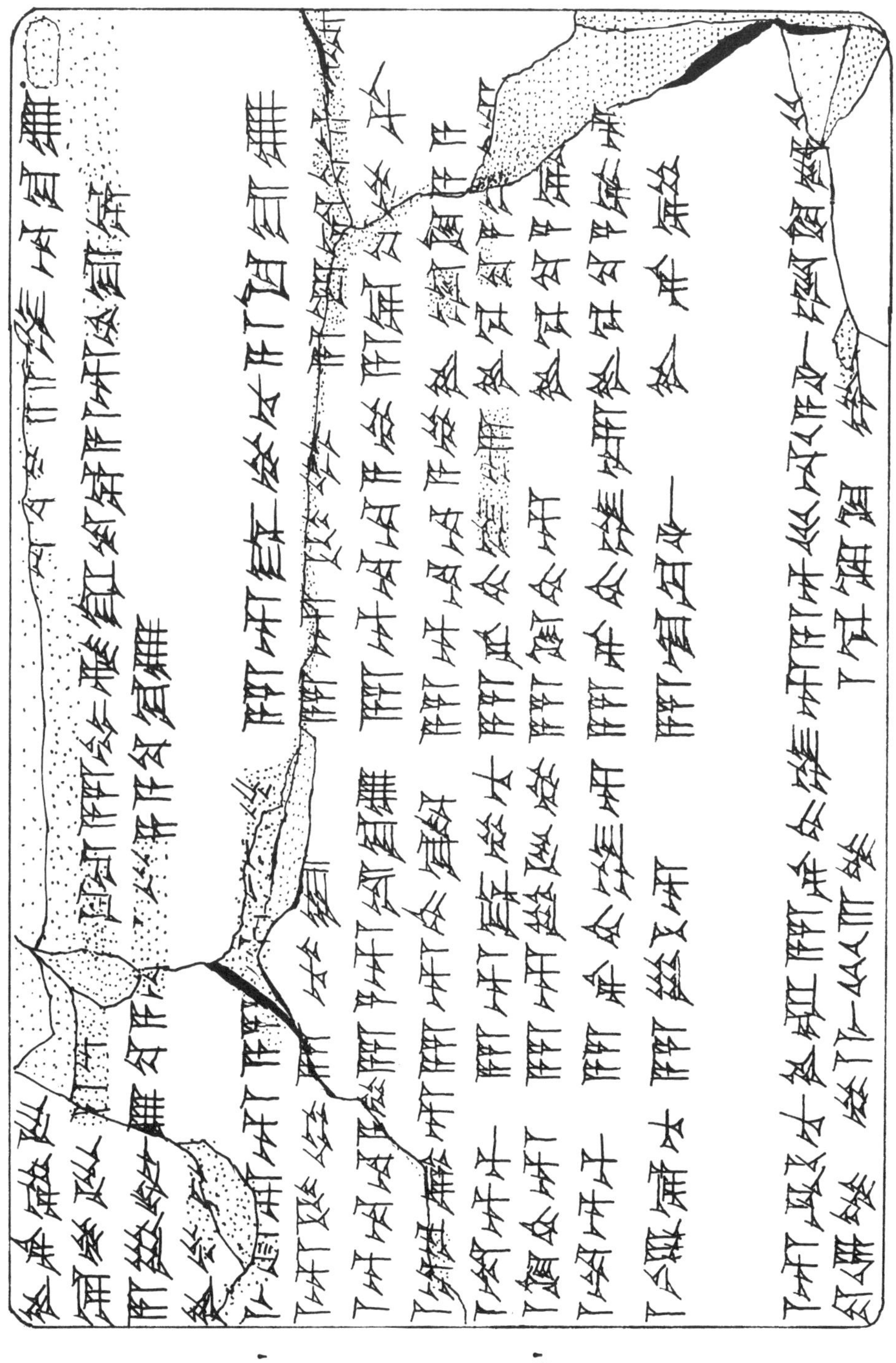

5'

10'

23

Le.E.

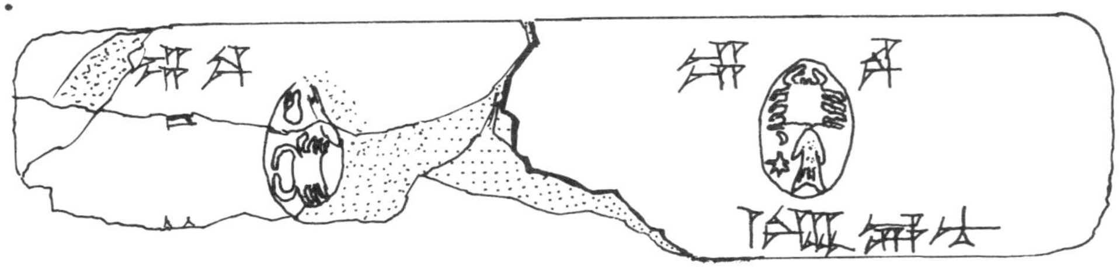

Lo.E.

PN at lower left

(Rest destroyed)

PN at lower right

23

R.E.

(Rest destroyed)

U.E.

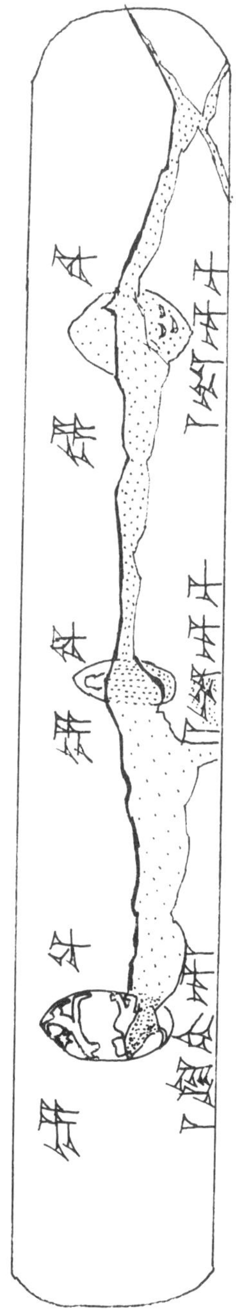

24

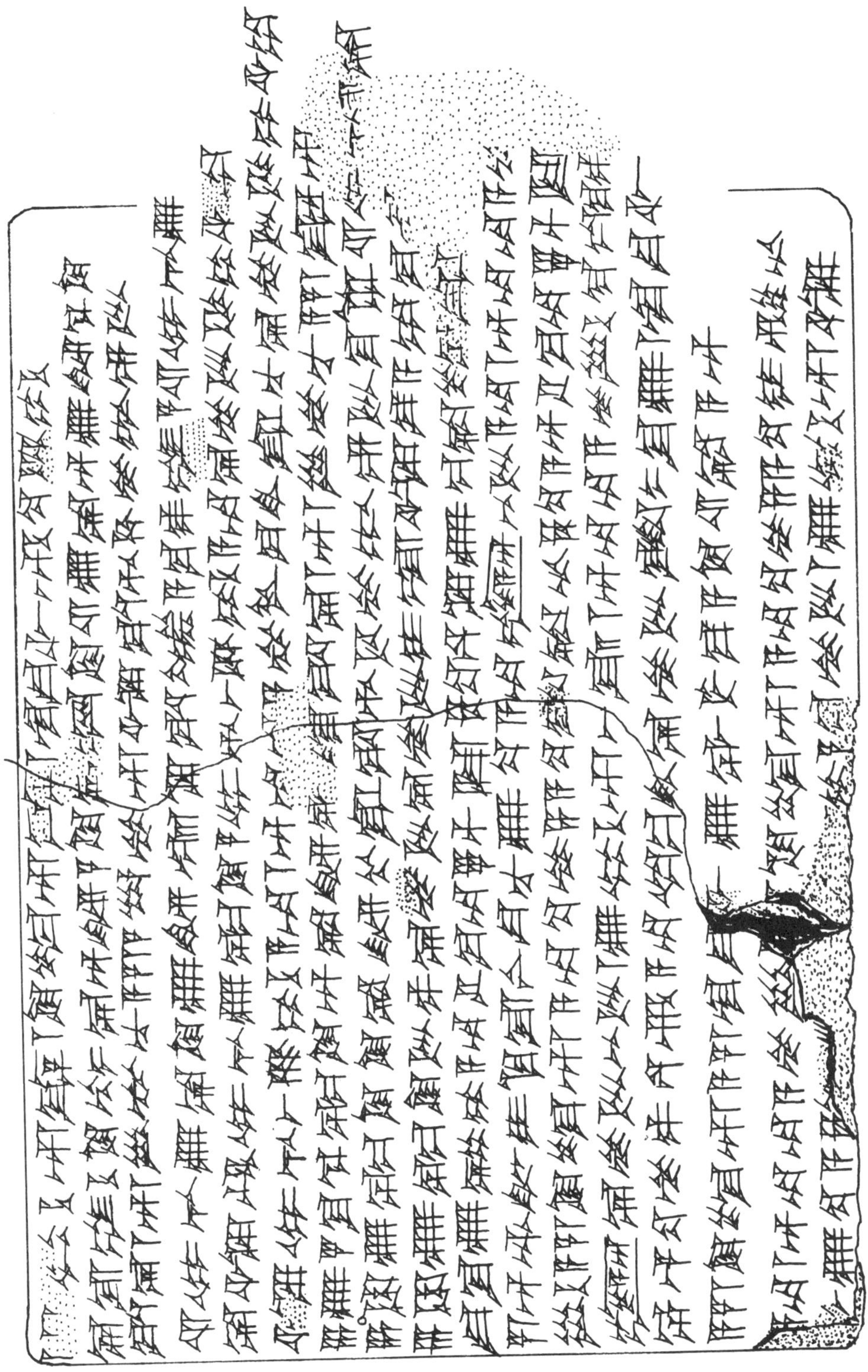

O.

(Reverse destroyed)

°for [sign] °for [sign]

24

Le.E.

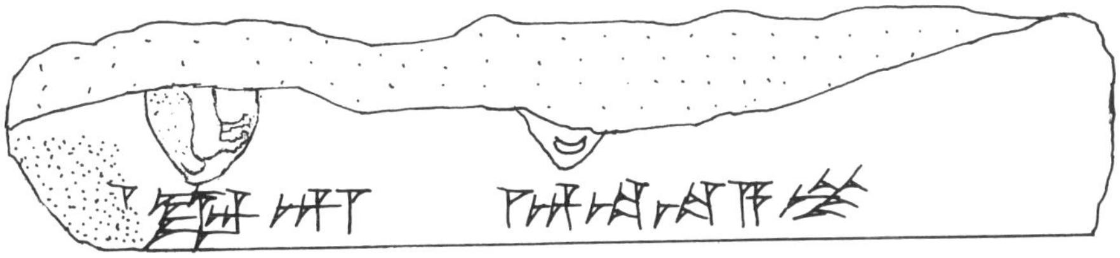

Lo.E.

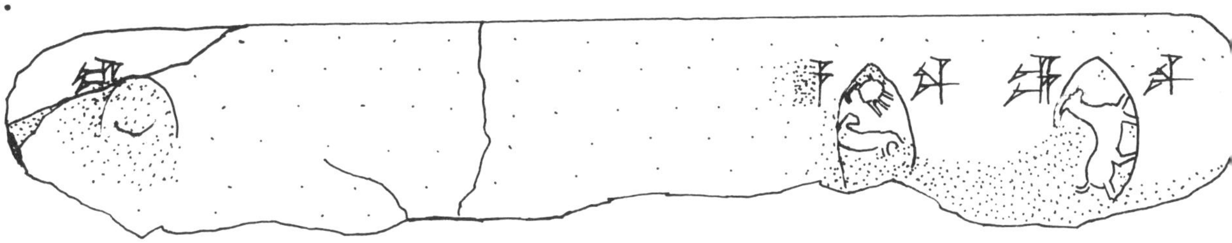

U.E.

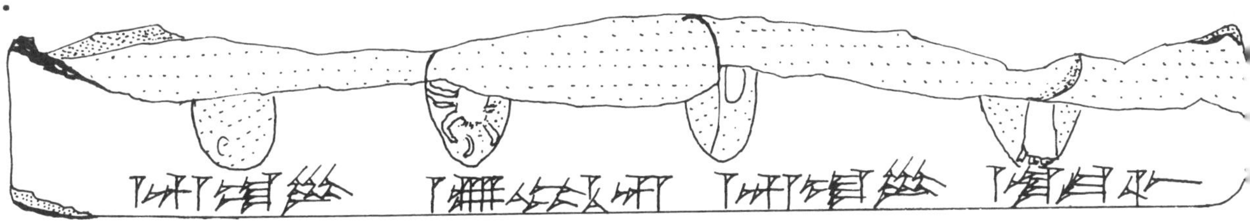

R.E.

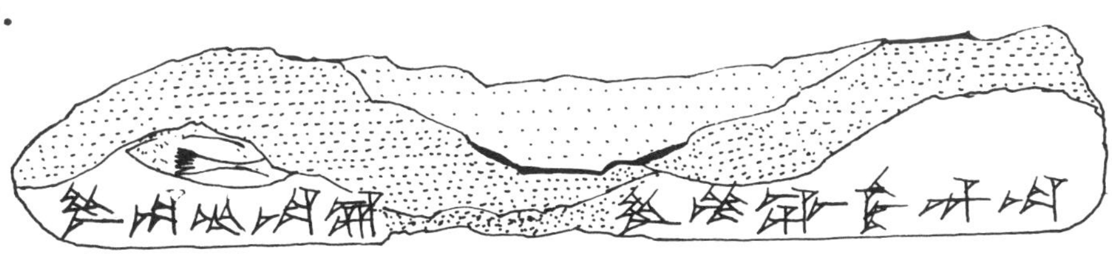

25

O.

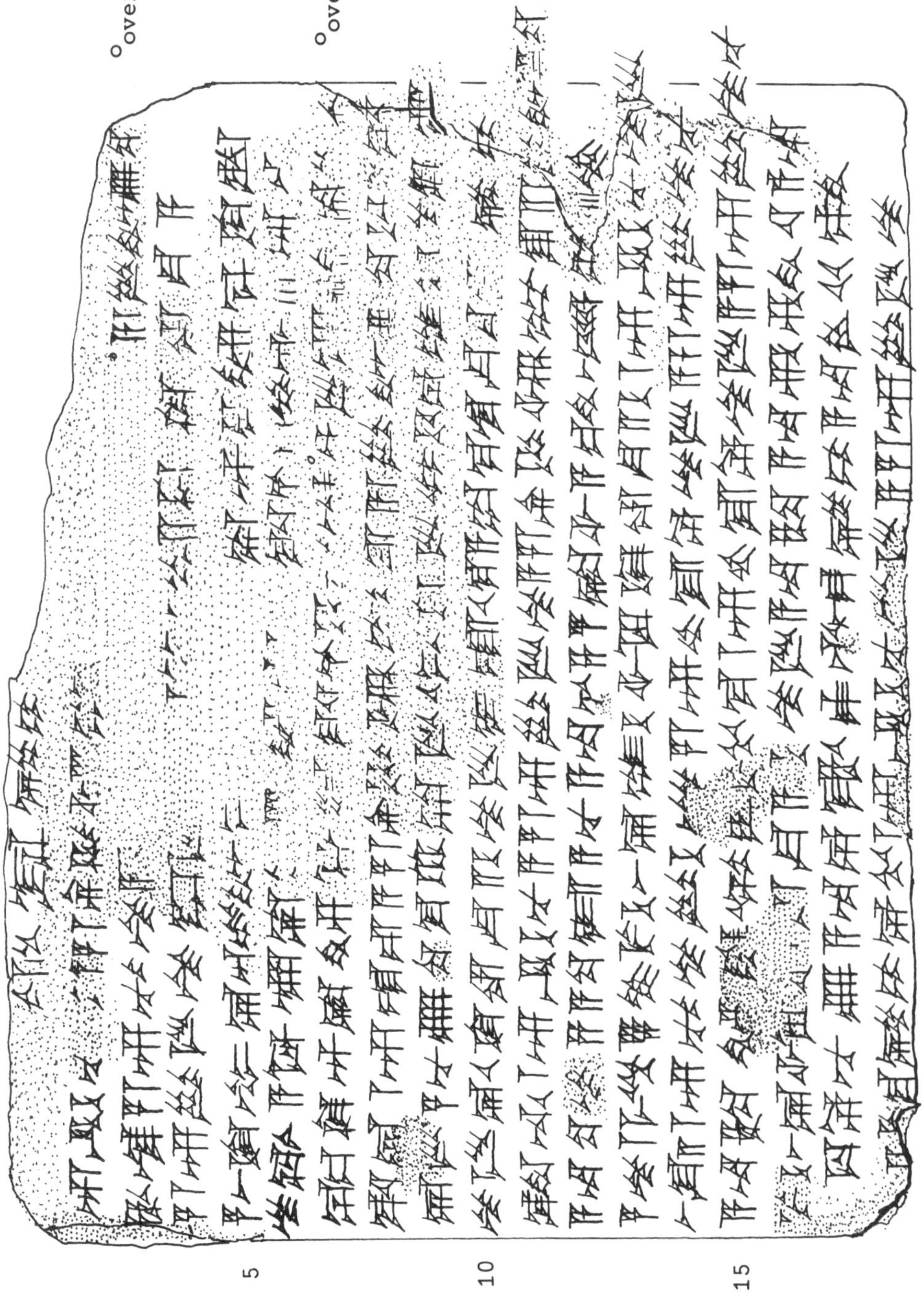

25

R.

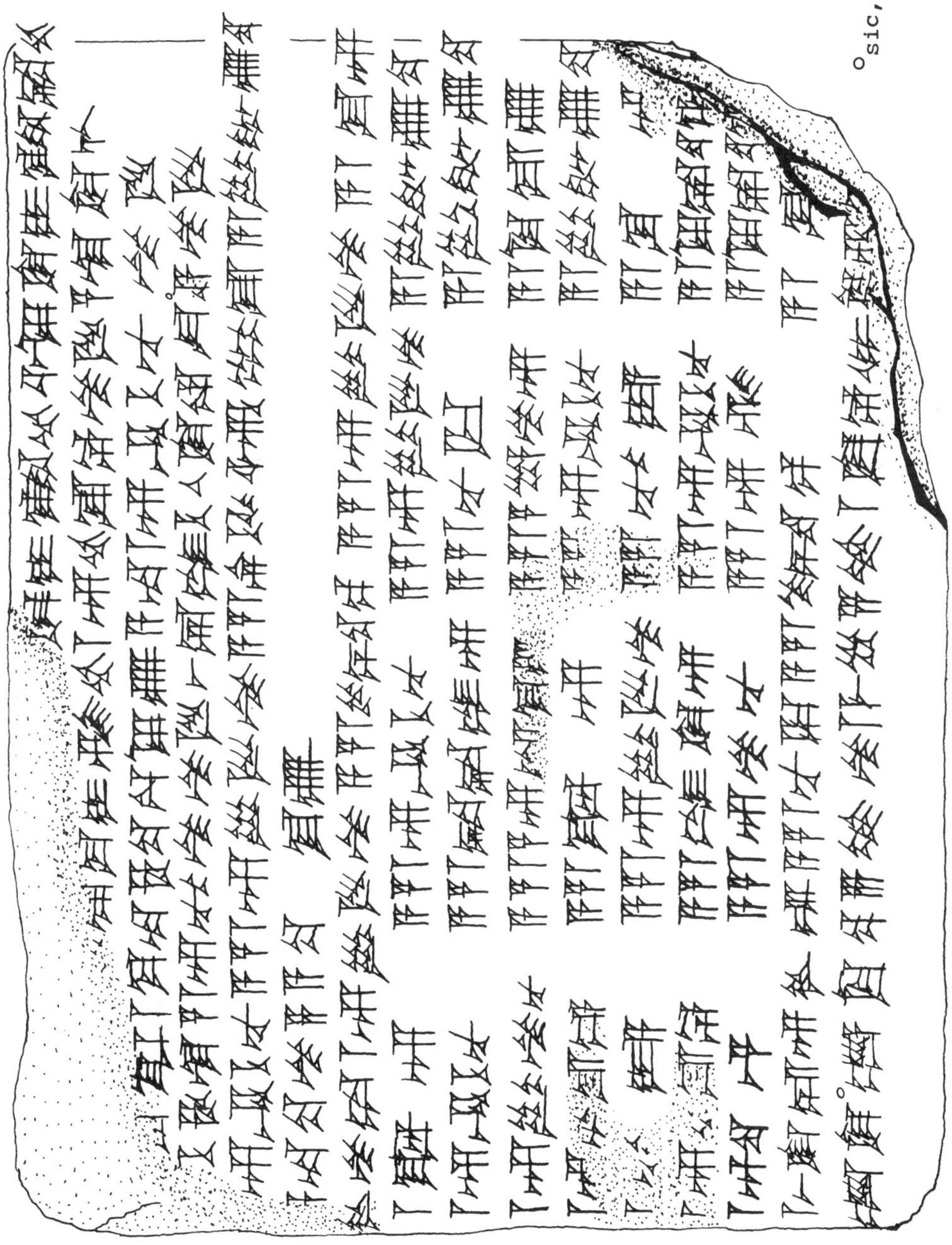

°over erasures

°sic, for

PLATE 60

25

°erasure

Le.E.

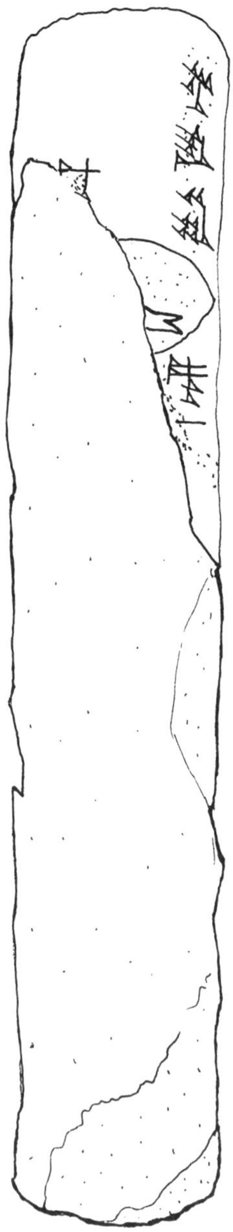

Lo.E.

25

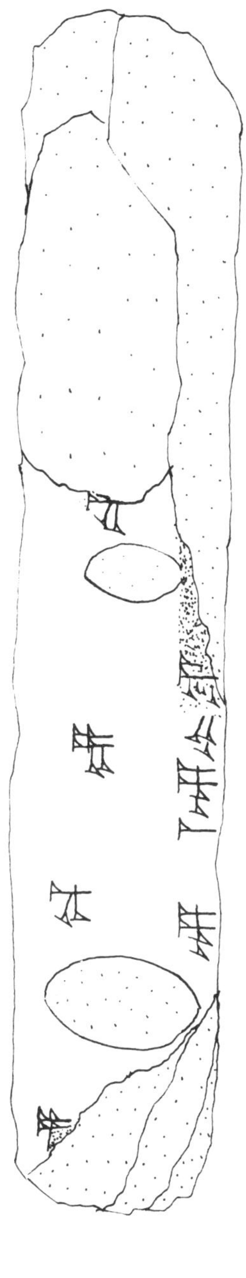

U.E.

R.E.

PLATE 62

26

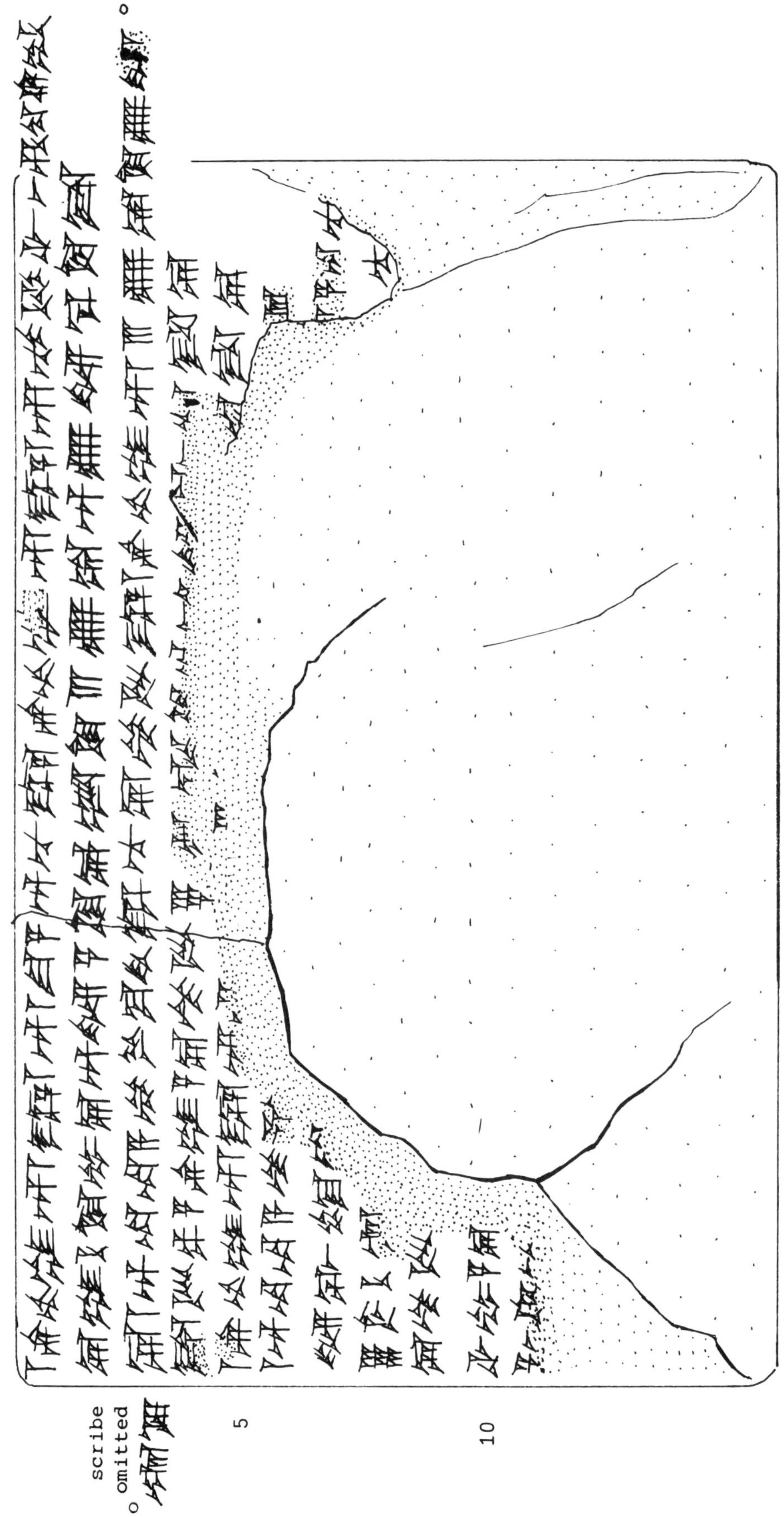

26

R.

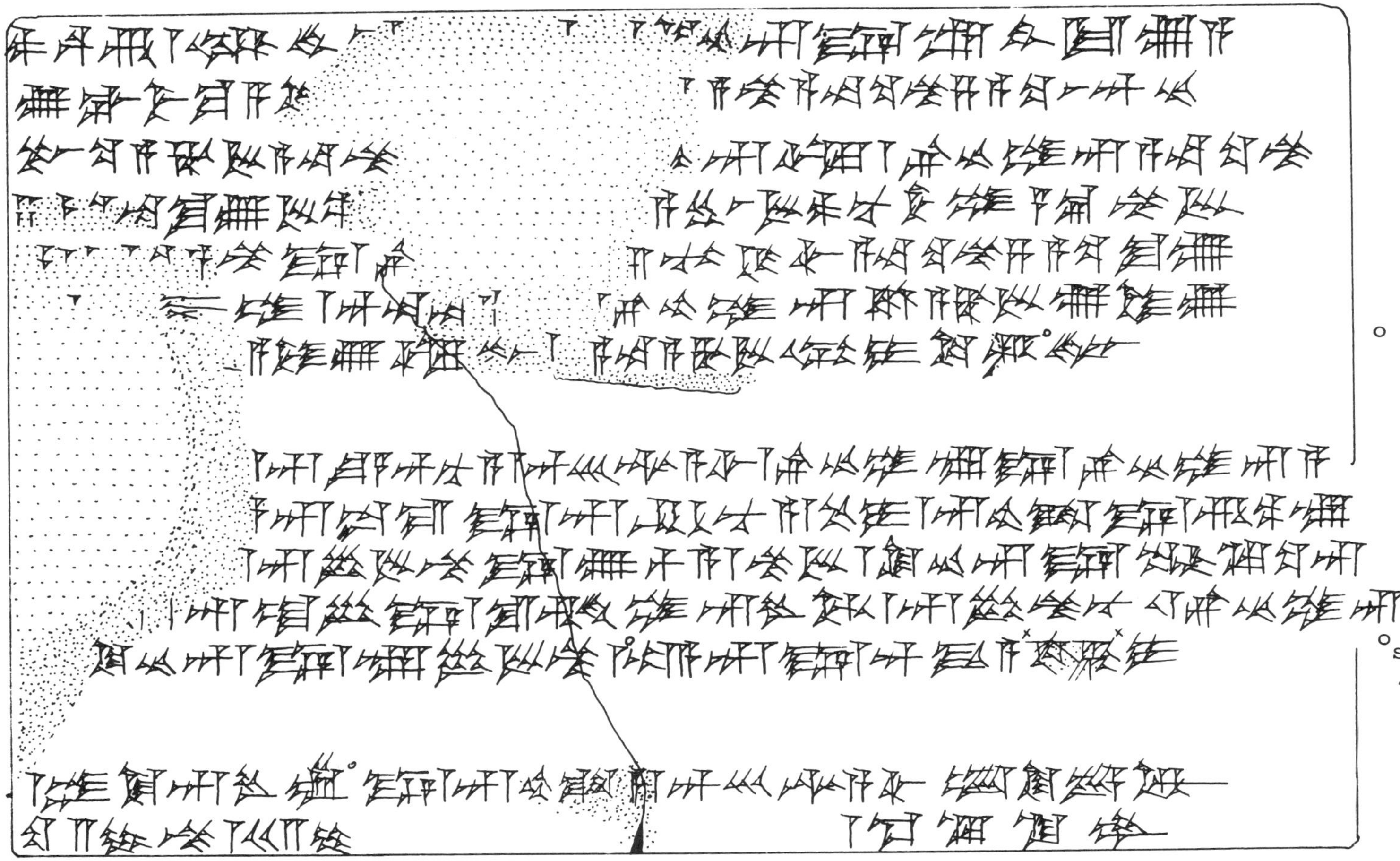

° over erasure

°sic, for ?

x sic, for ^{ld}GAŠAN.A.<MU> A ^{I}KUR-i?x

° over erasure

PLATE 64

26

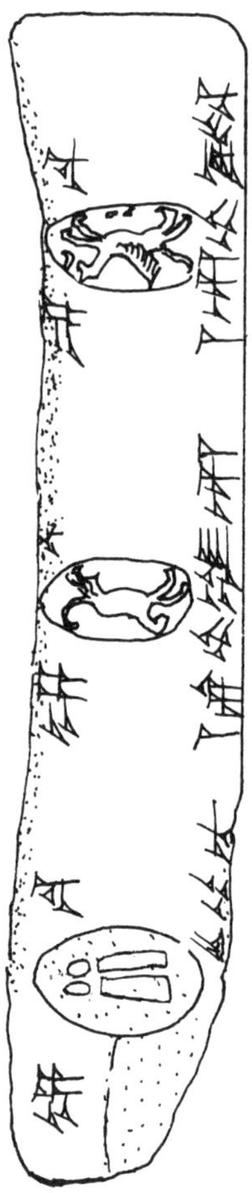

Le.E.

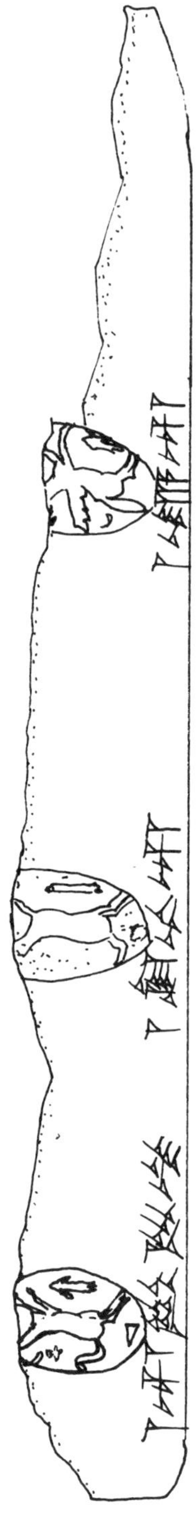

Lo.E.

26

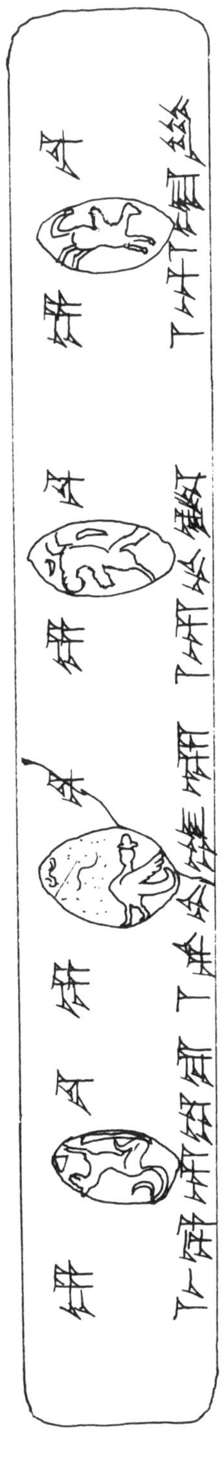

U.E.

R.E.

27

O.

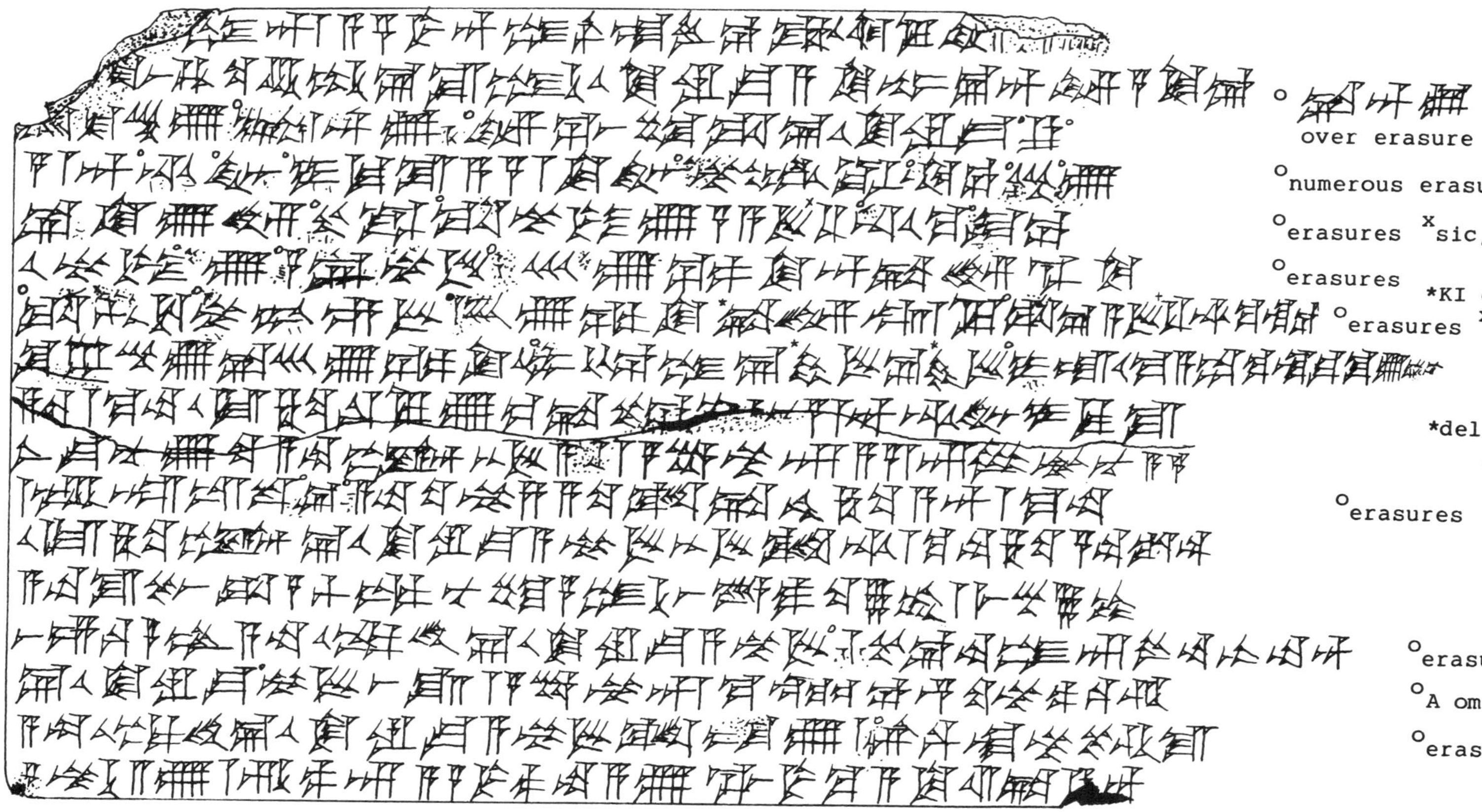

° over erasure ° ° over erasure °

° numerous erasures

° erasures ˣ sic, for [sign]

° erasures *KI omitted +sic, for [sign]

° erasures ˣ SIL. ● 30? dup. 40

° erasures

*delete? or read: ḪI.A?

° erasures

° erasures

° A omitted

° erasure

°erasures

° [signs] over erasures°

x dittography x

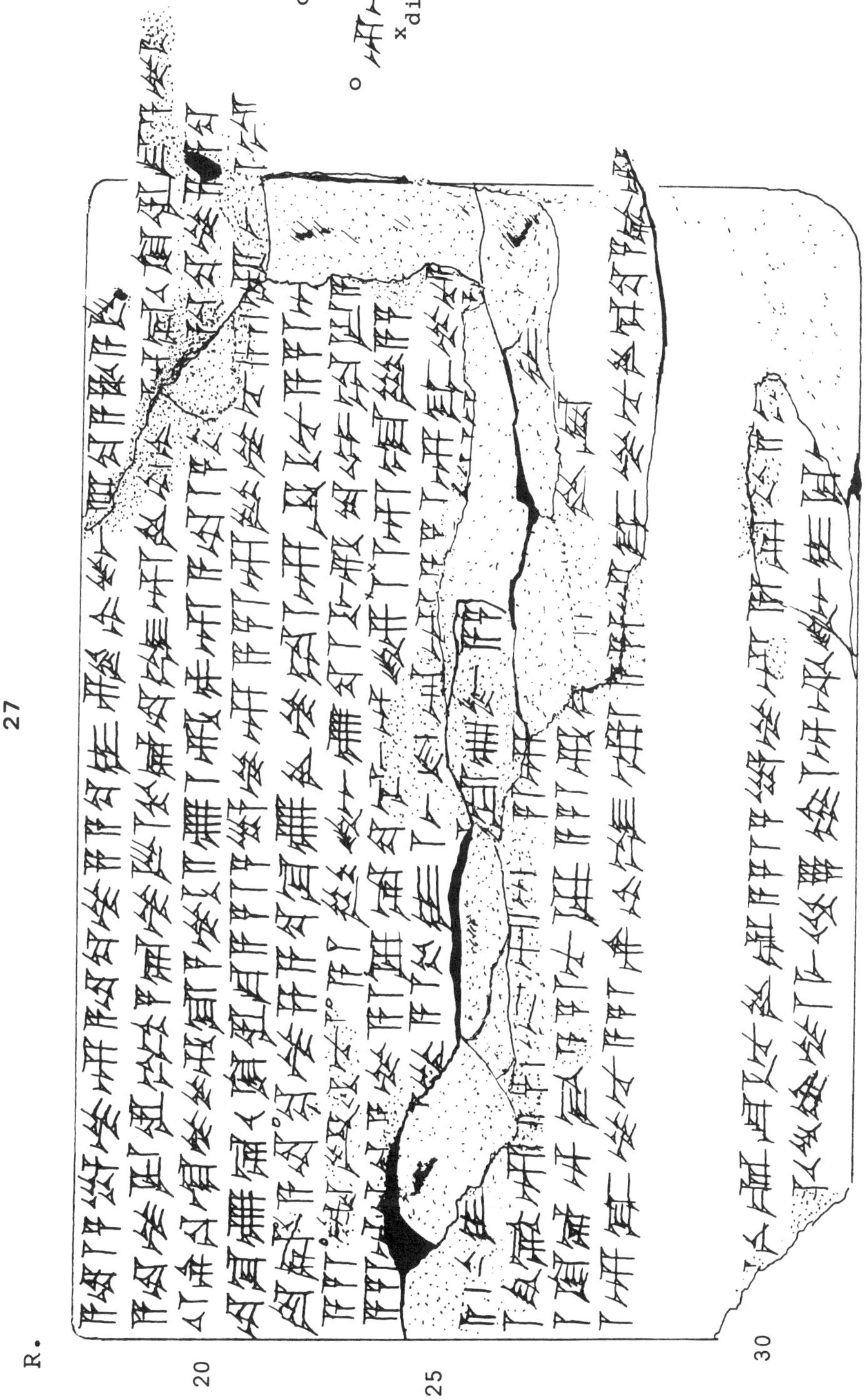

PLATE 68

27

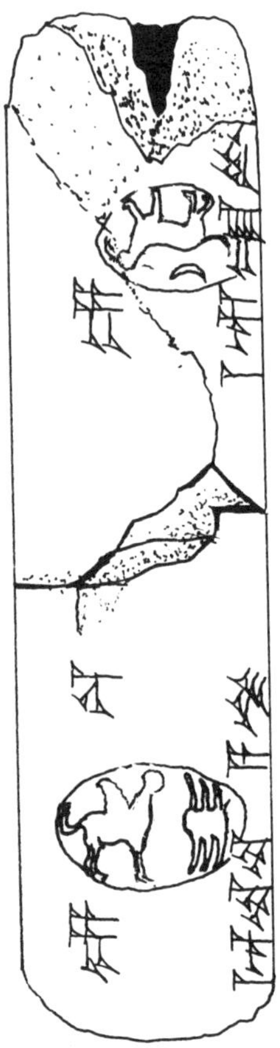

Le.E.

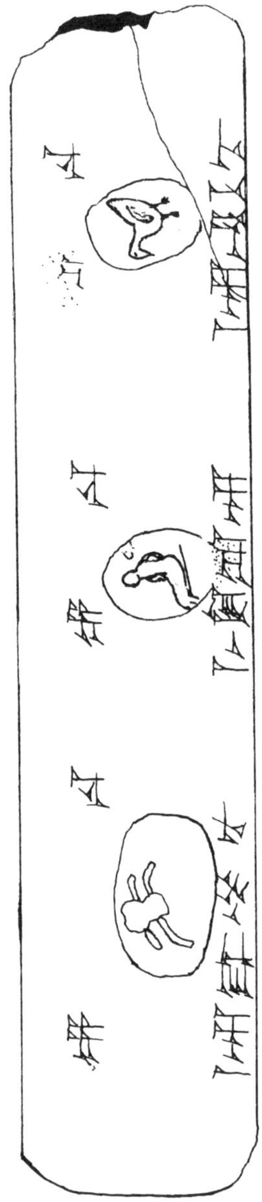

Lo.E.

27

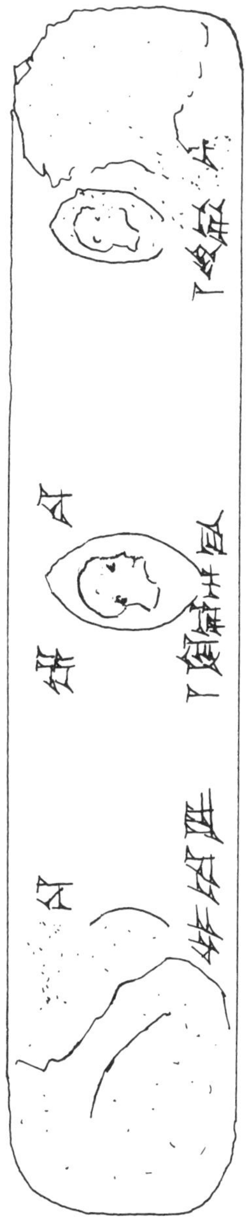

U.E.

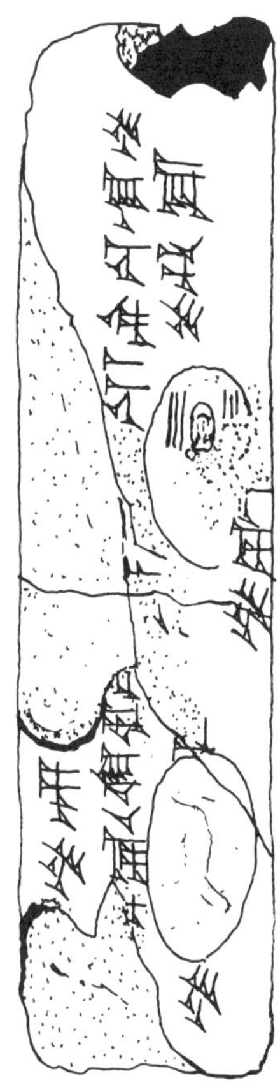

R.E.

28

O.

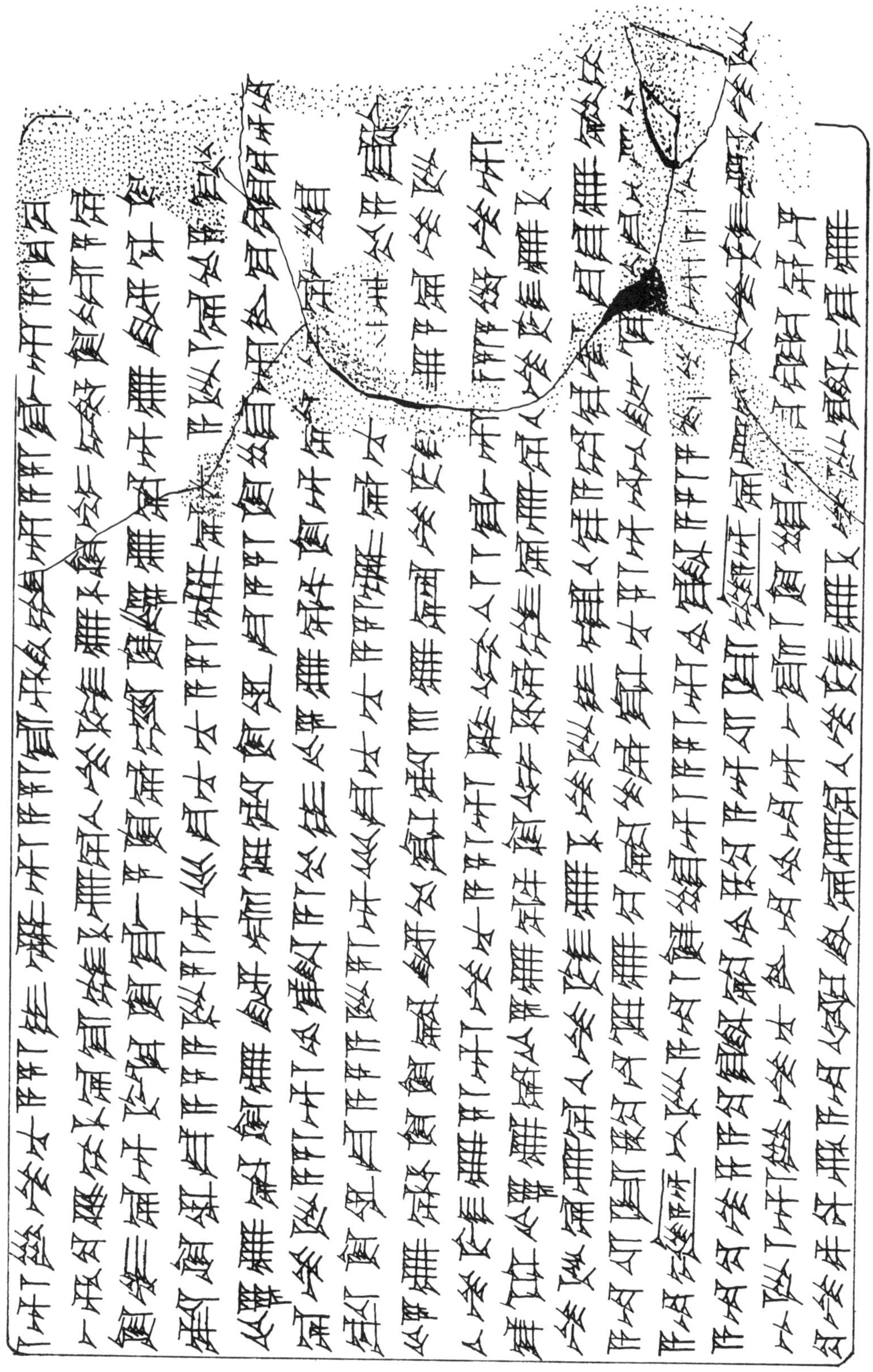

28

R.

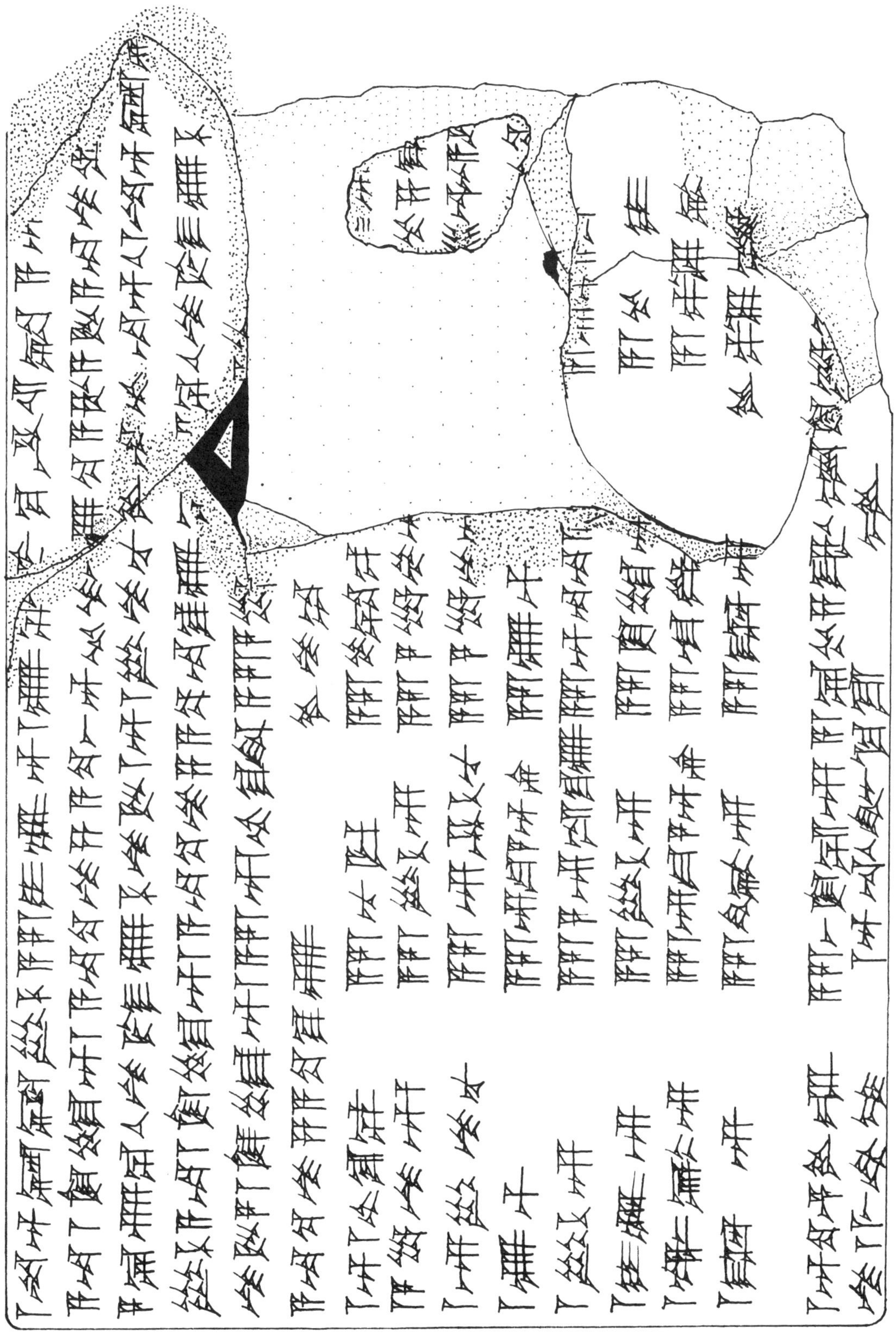

28

Le.E.

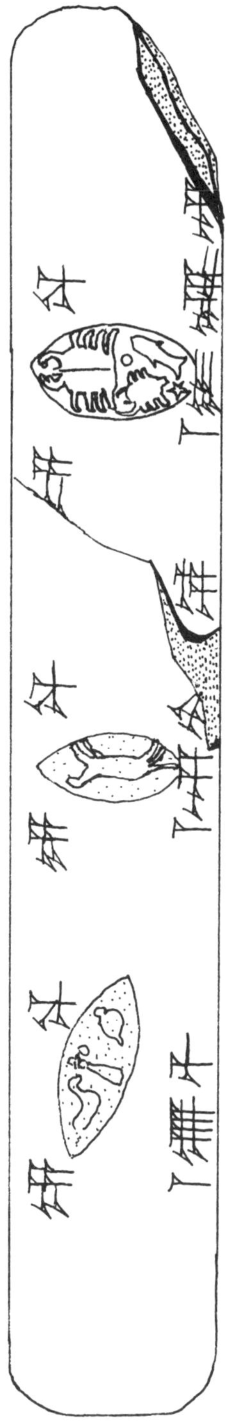

Lo.E.

28

U.E.

R.E.

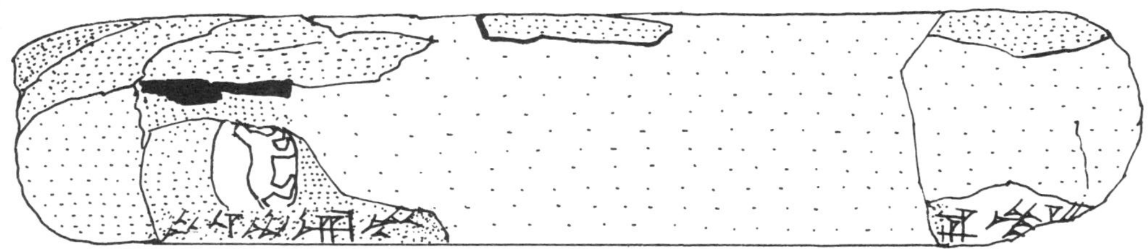

Four unplaced fragments

29

O.

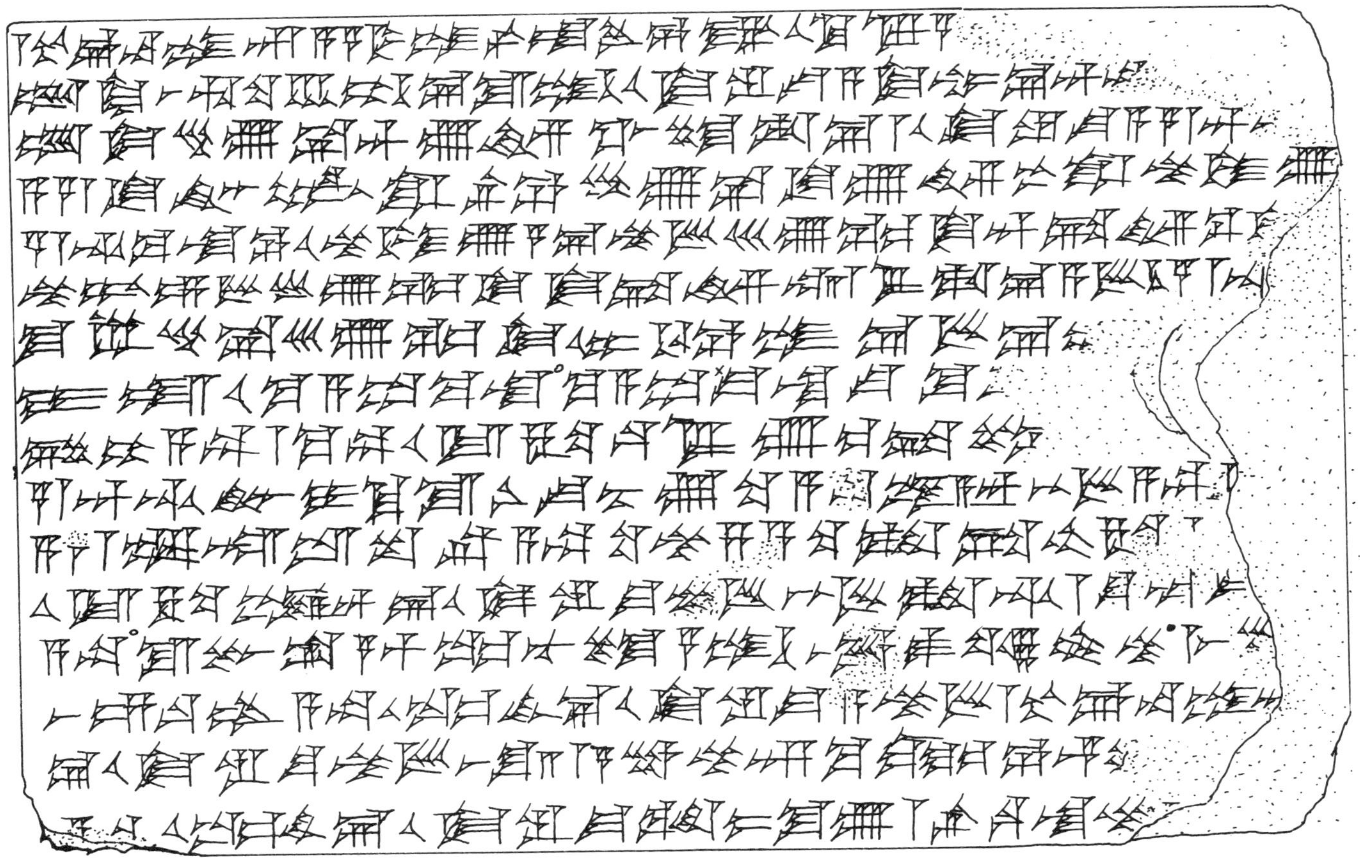

° sic ˣ sic

° sic, for ṣu-bu-ta
• sic for <1>

29

R.

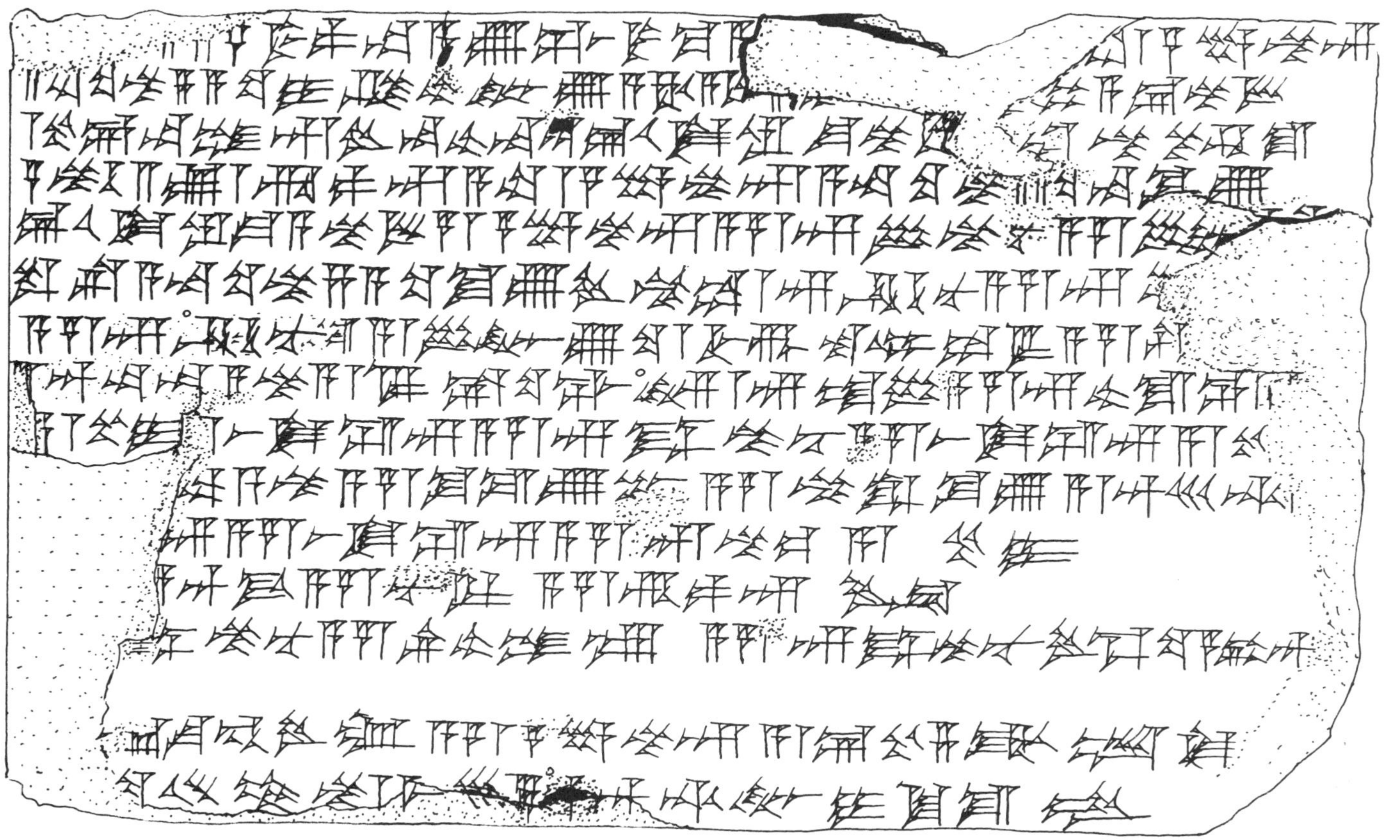

°EN-šú-nu over erasures

°<d>

°<KÁM>

PLATE 76

29

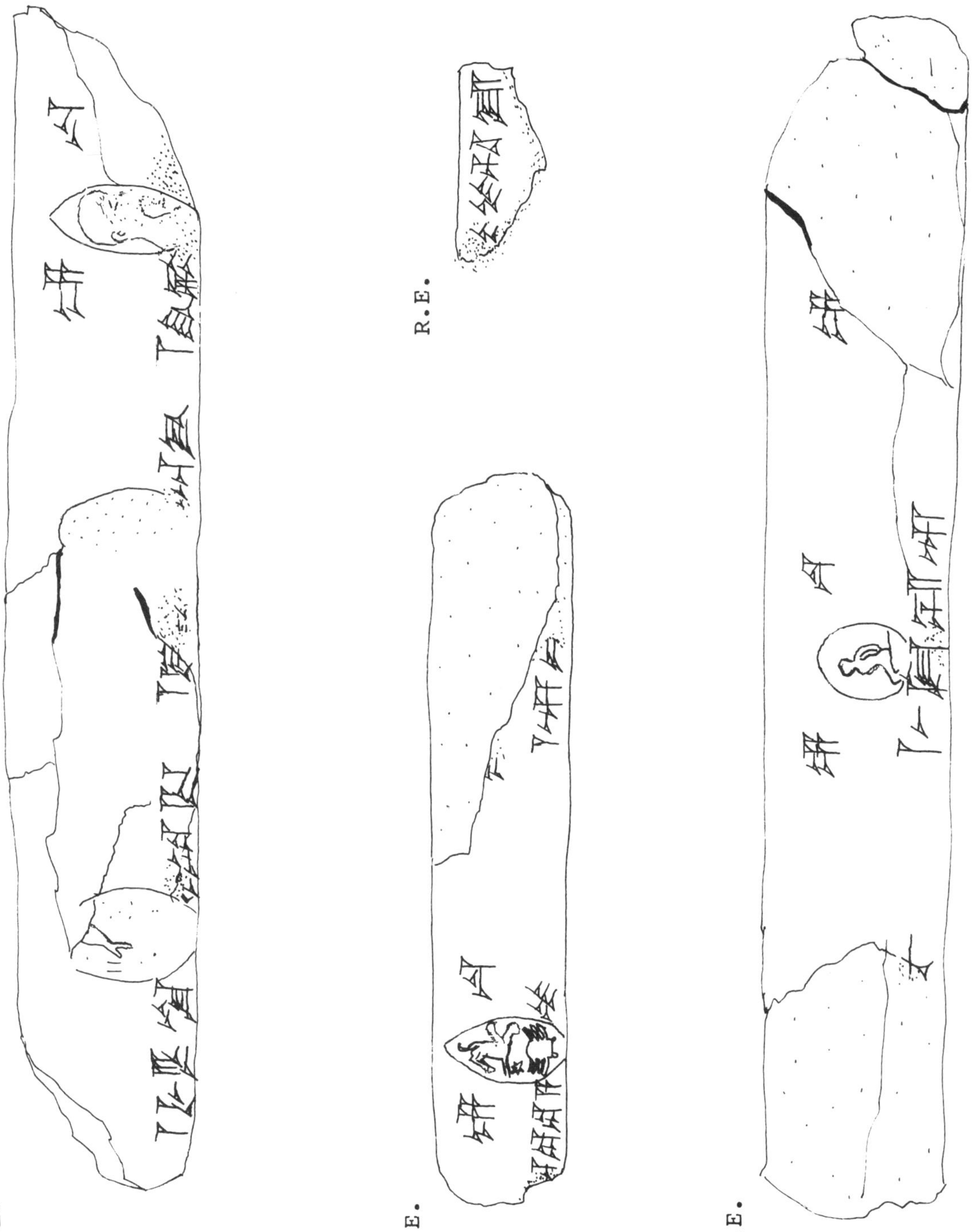

U.E.

Le.E.

R.E.

Lo.E.

30

O.

30

R.

1'

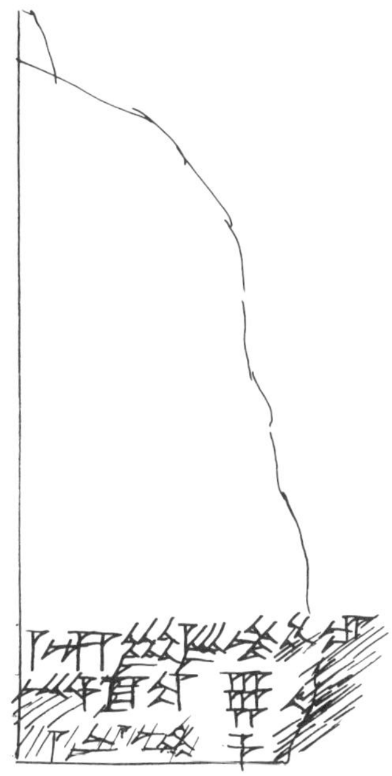

U.E.

seal impression

31

O.

° 𒐀 over erasure

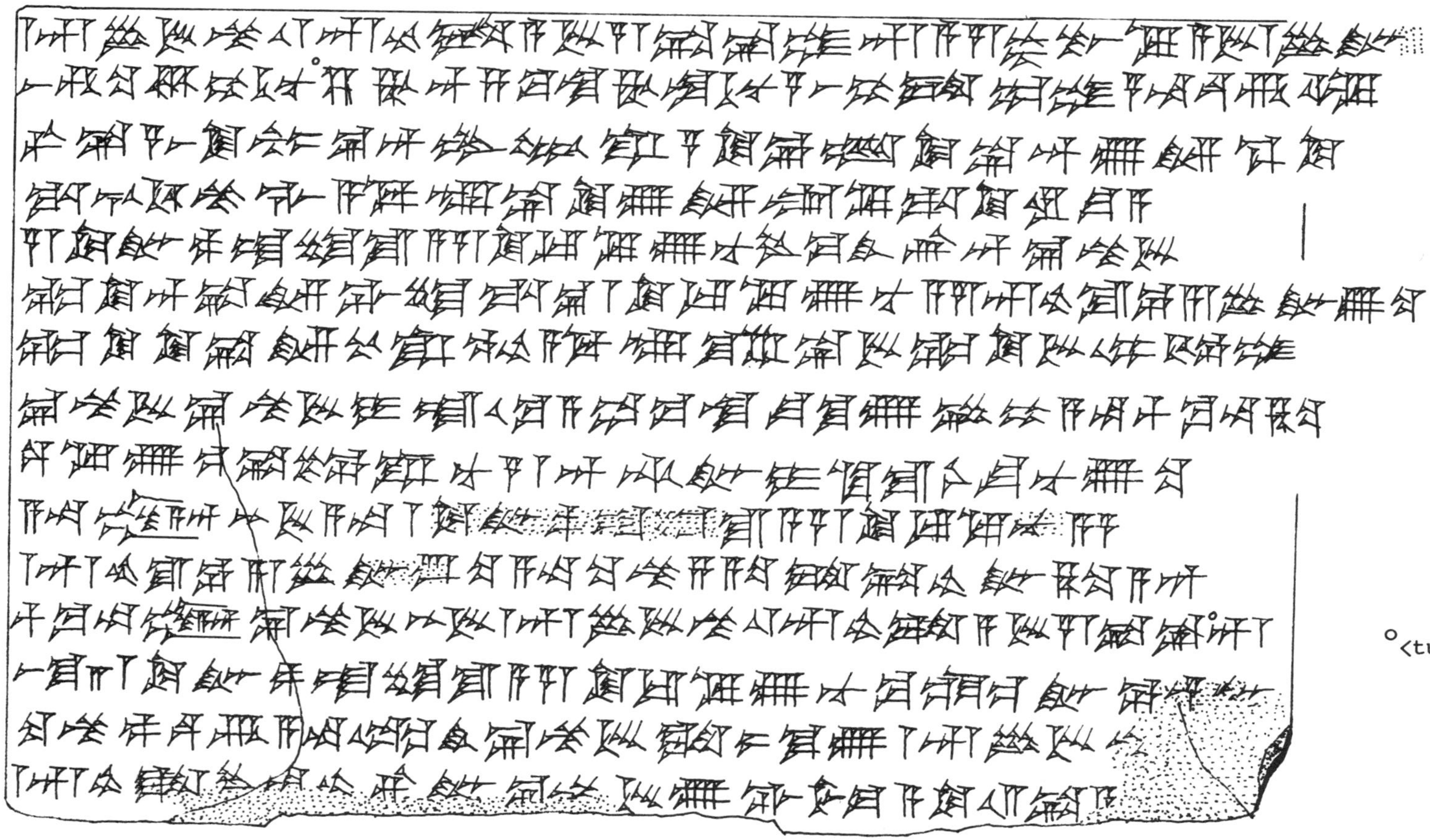

°⟨tum⟩

(Reverse destroyed)

31

Le.E.

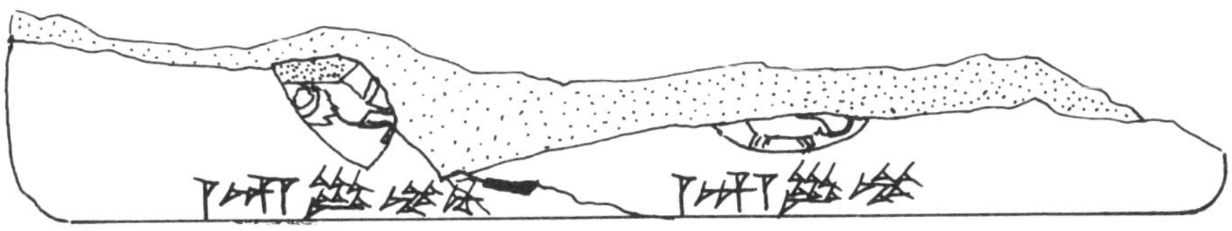

U.E.

(at lower left)

(Rest destroyed)

Lo.E.

(at upper left)

R.E.

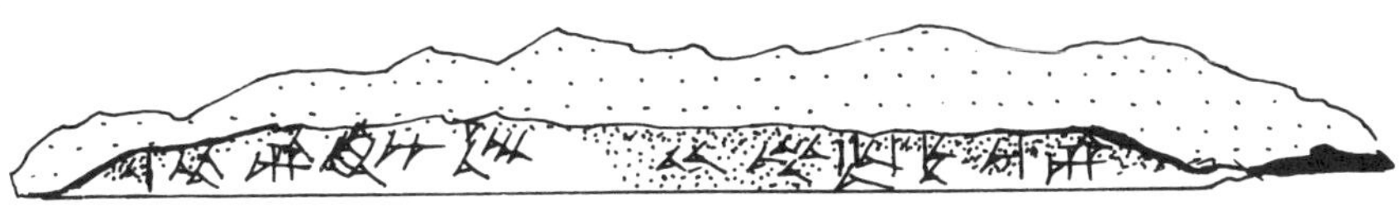

PLATE 80

32

O.

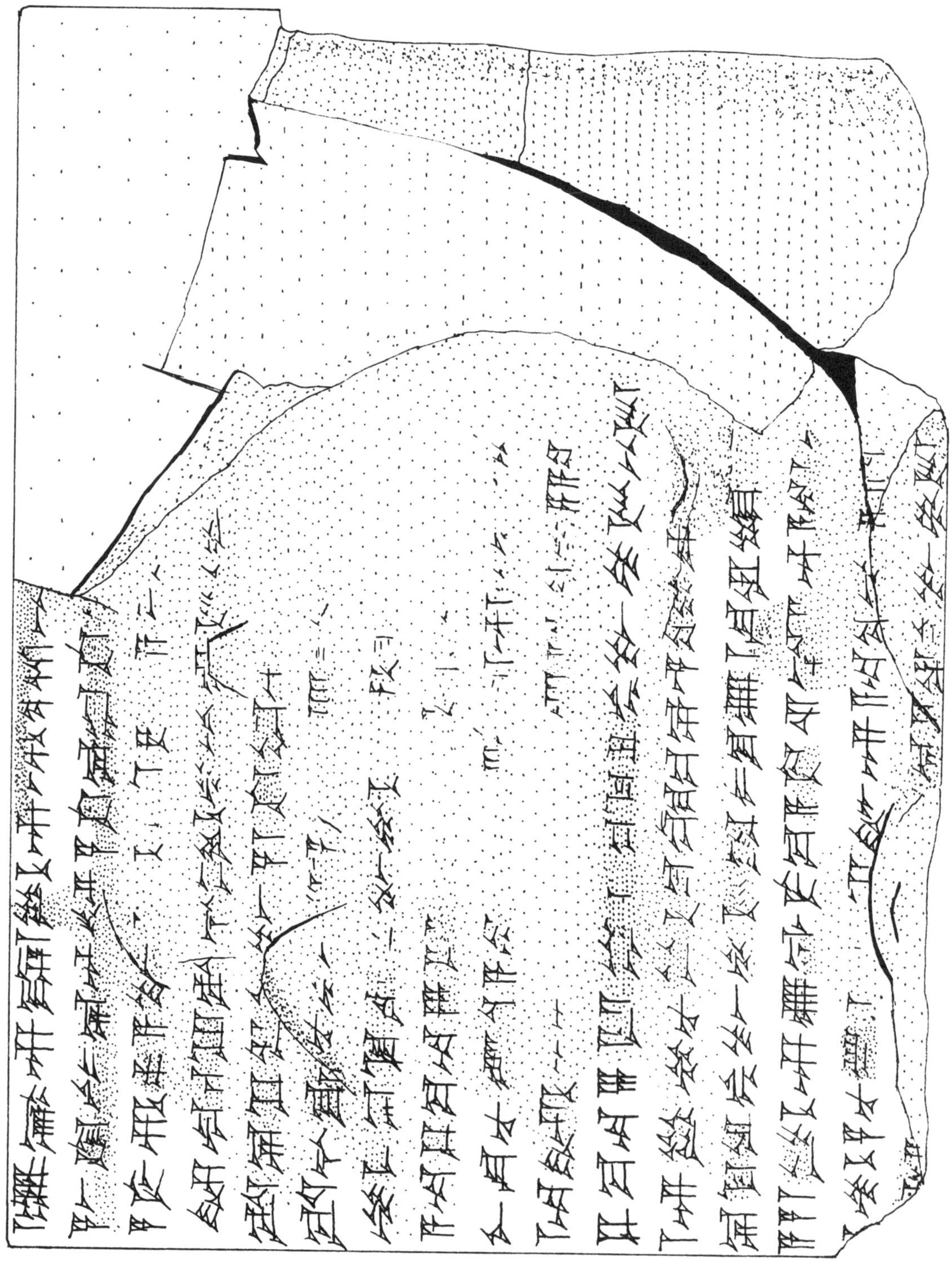

32

R.

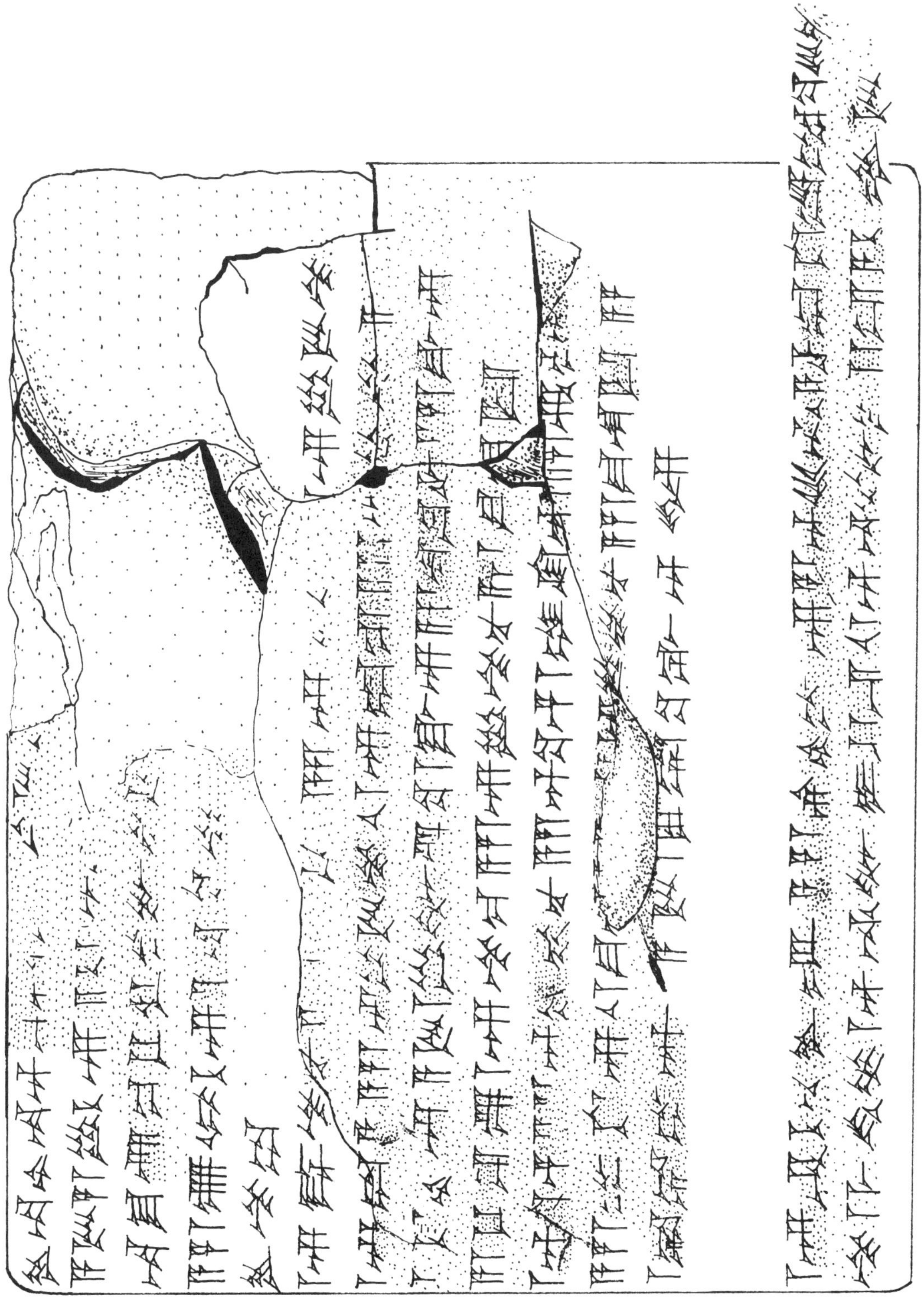

32

Le.E.

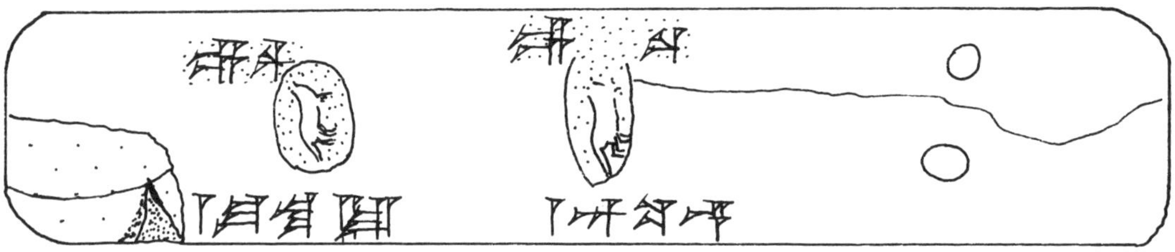

Nothing missing in right part of Le.E.

(Lo.E. destroyed)

32

U.E.

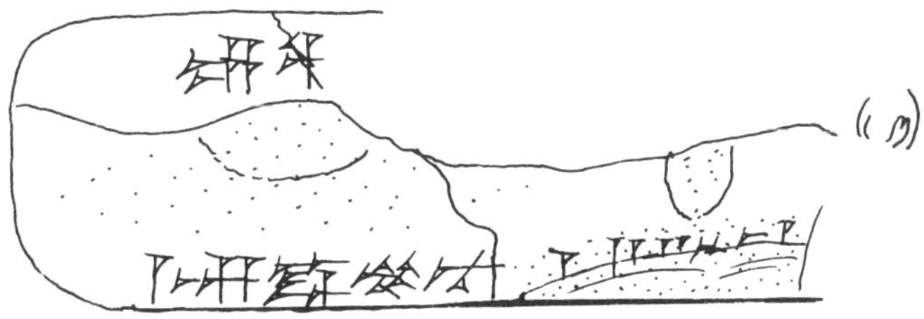

(Rest destroyed)

R.E.

(Rest destroyed)

Four unplaced fragments

33

O.

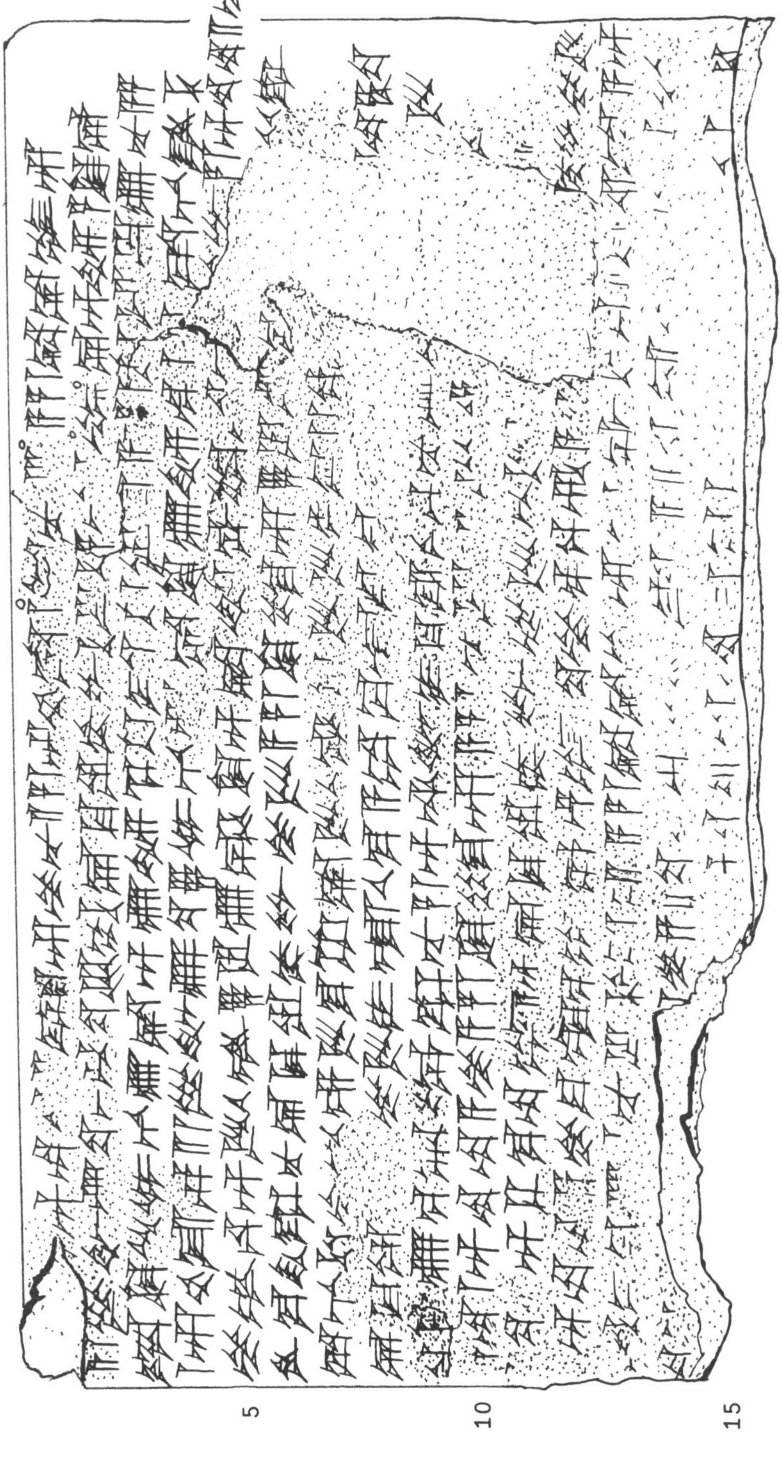

33

R.

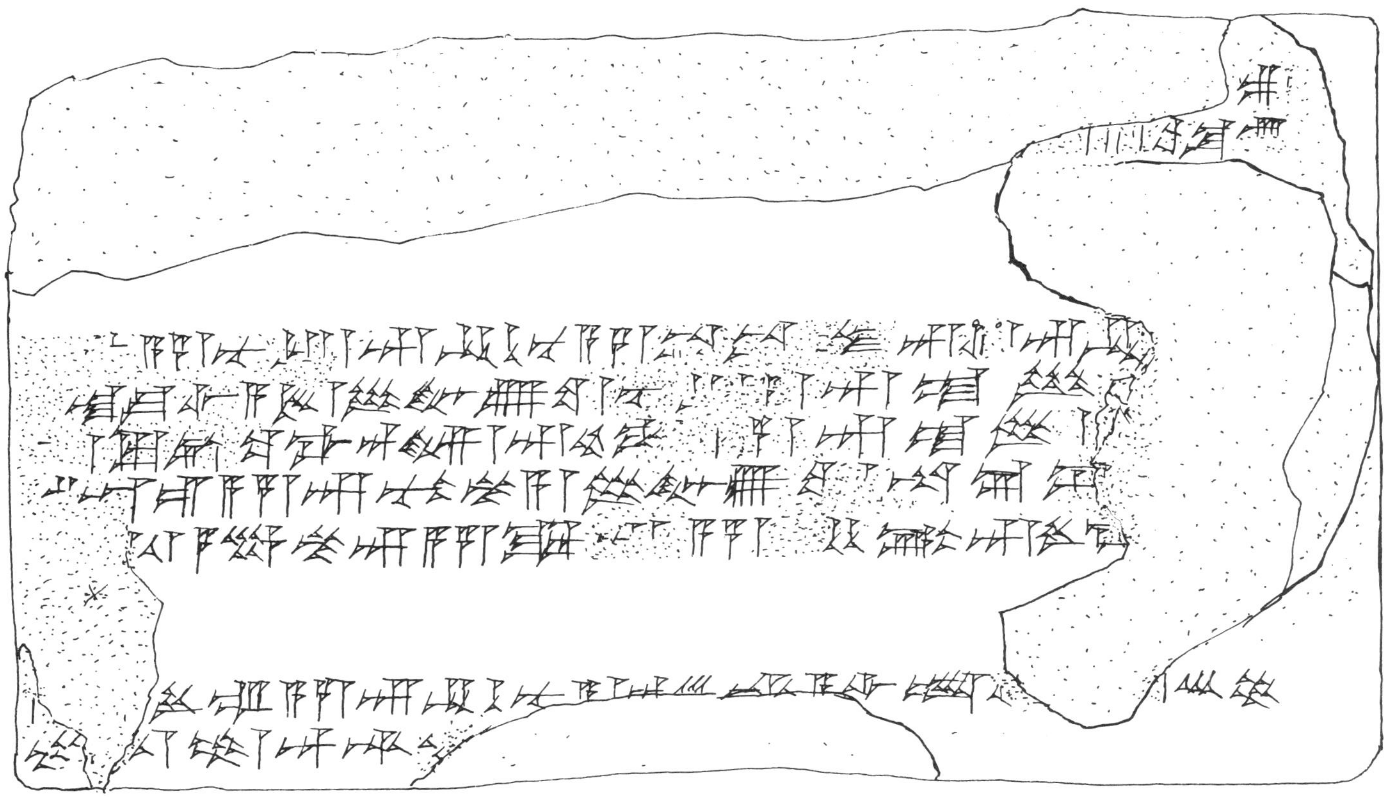

° [sign] over erasure°

PLATE 86

33

Le.E.

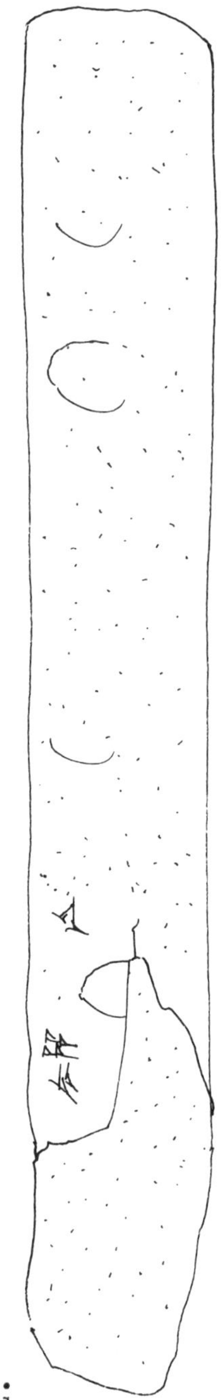

Lo.E.

33

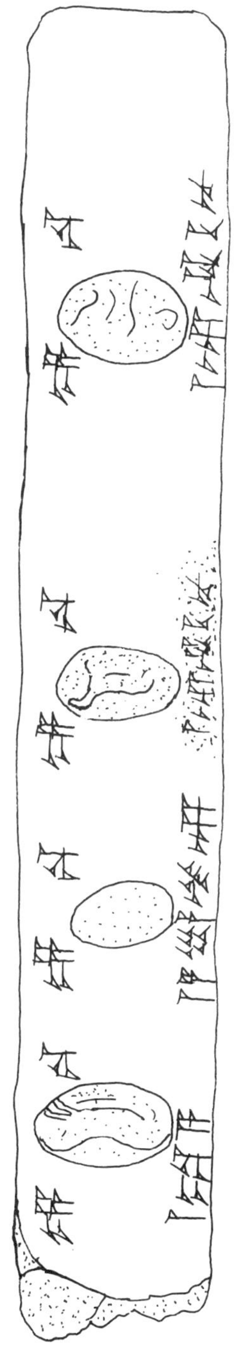

U.E.

R.E.

34

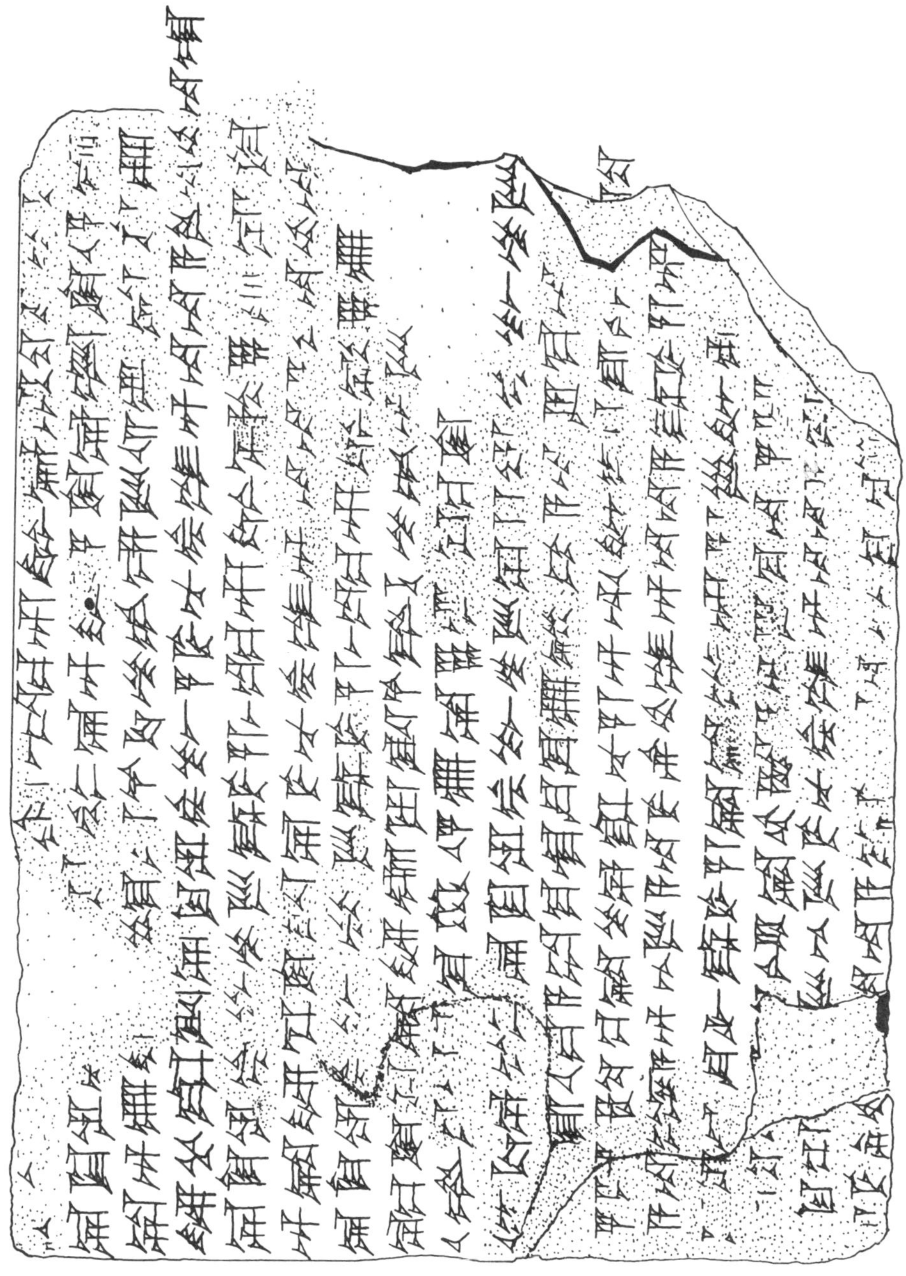

O.

34

R.

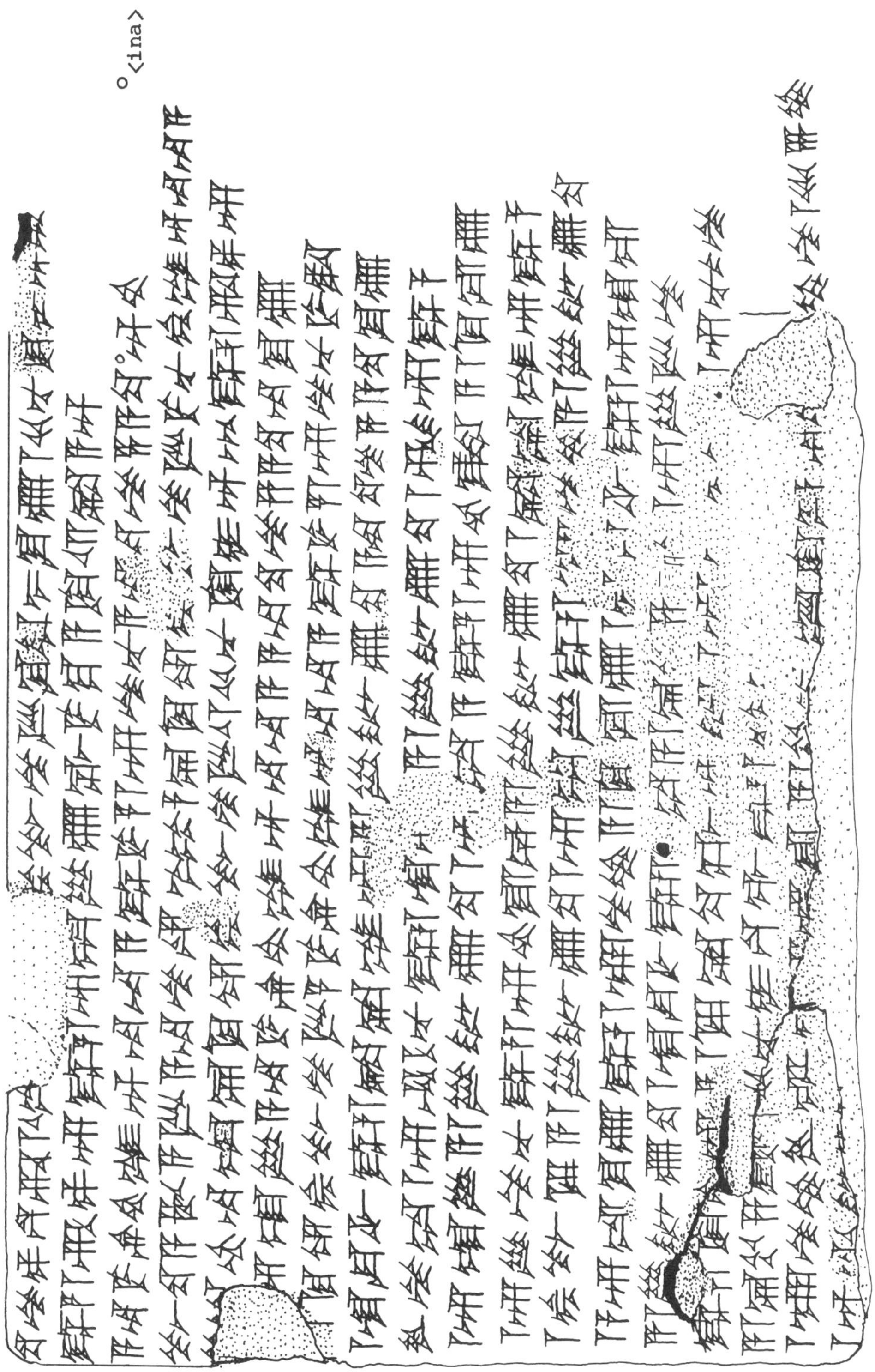

20

25

30

35

34

Le.E.

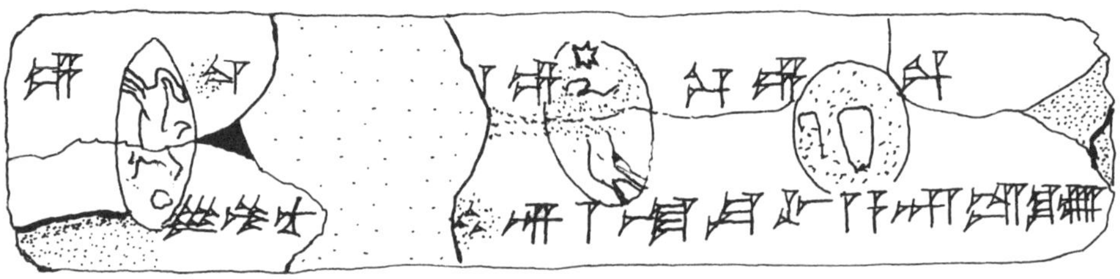

Lo.E.

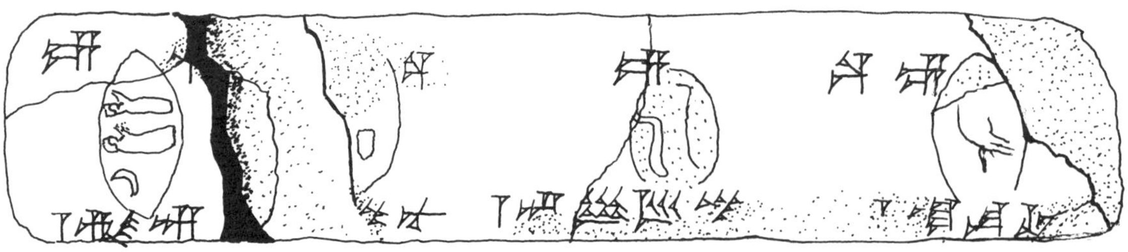

34

U.E.

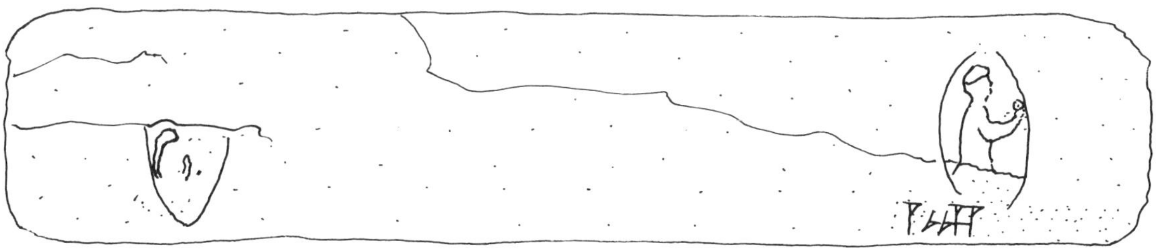

R.E.

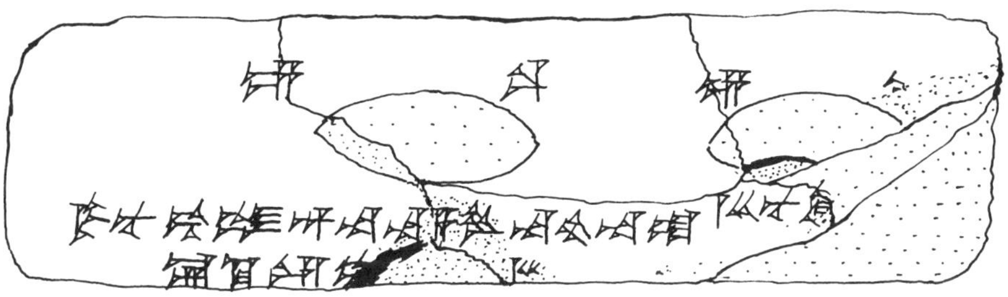

Unplaced Fragment

PLATE 92

35

O.

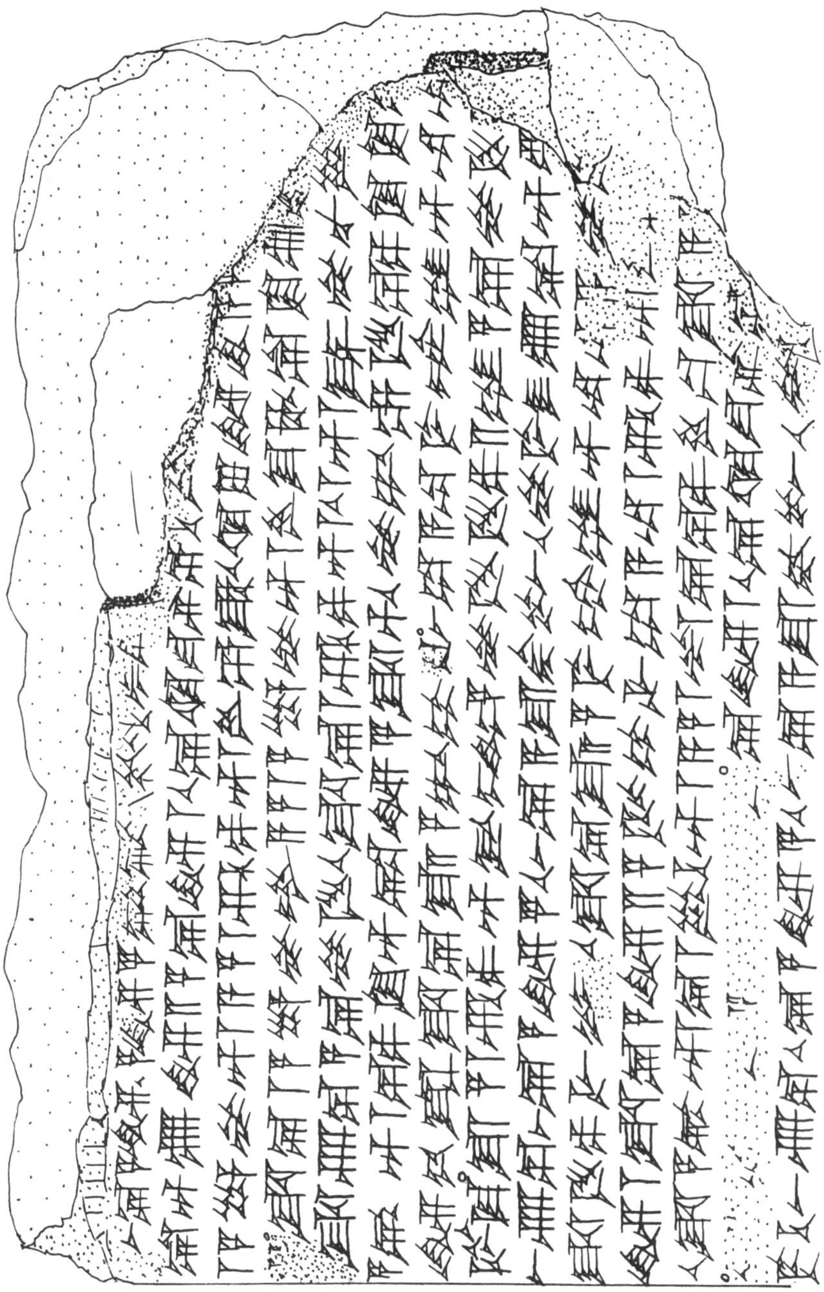

°over erasures

°erasure

°IGI over erasure

°NIN error for

°erasure°

°over erasures

R.

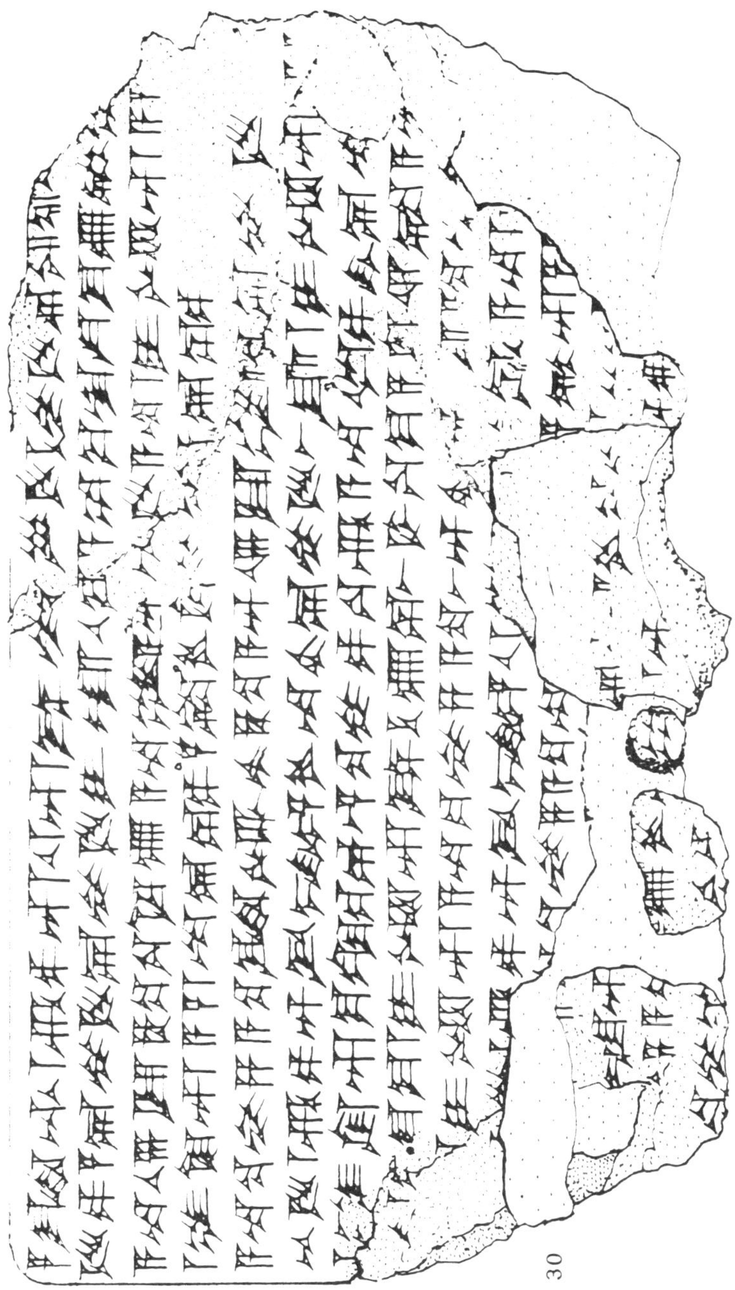

PLATE 94

35

Le.E.

°sic, for tu

Lo.E.

19

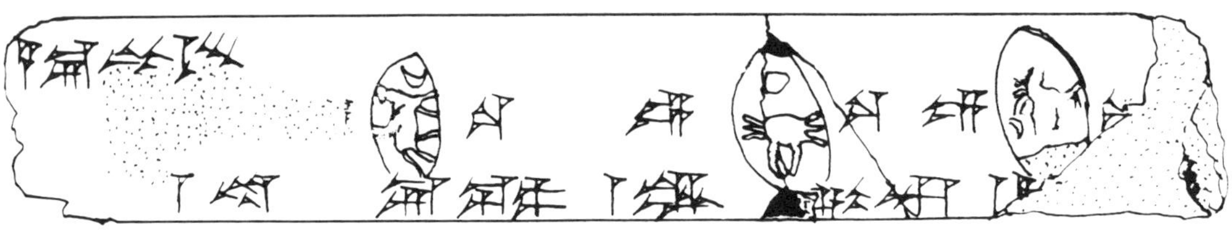

(U.E. and R.E. destroyed)

36

O.

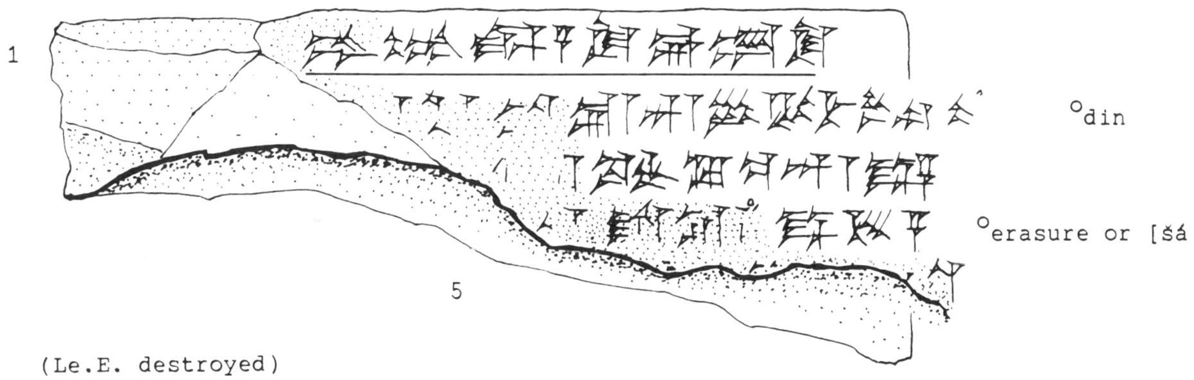

(Le.E. destroyed)

R.

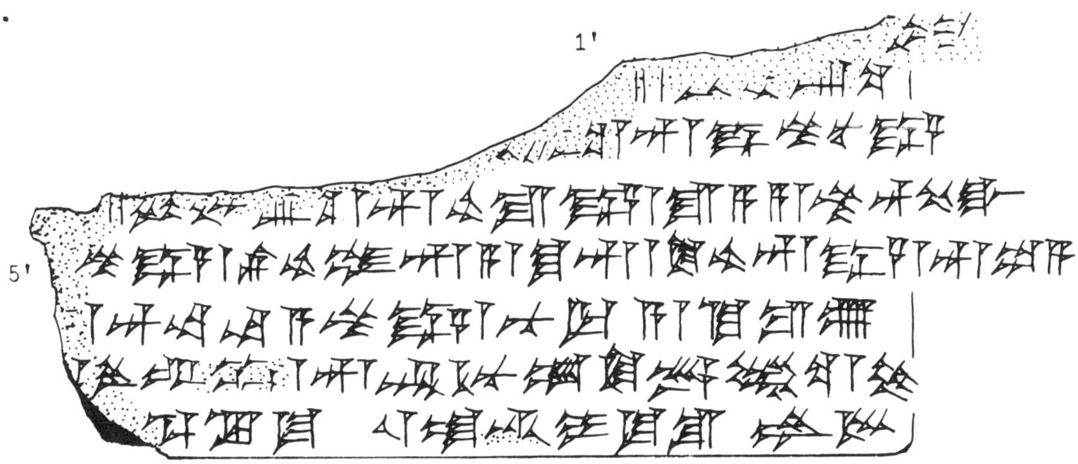

R.E.

Writing from lines 4 and 5 of R. intrudes here.

U.E.

(Lo.E. destroyed)

37

O.

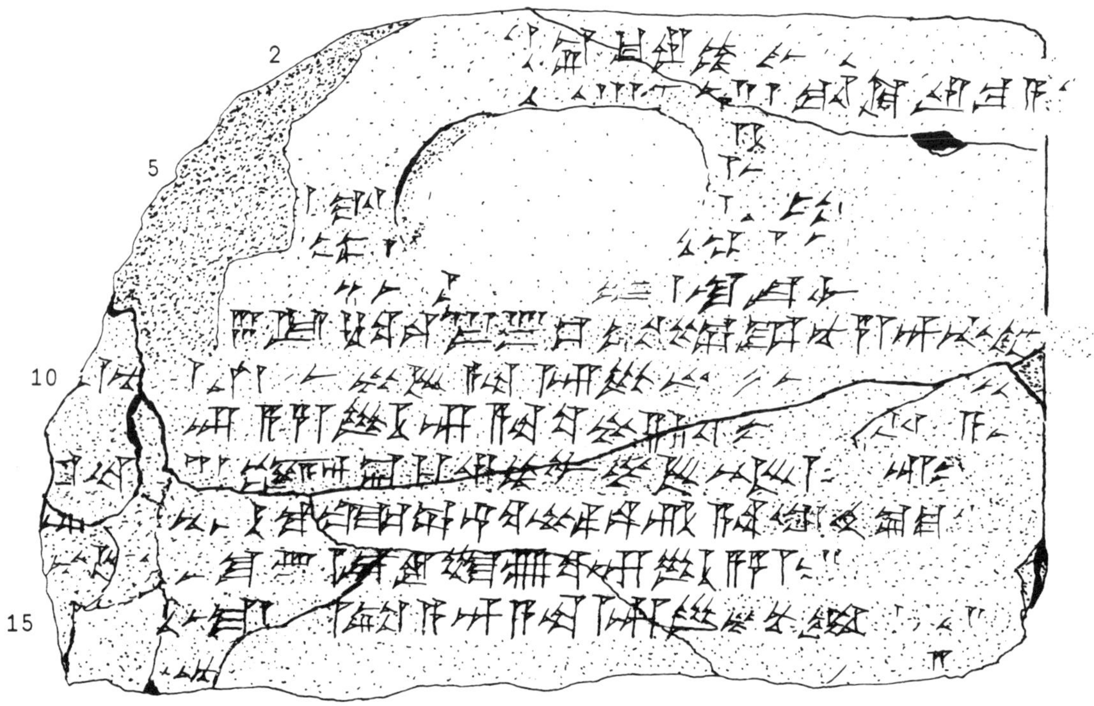

(Lo.E. and L.E. destroyed)

37

R.

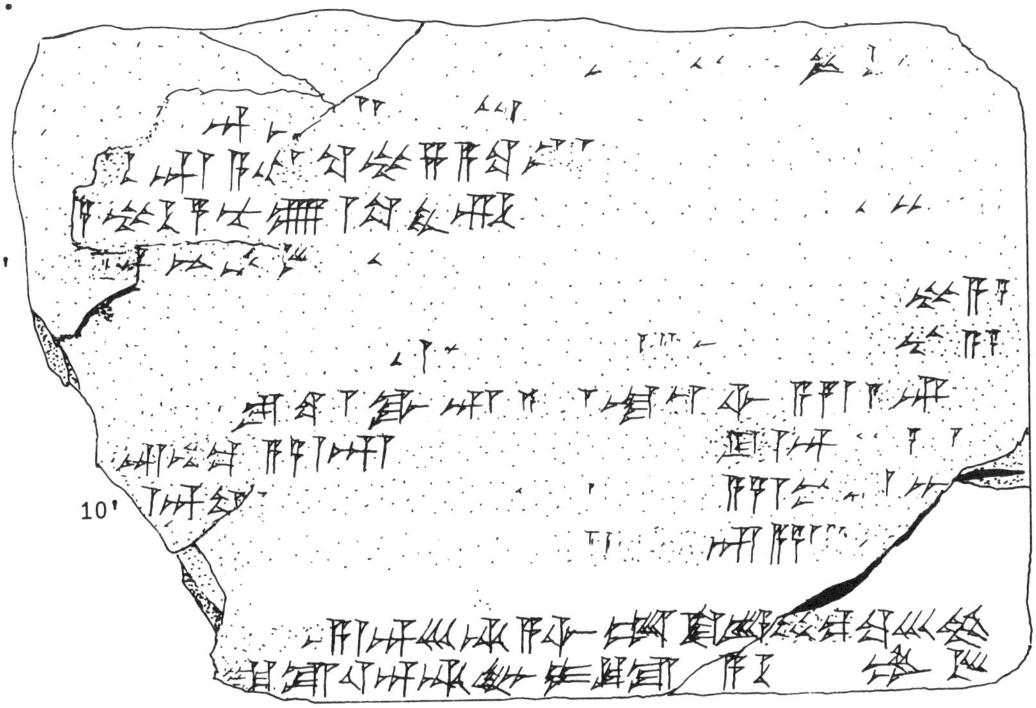

Outline of one seal and trace of one witness' name appears on U.E.

R.E. preserves only 

38

O.

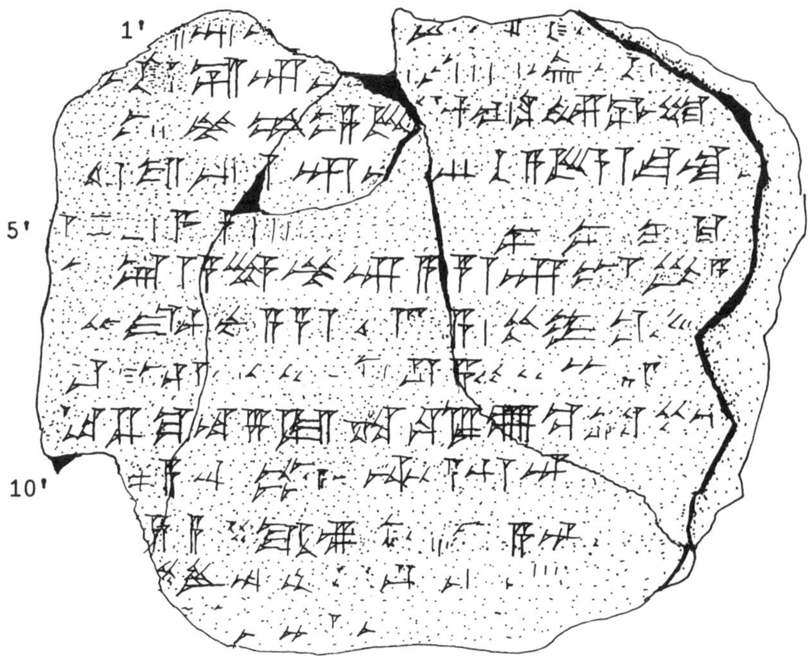

(Rest destroyed)

39

Le.E.

O.

1

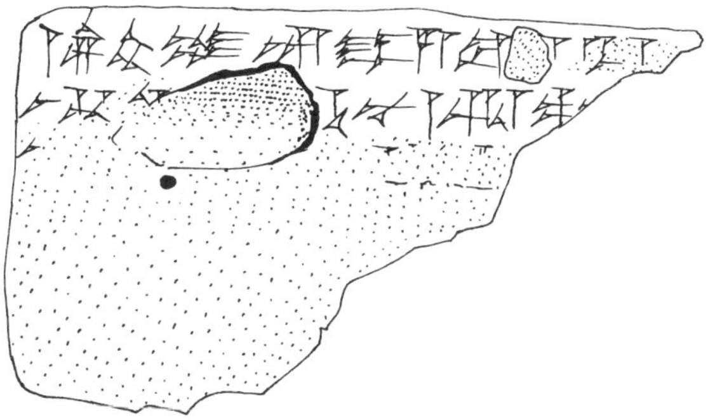

R.

1'
2'
5'

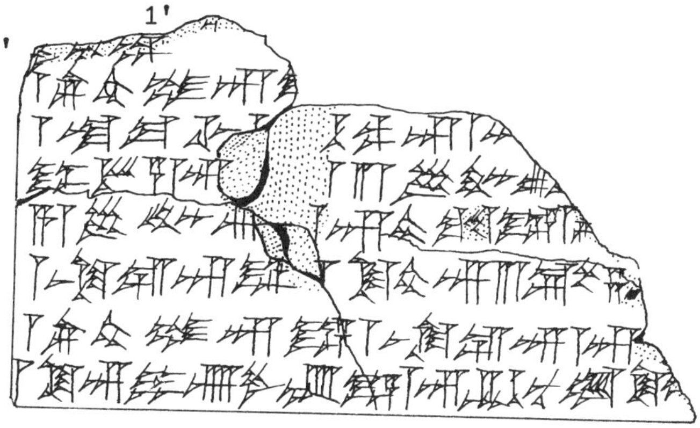

U.E.

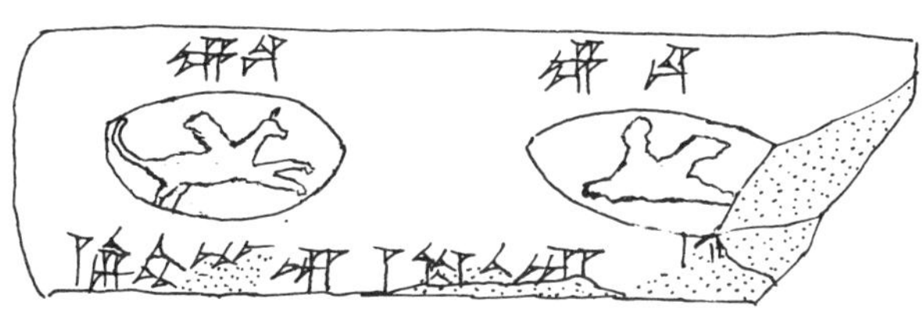

40

O.

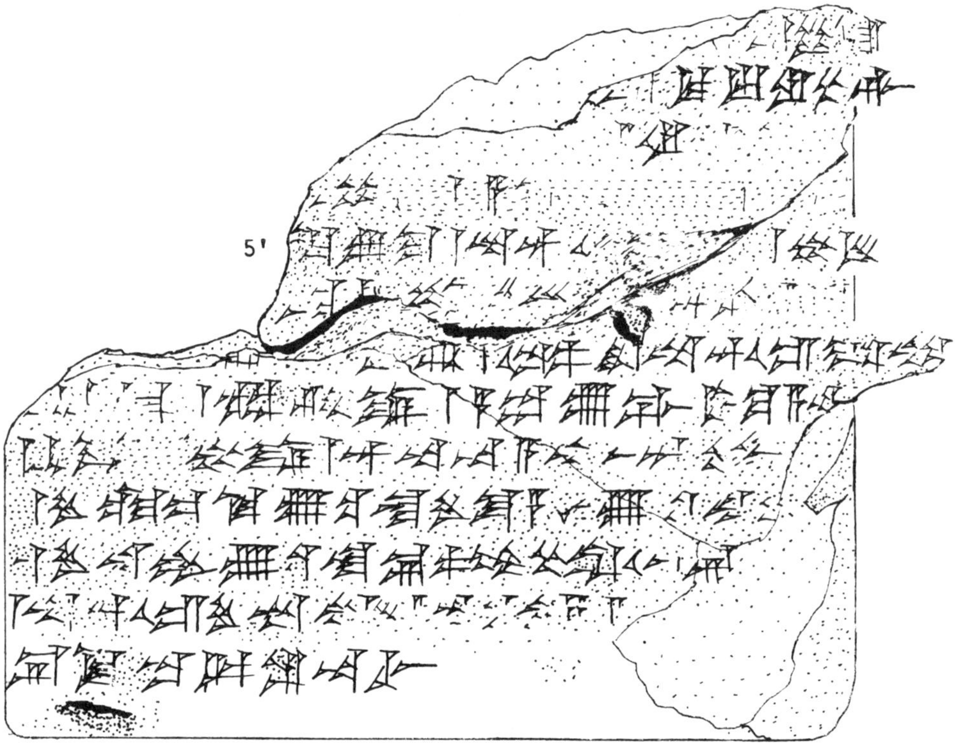

Lo.E.

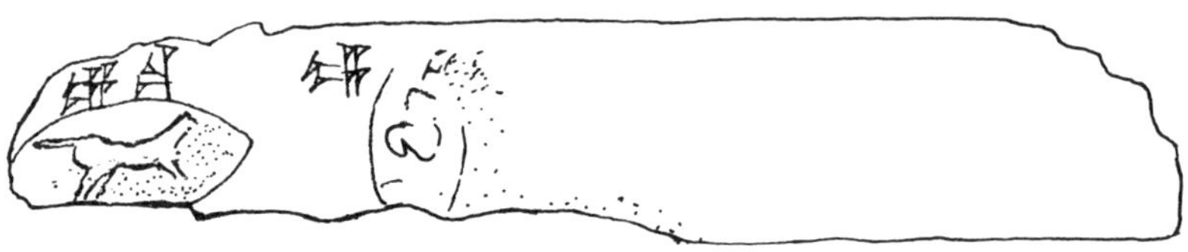

Le.E.

40

R.

1'

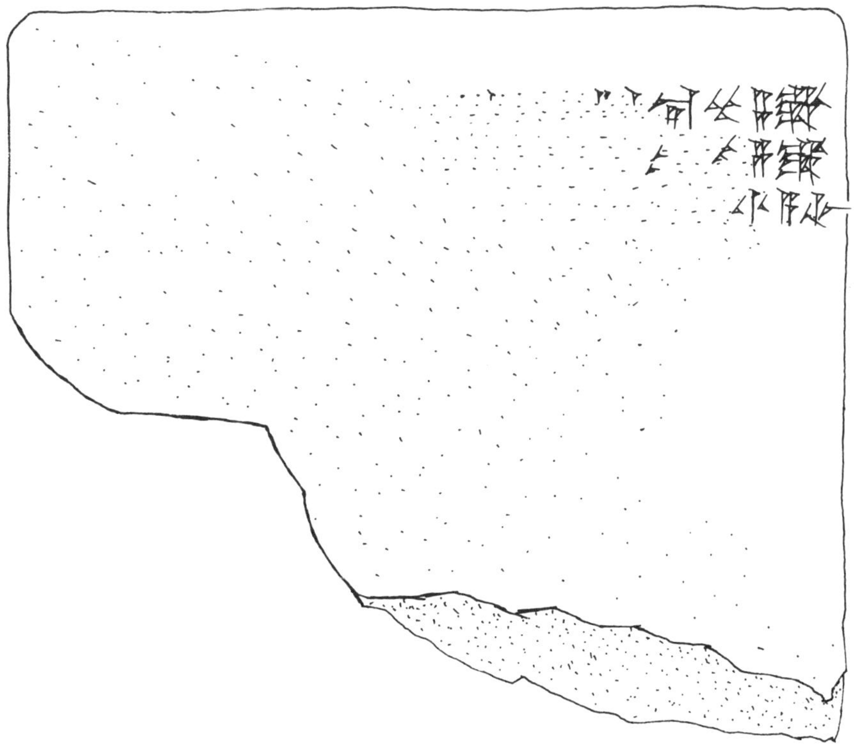

R.E.

°LÚ omitted

(U.E. destroyed)

PLATE 102

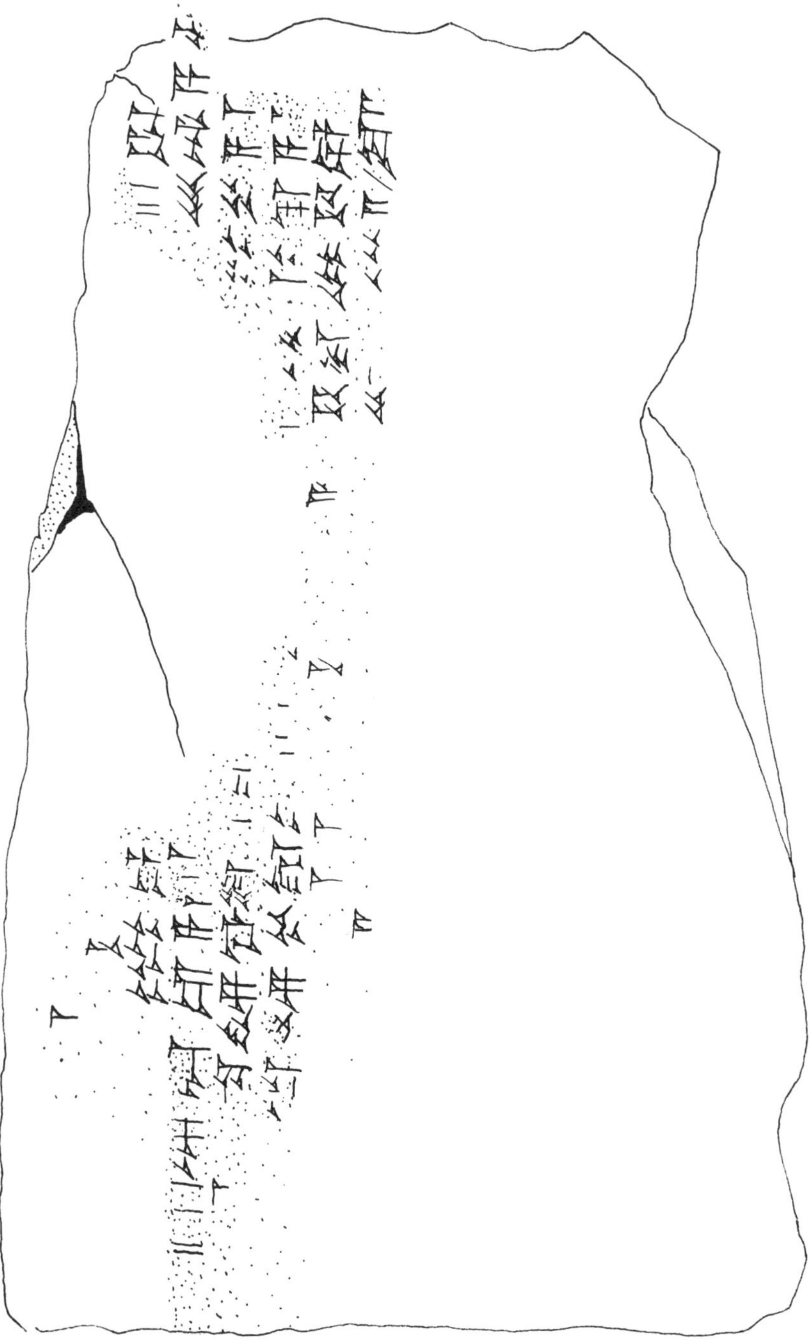

O.

2' 3' 4' 5' 6' 7' 8' 9'

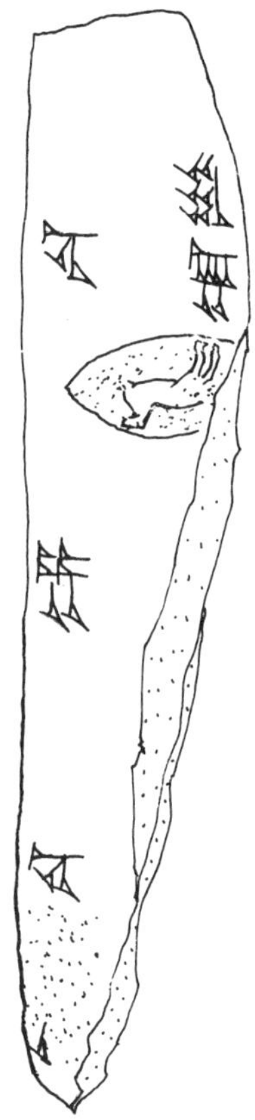

Le.E.

U.E.

41

R.

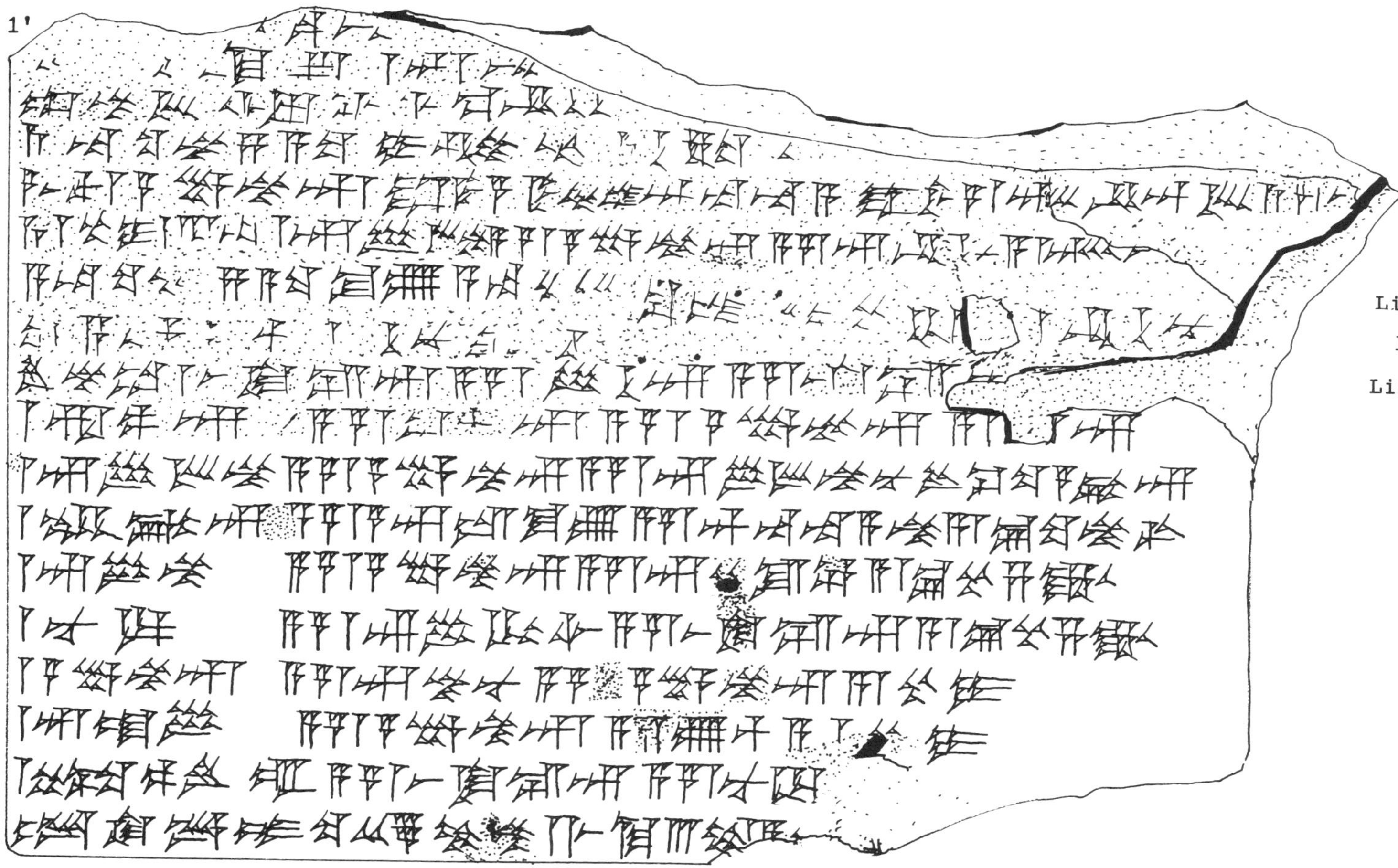

Line 7 runs into line below's space.

Line 8: 1/2 line

R.E.

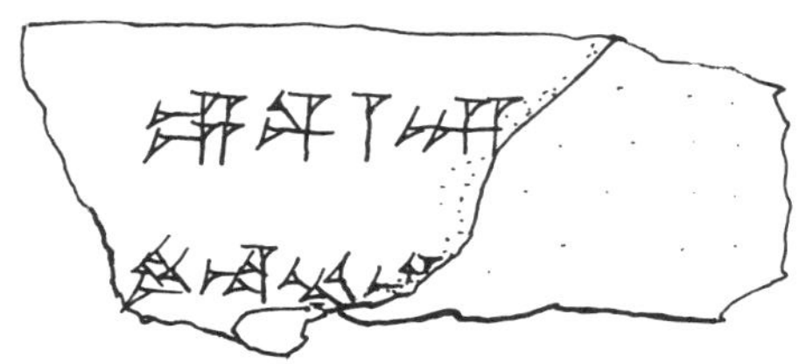

(Lo.E. destroyed)

PLATE 104

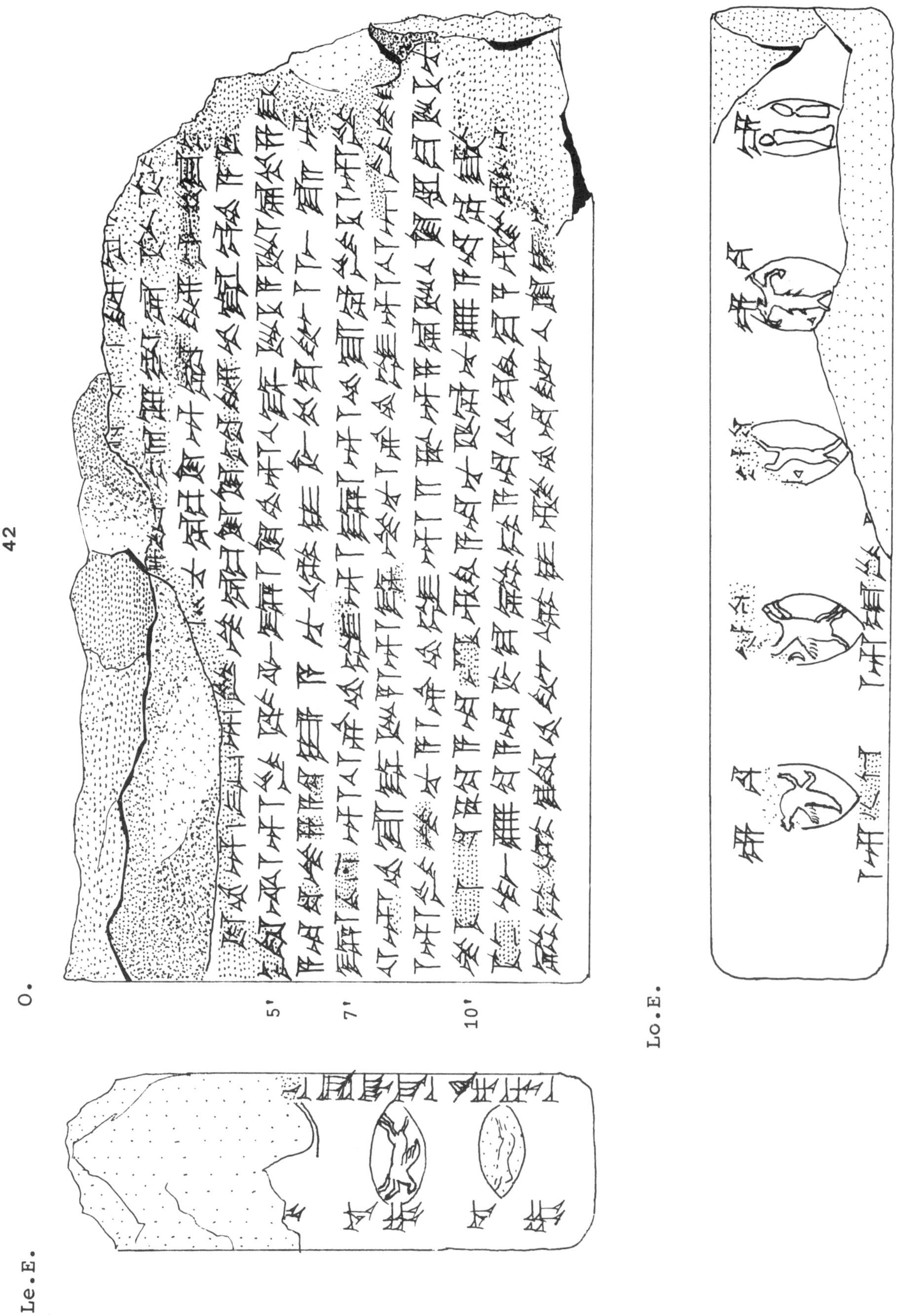

42

R.E.

R.

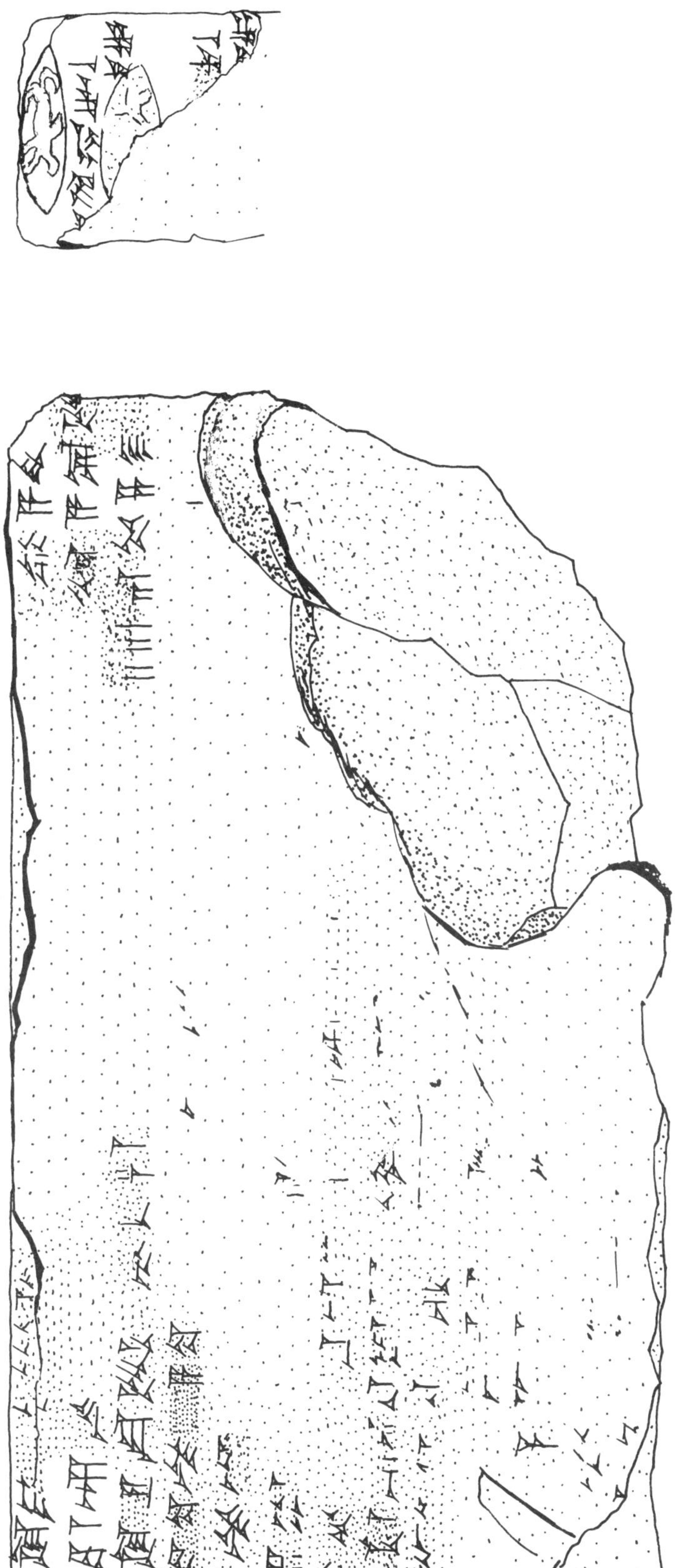

(U.E. destroyed)

43

O.

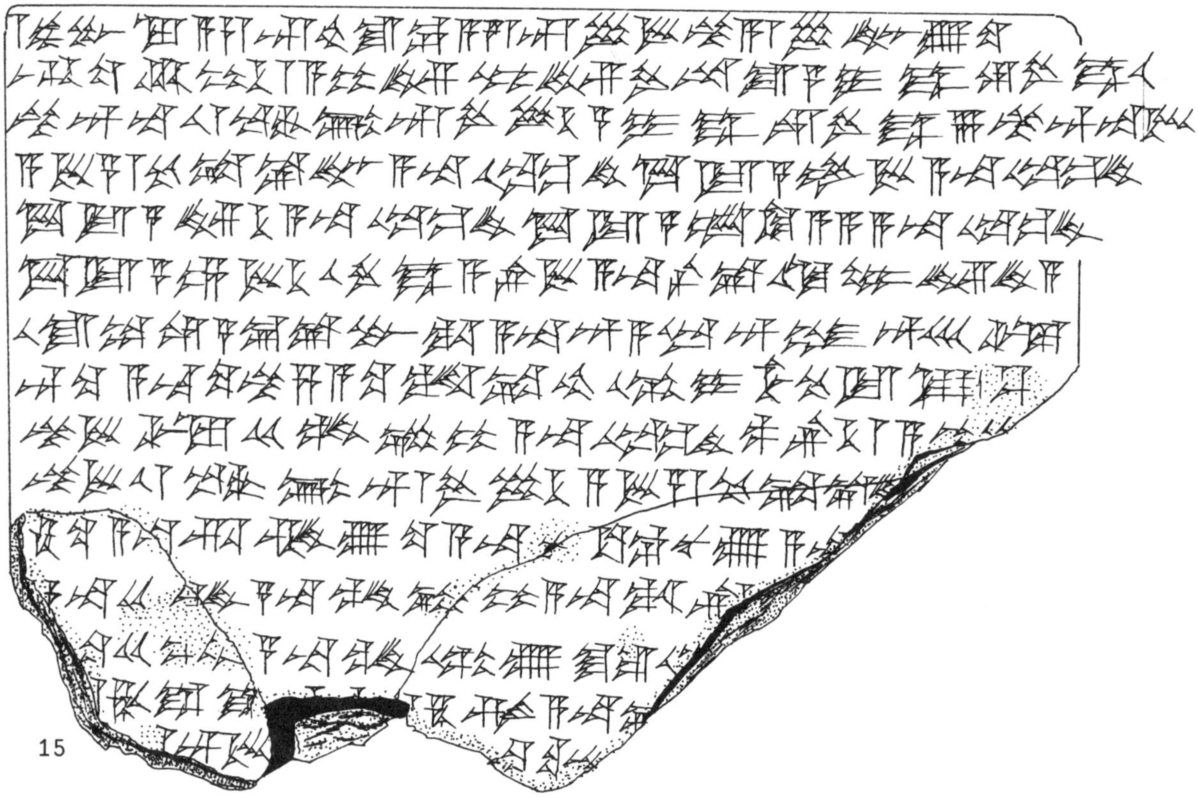

(Lo.E. destroyed)

Le.E.

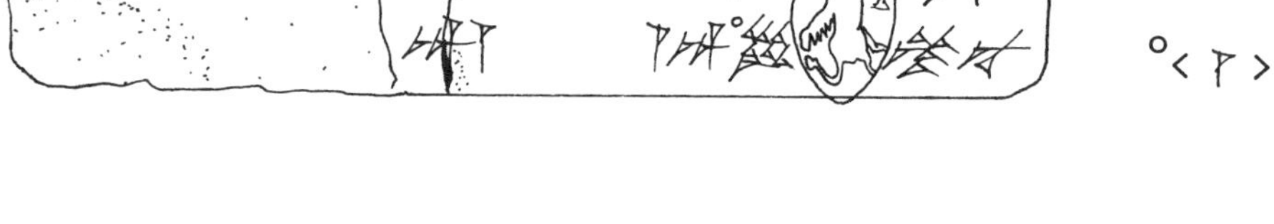

43

R.

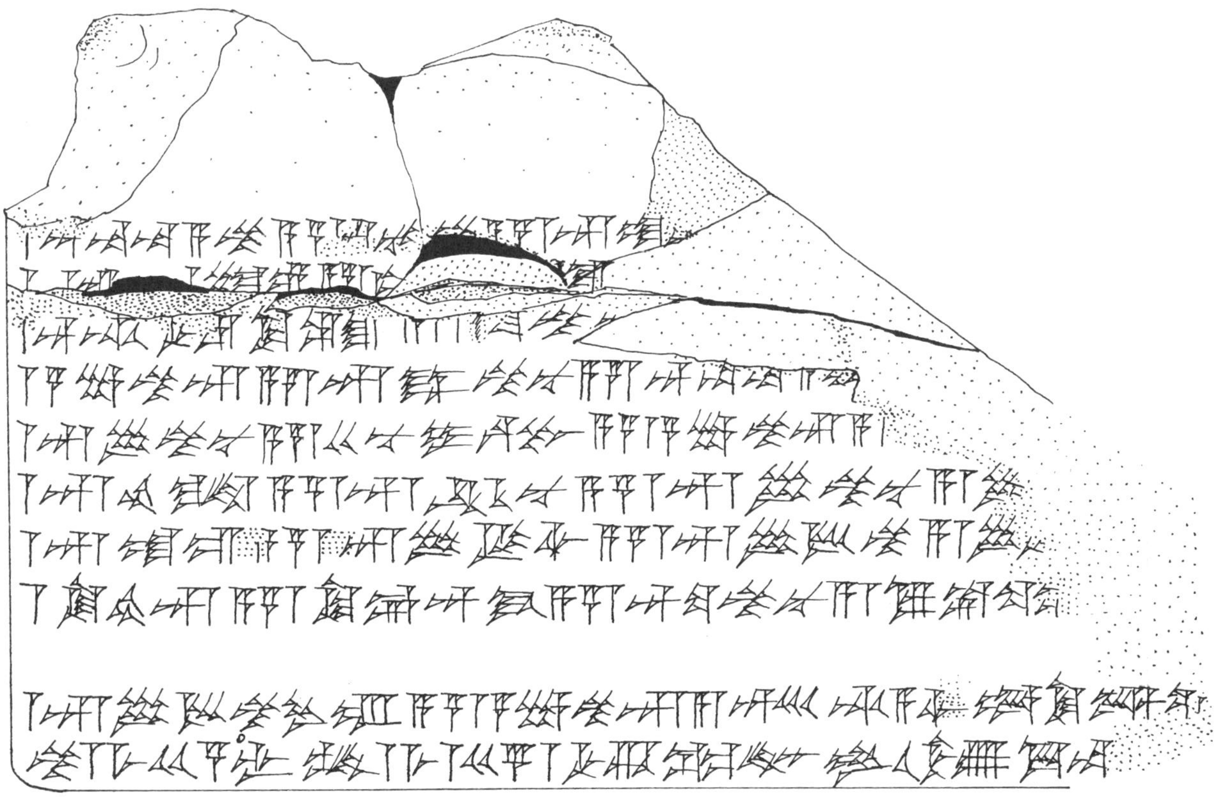

°sic, for ši?

U.E.

R.E.

44

O.

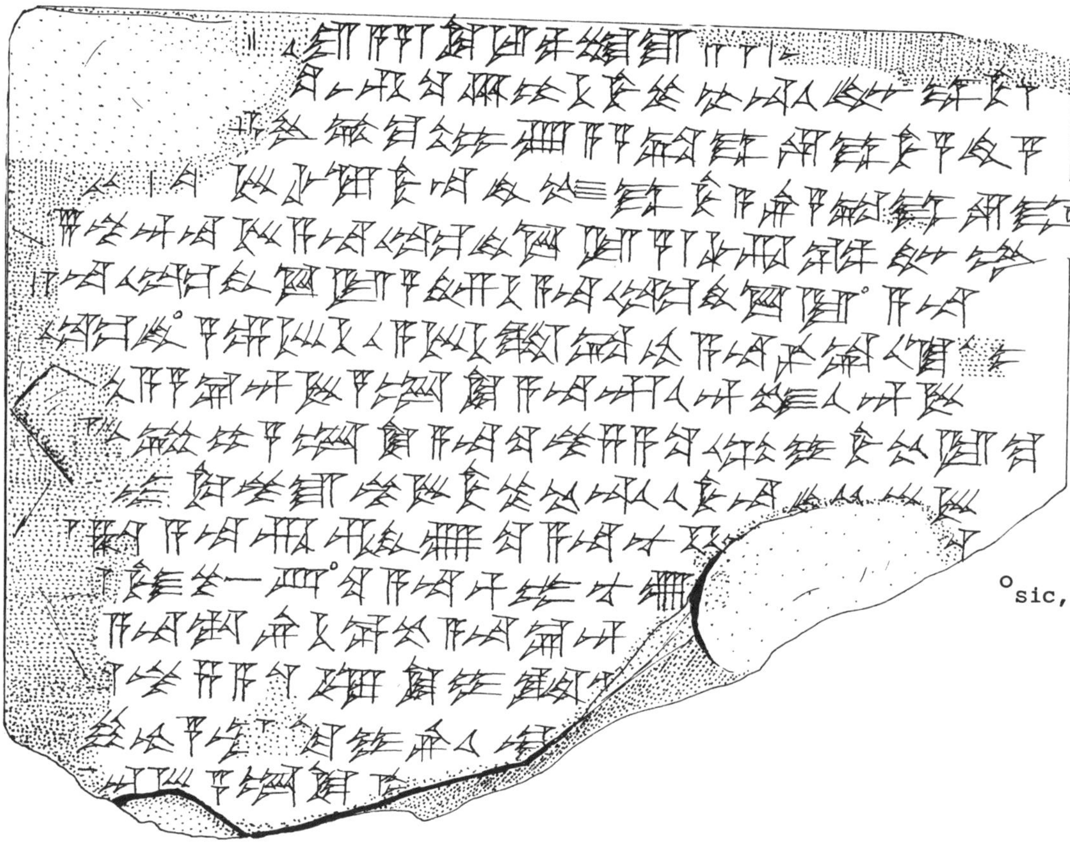

°<šá UNUG.KI-a-a>

°<bulṭu>

°sic, for

(Lo.E. destroyed)

Le.E.

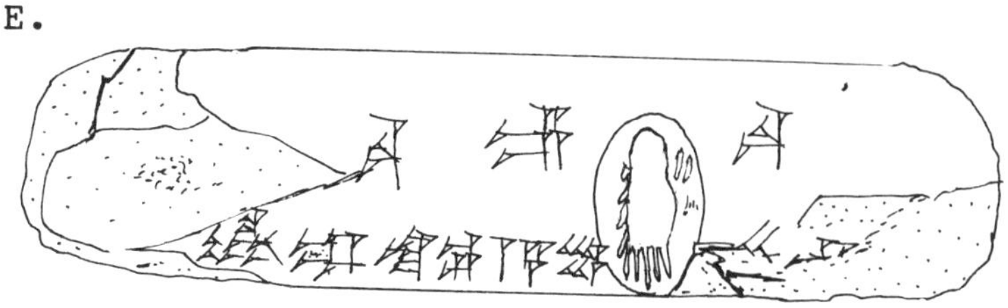

44

R.

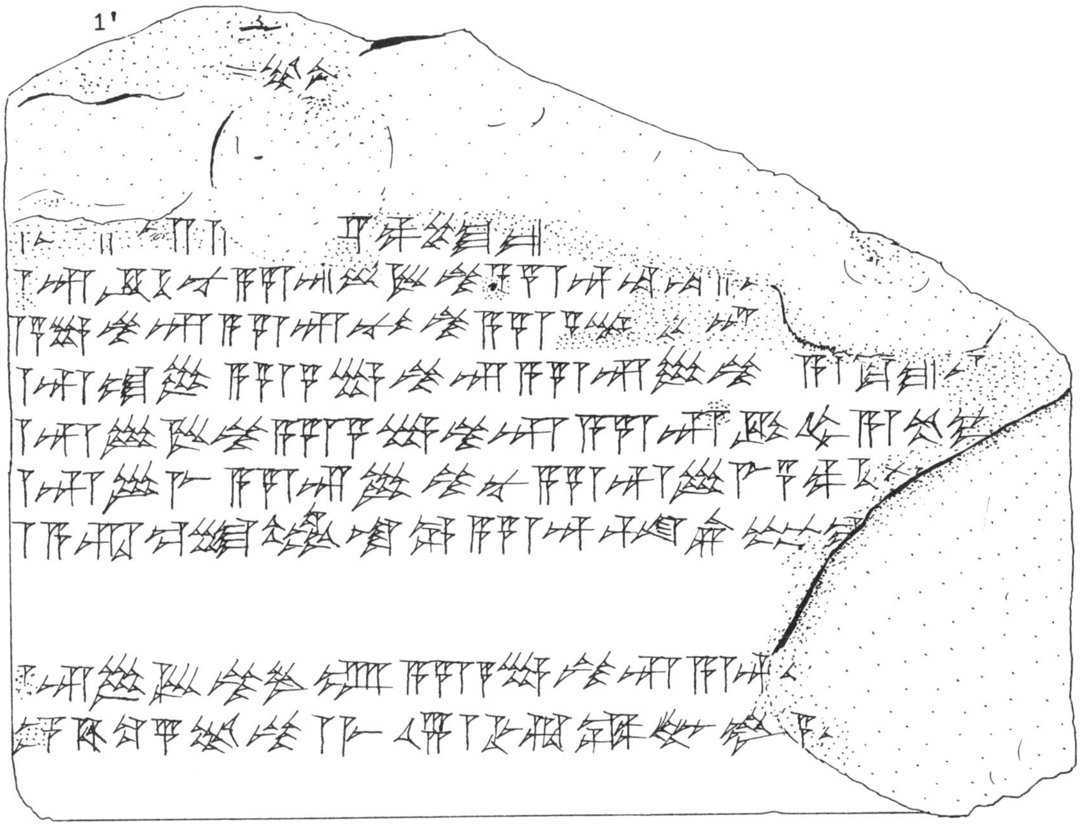

U.E.

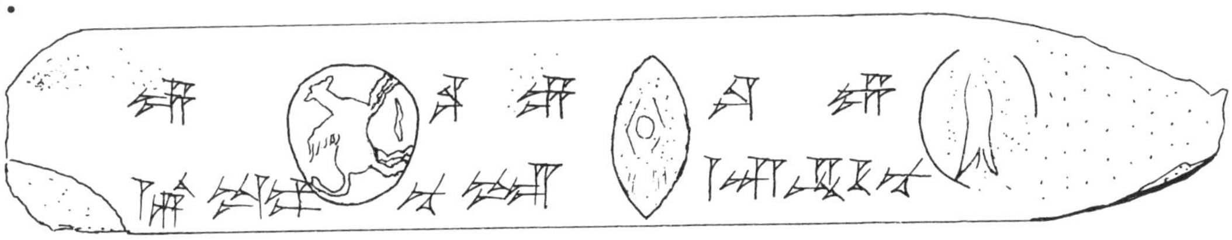

R.E.

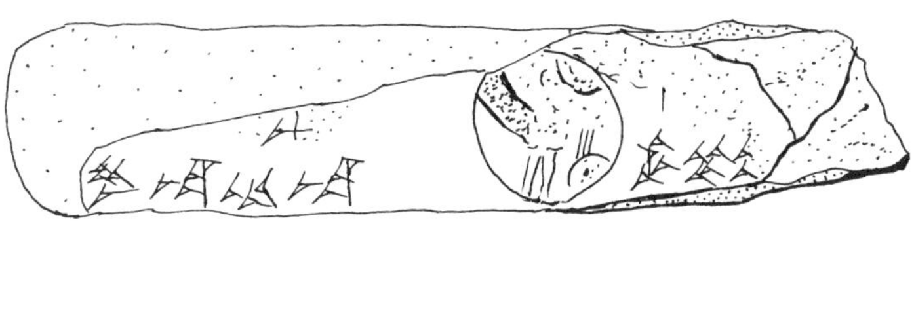

45

O.

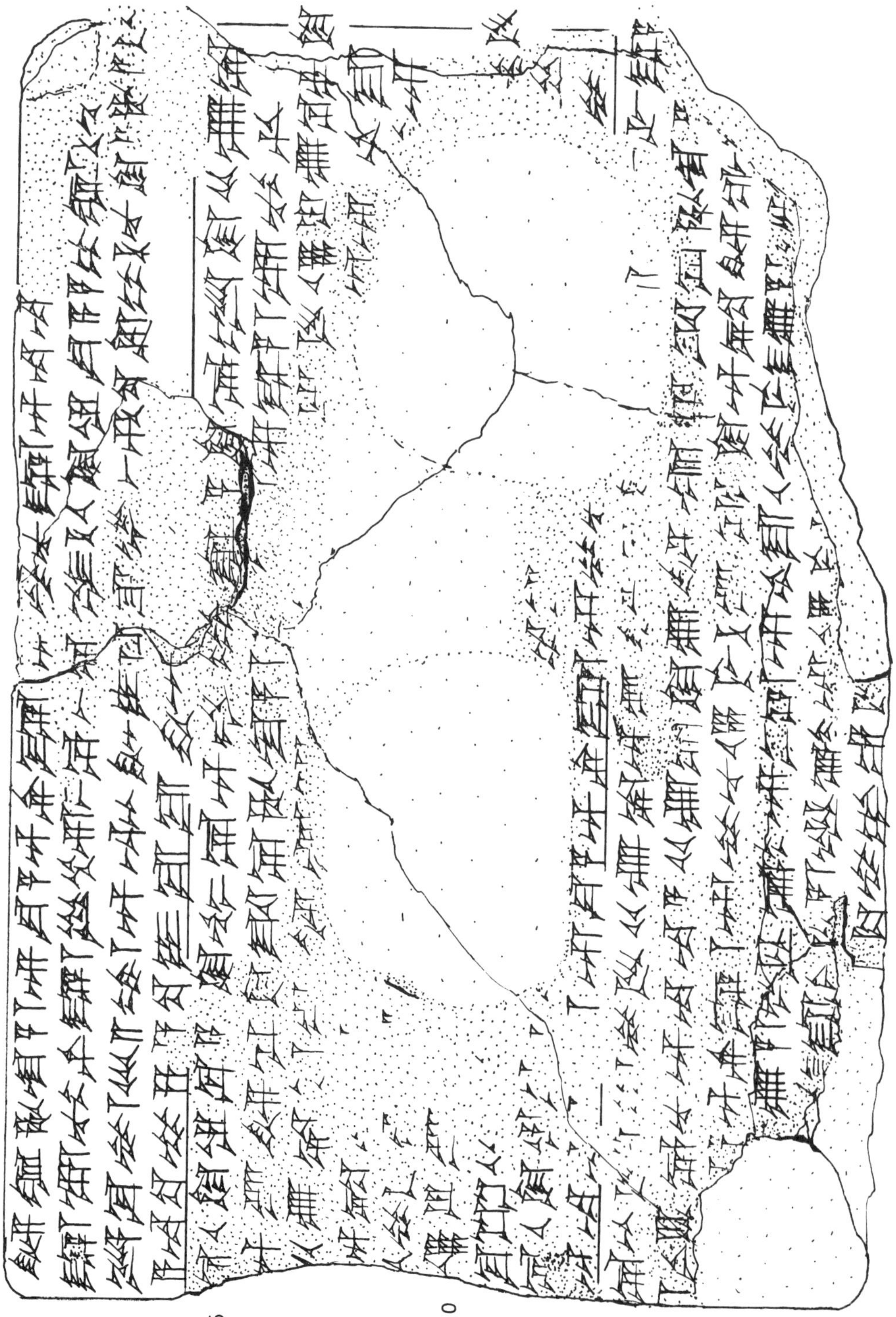

45

R.

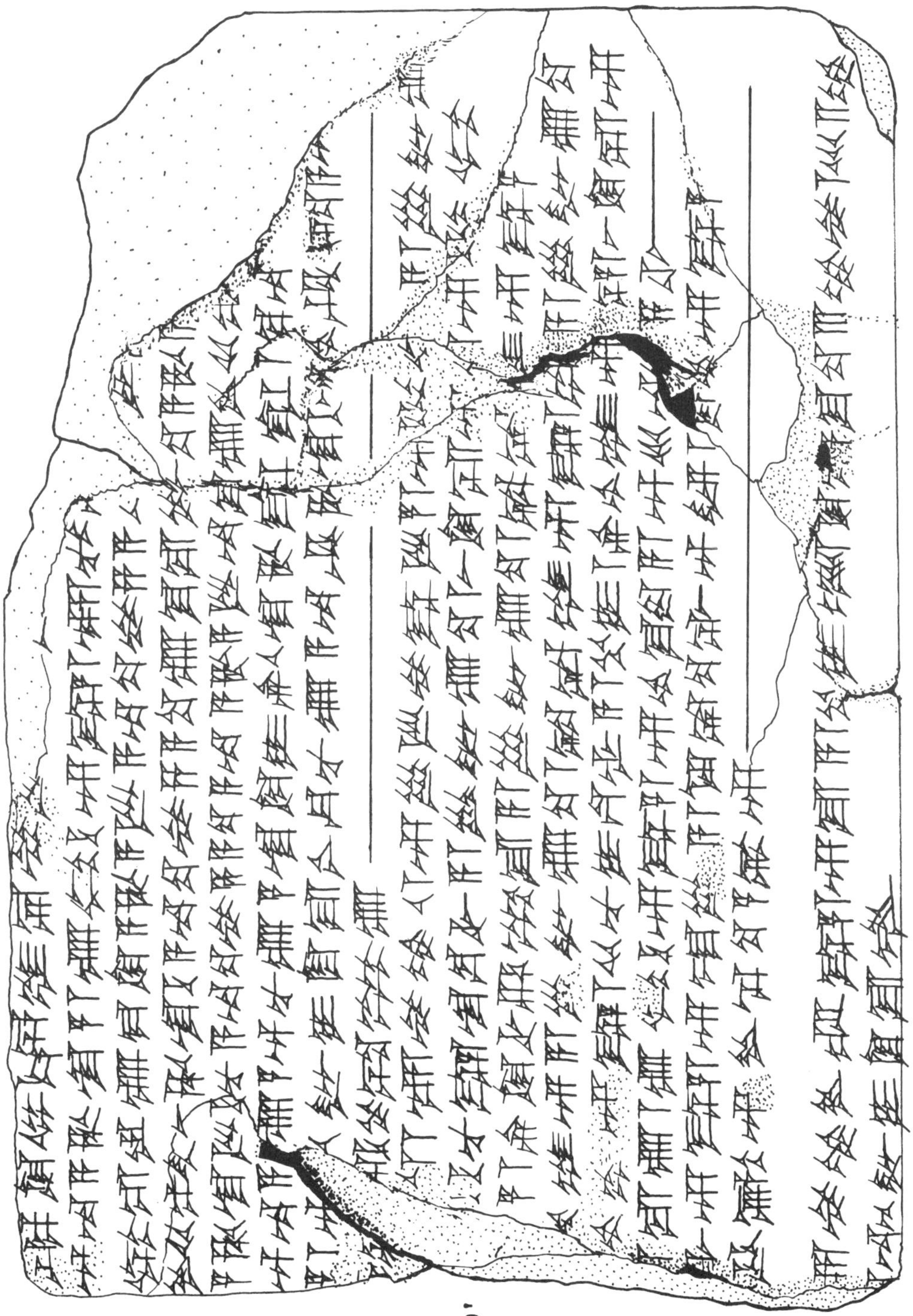

PLATE 112

45

Le.E.

Lo.E.

45

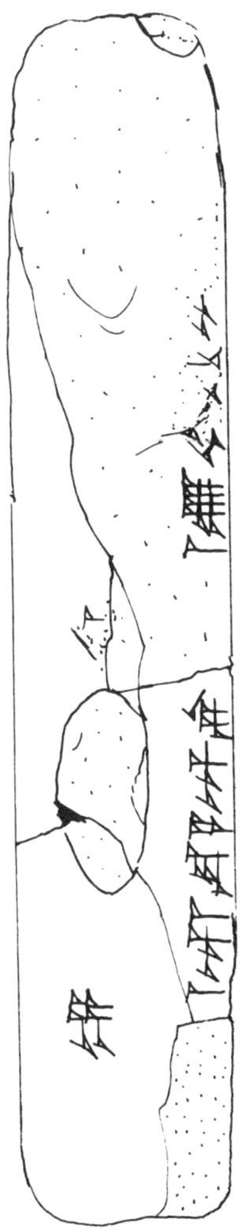

R.E.

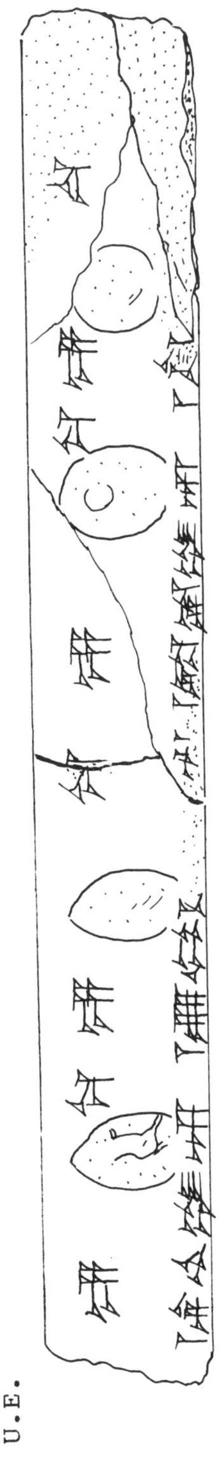

U.E.

46

O.

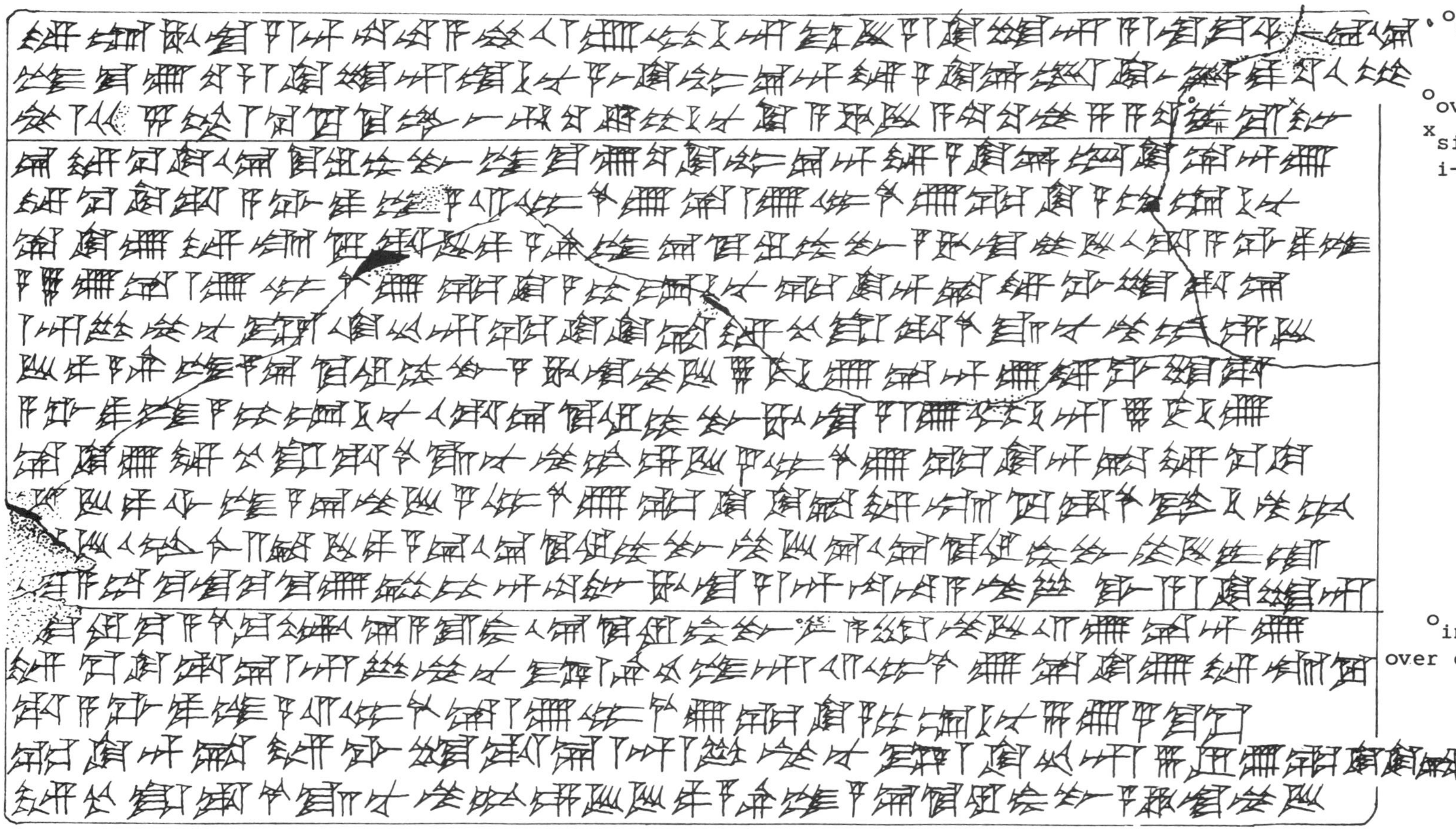

°continued on R.E.

°over erasure

ˣsic for i-zu-zu-'

°ina over erasure

continuation of line 1 on R.E.  °

°possibly erasure or MEŠ

46

R.

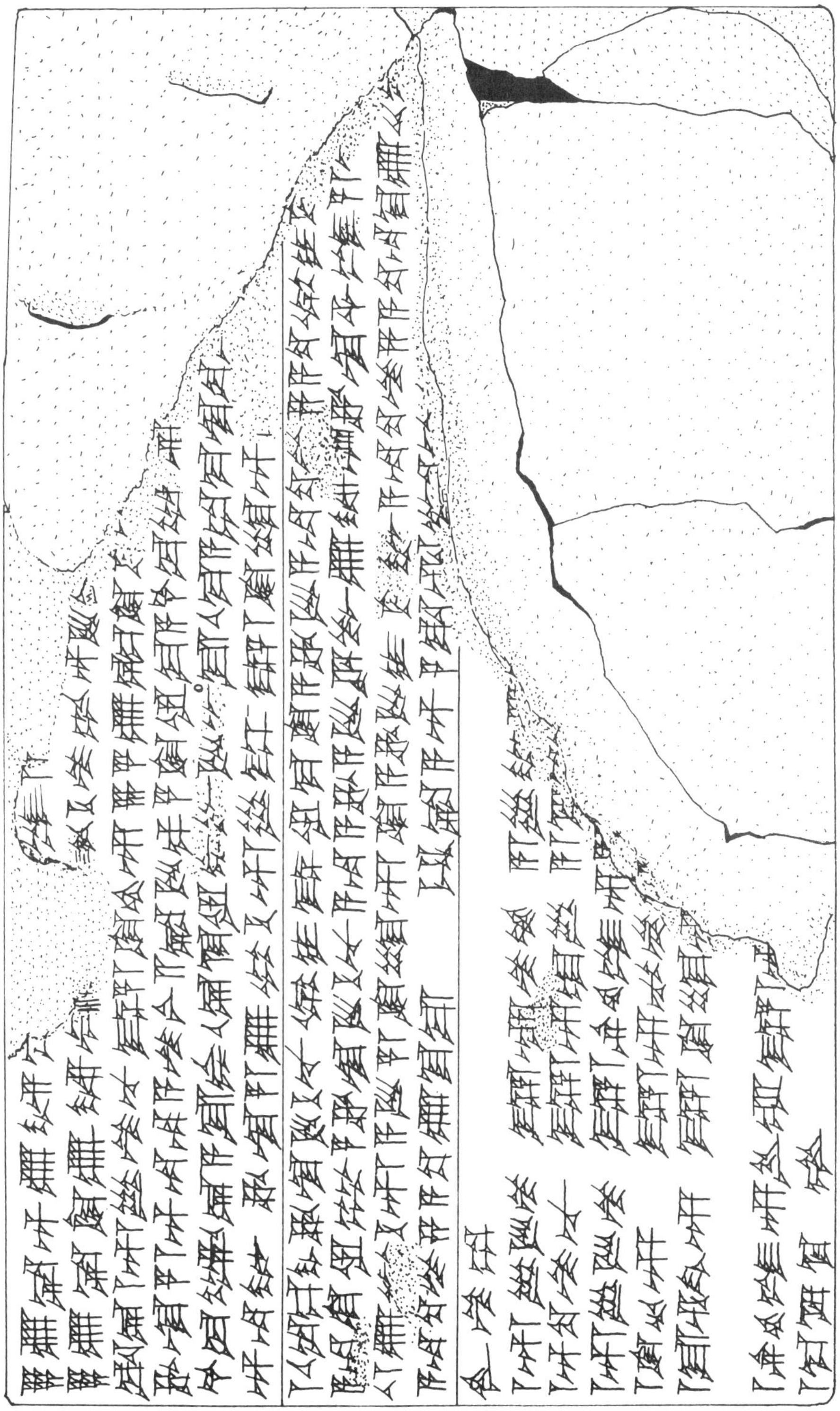

°error for

PLATE 116

46

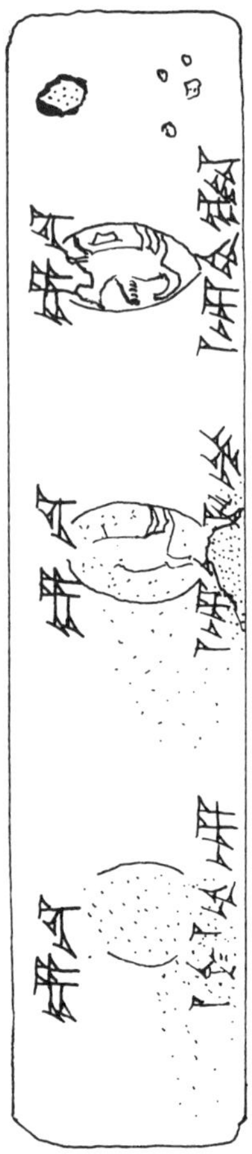

Le.E.

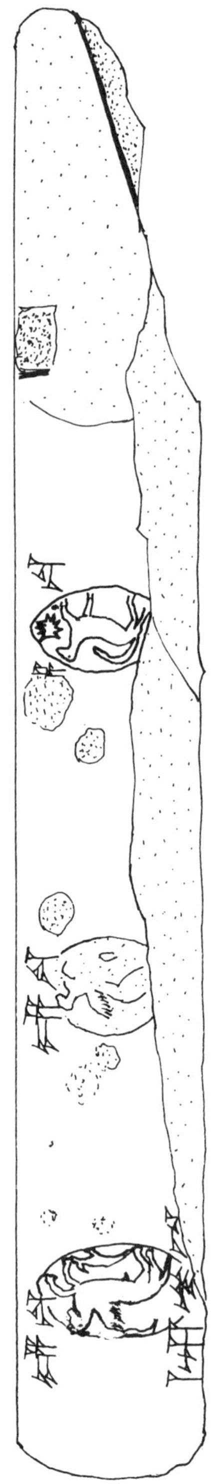

Lo.E.

46

o<mu>

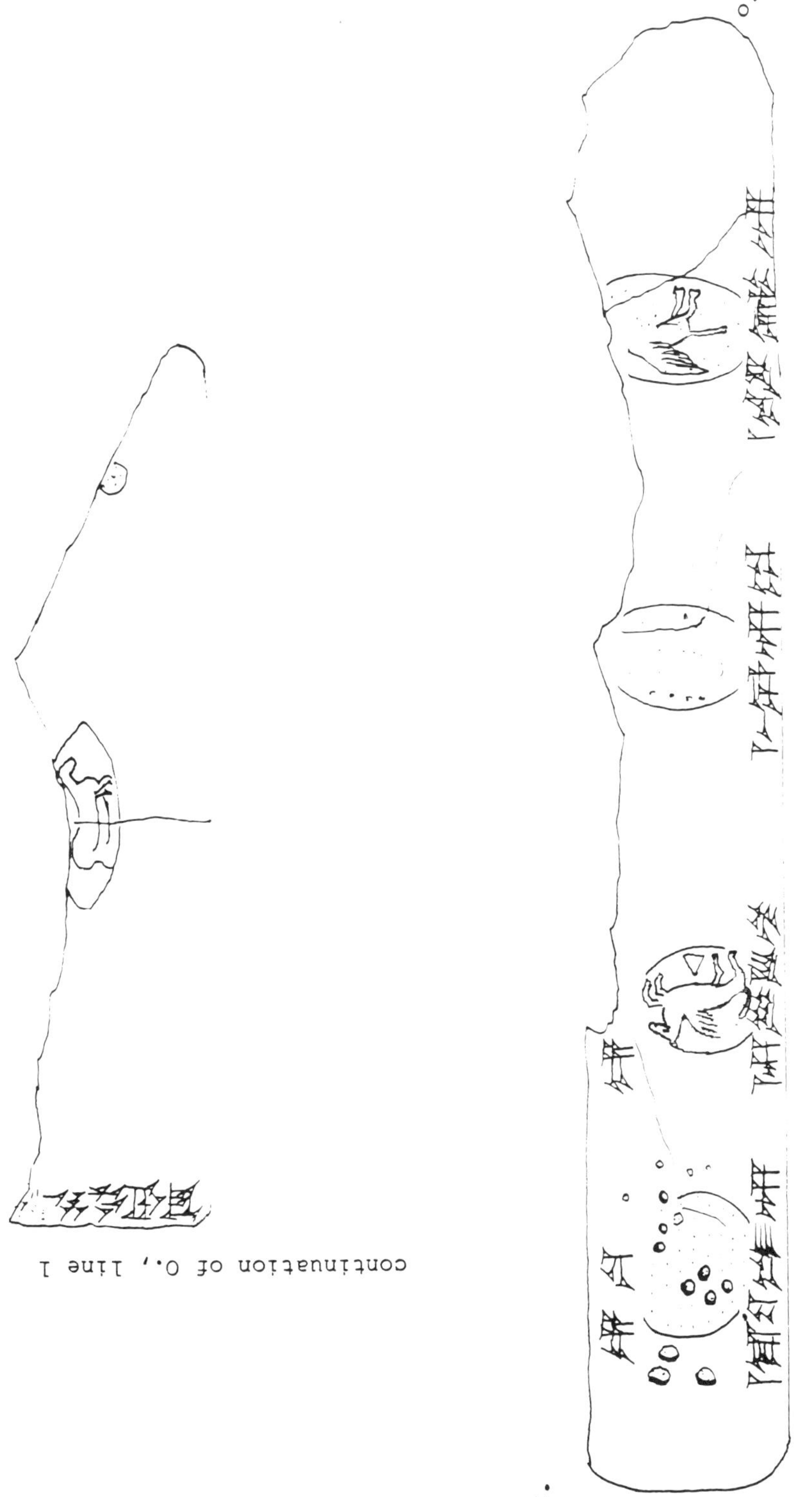

R.E.

continuation of O., line 1

U.E.

PLATE 118

47

O.

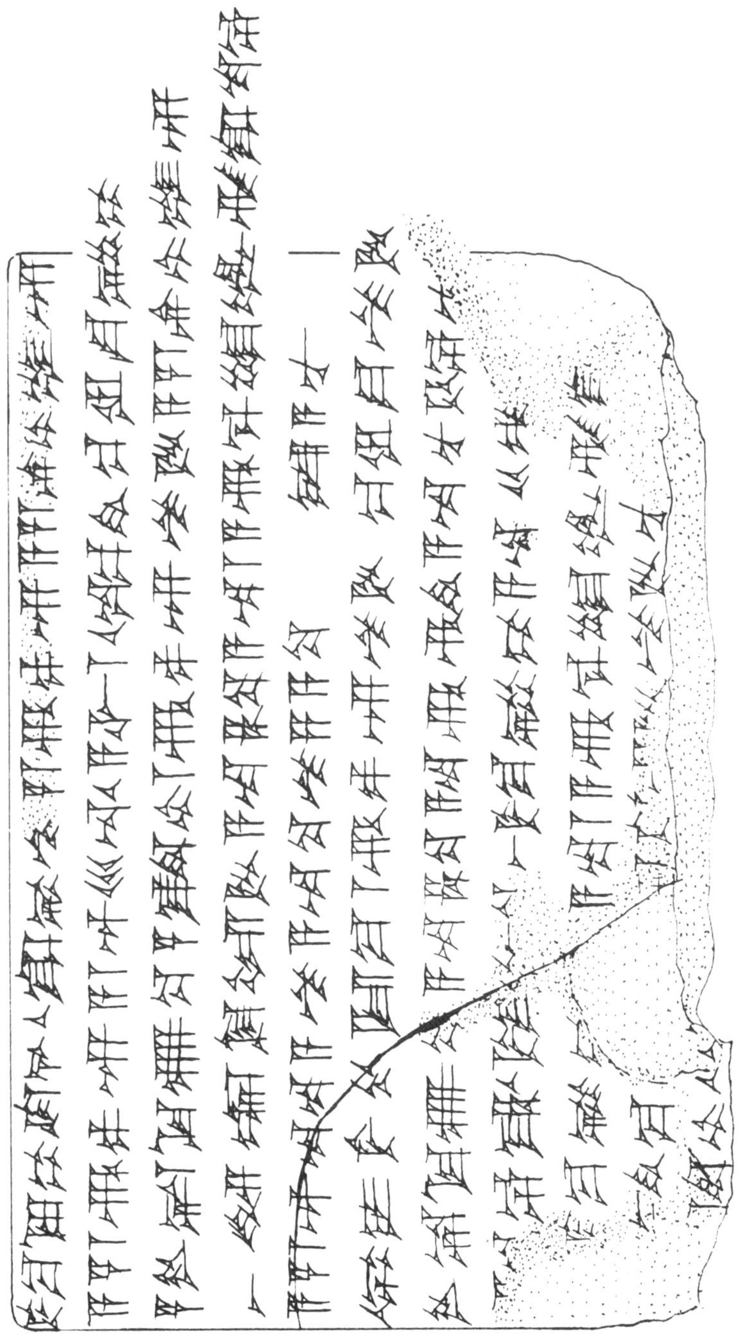

(Reverse destroyed)

47

Le.E.

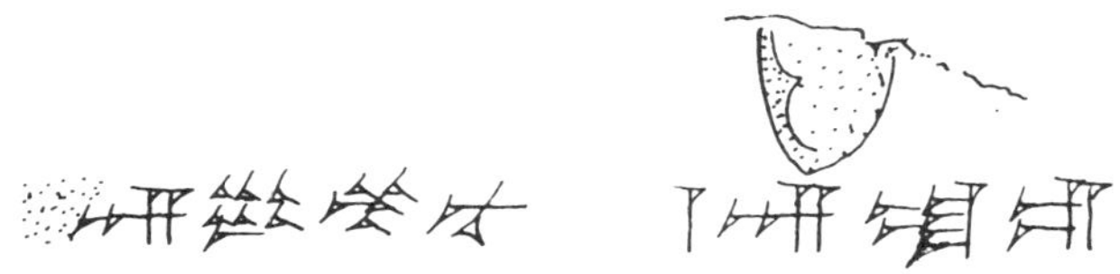

(Rest destroyed)

Lo.E.

(Rest destroyed)

U.E.

(Rest destroyed)

R.E.

(Rest destroyed)

48

O.

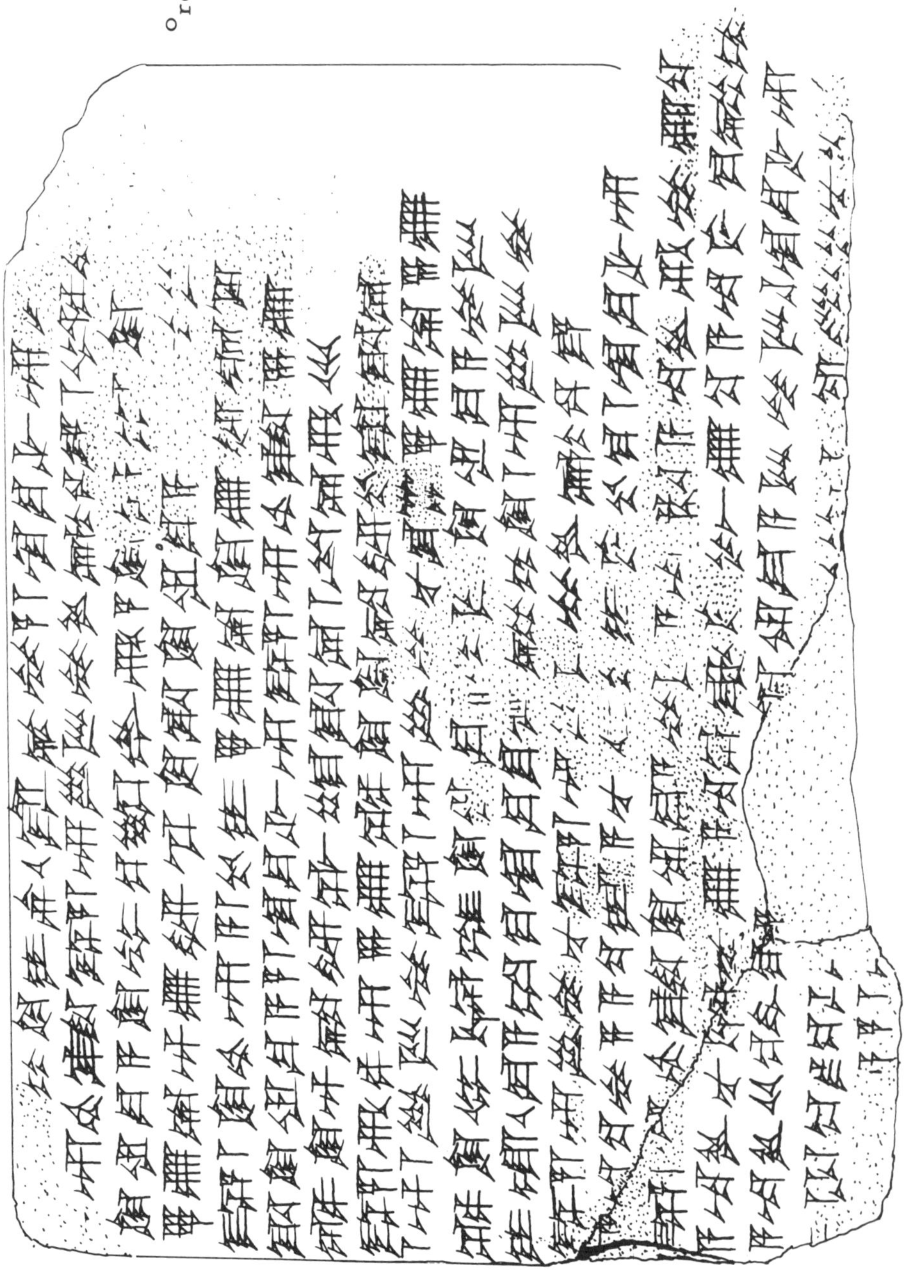

°reading uncertain

48

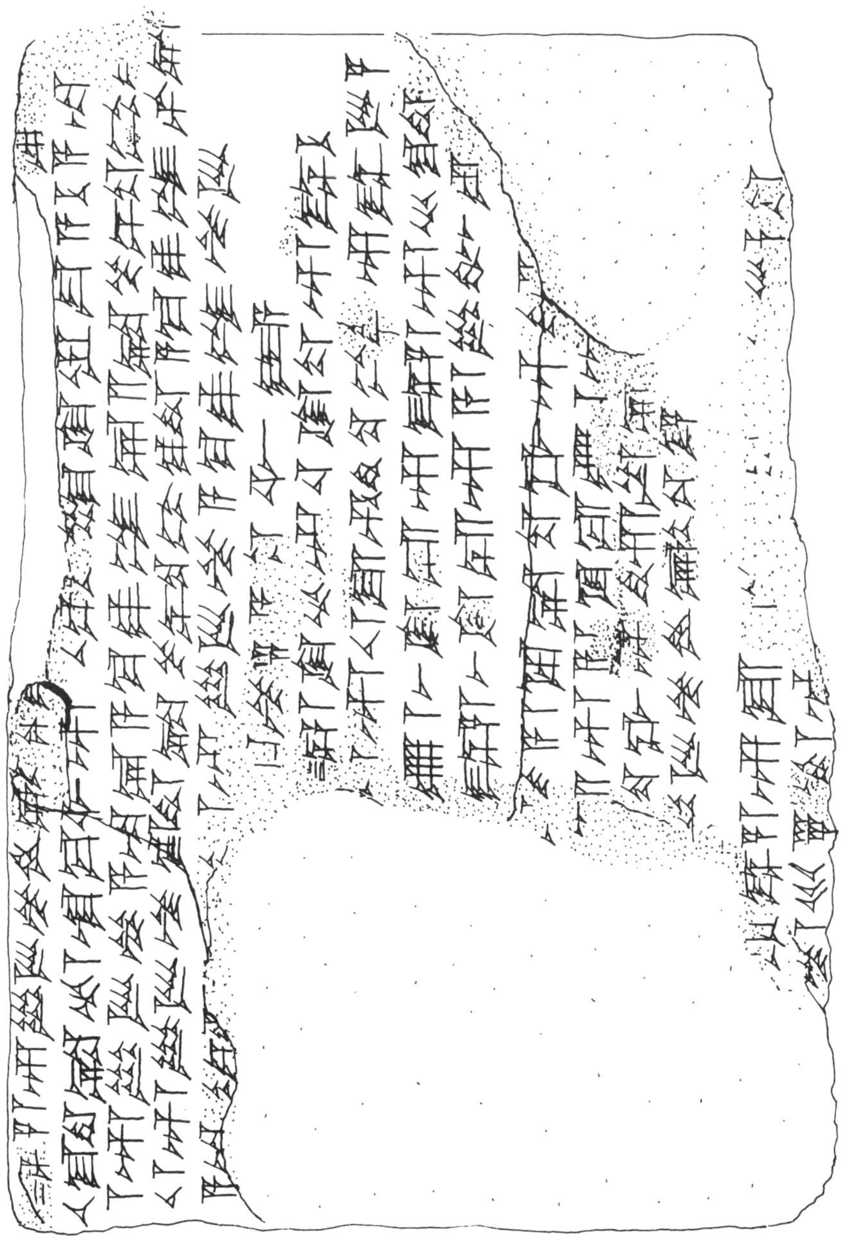

R.

19

25

30

48

U.E.

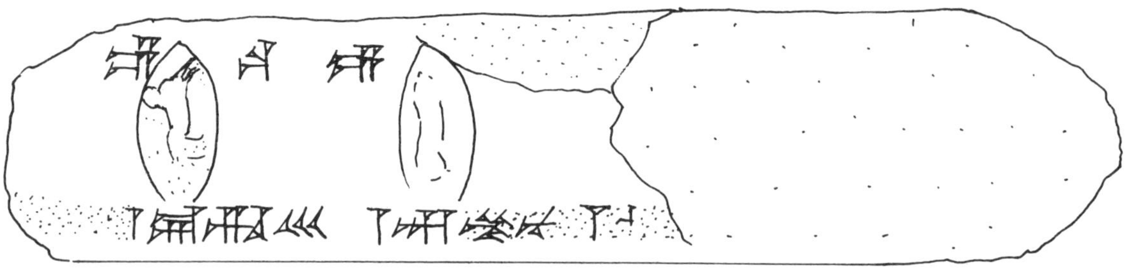

Le.E.

48

Lo.E.

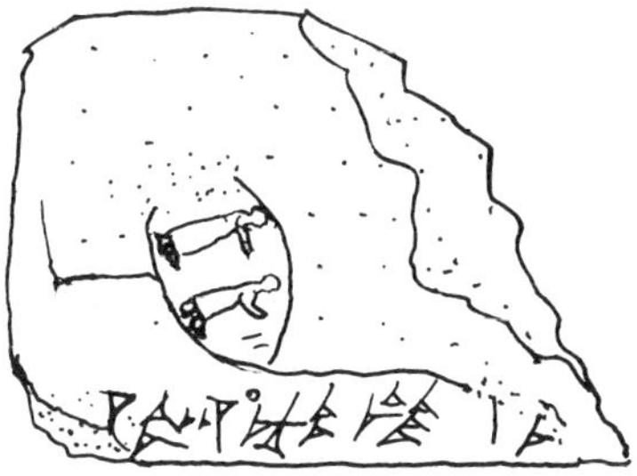

(Rest destroyed)

o  (^{1d}60 over erasure)

R.E.

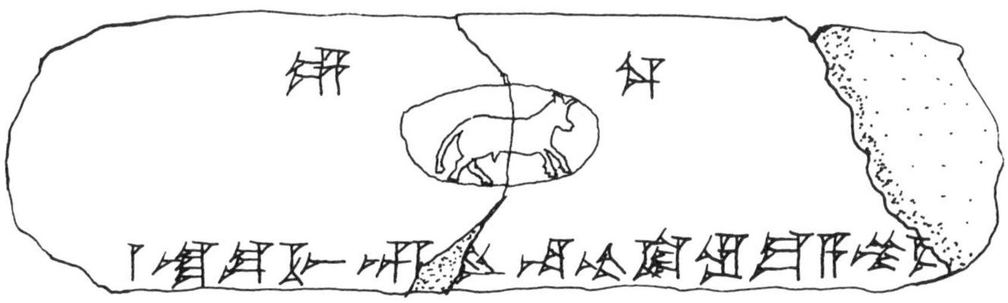

49

O.

1'

6'

7'

8'

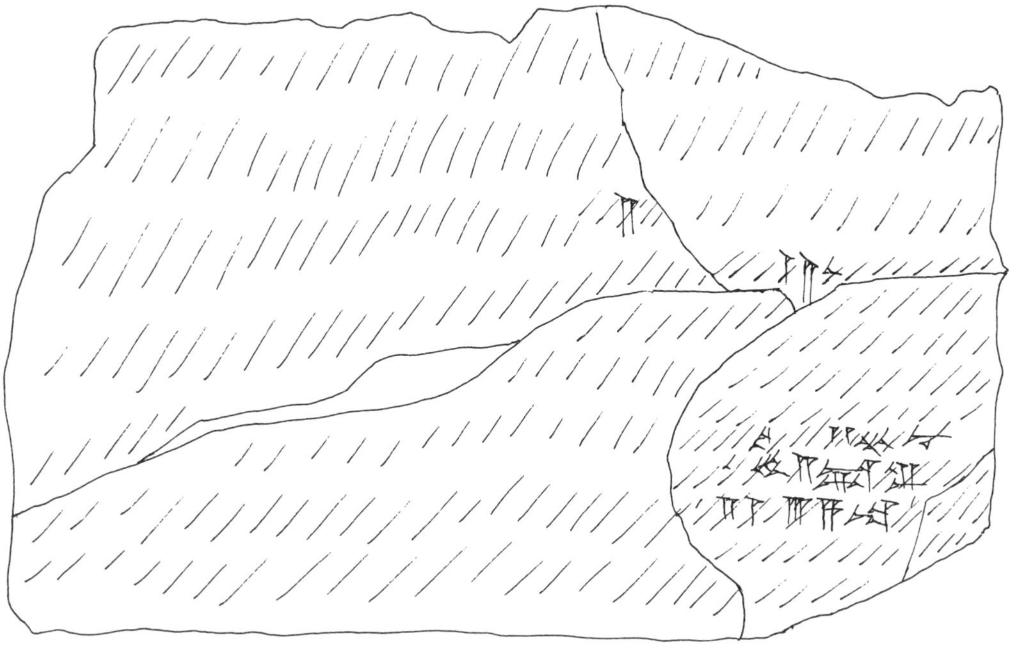

49

R.

A 3655

A 3493

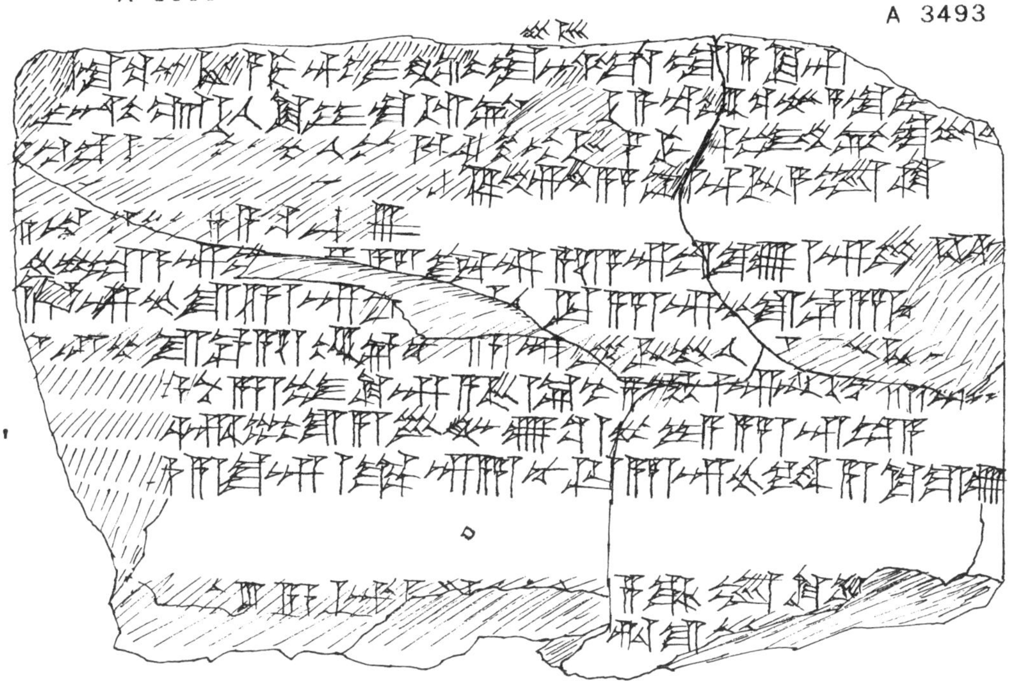

A 3489

A 3422

49

Le.E.

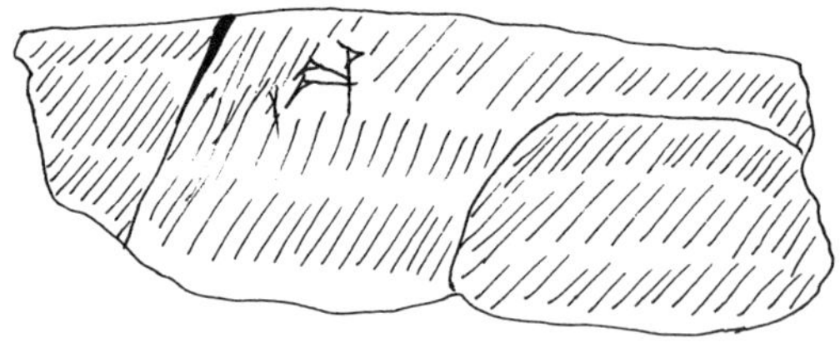

Lo.E.

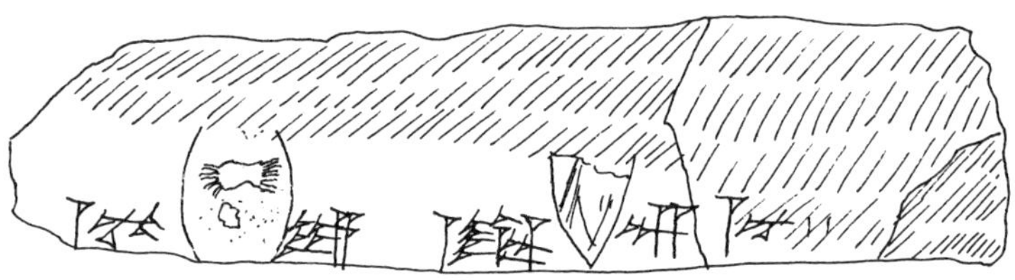

R.E.

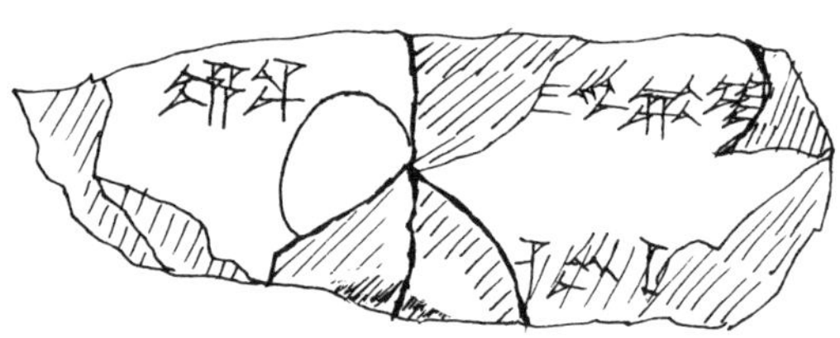

(U.E. destroyed)

50

O.

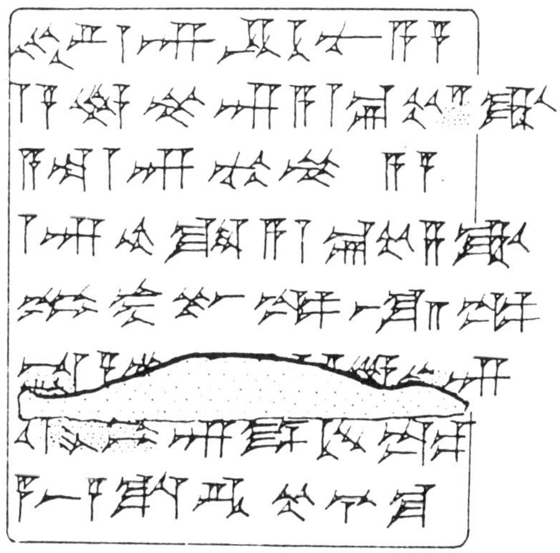

R.

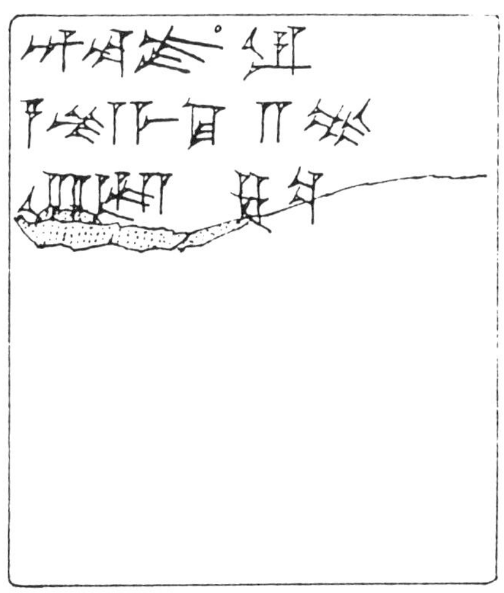

°sic

PLATE 128

51

U.E.

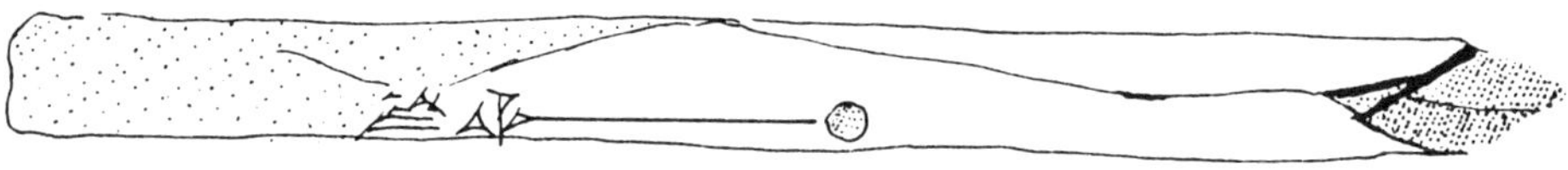

O.

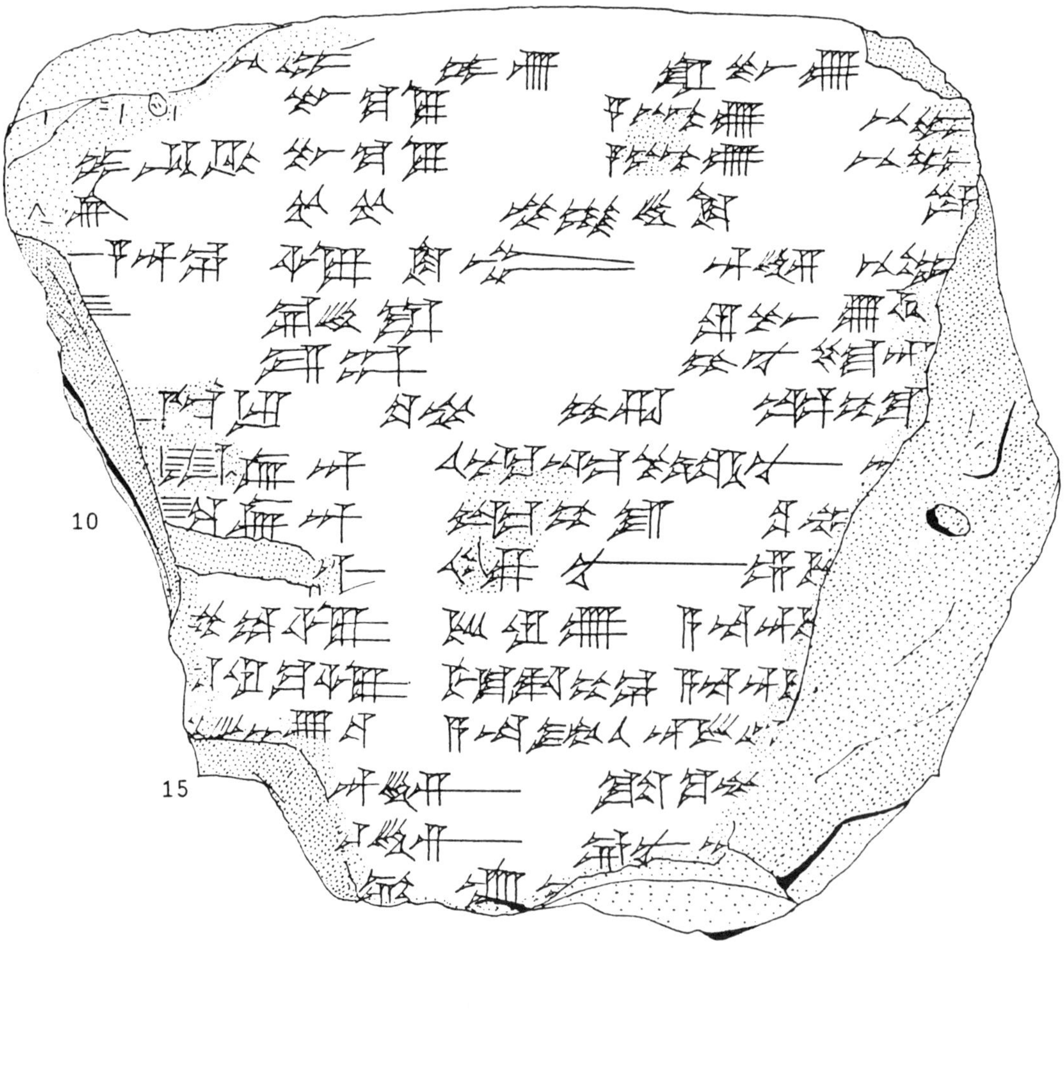

51

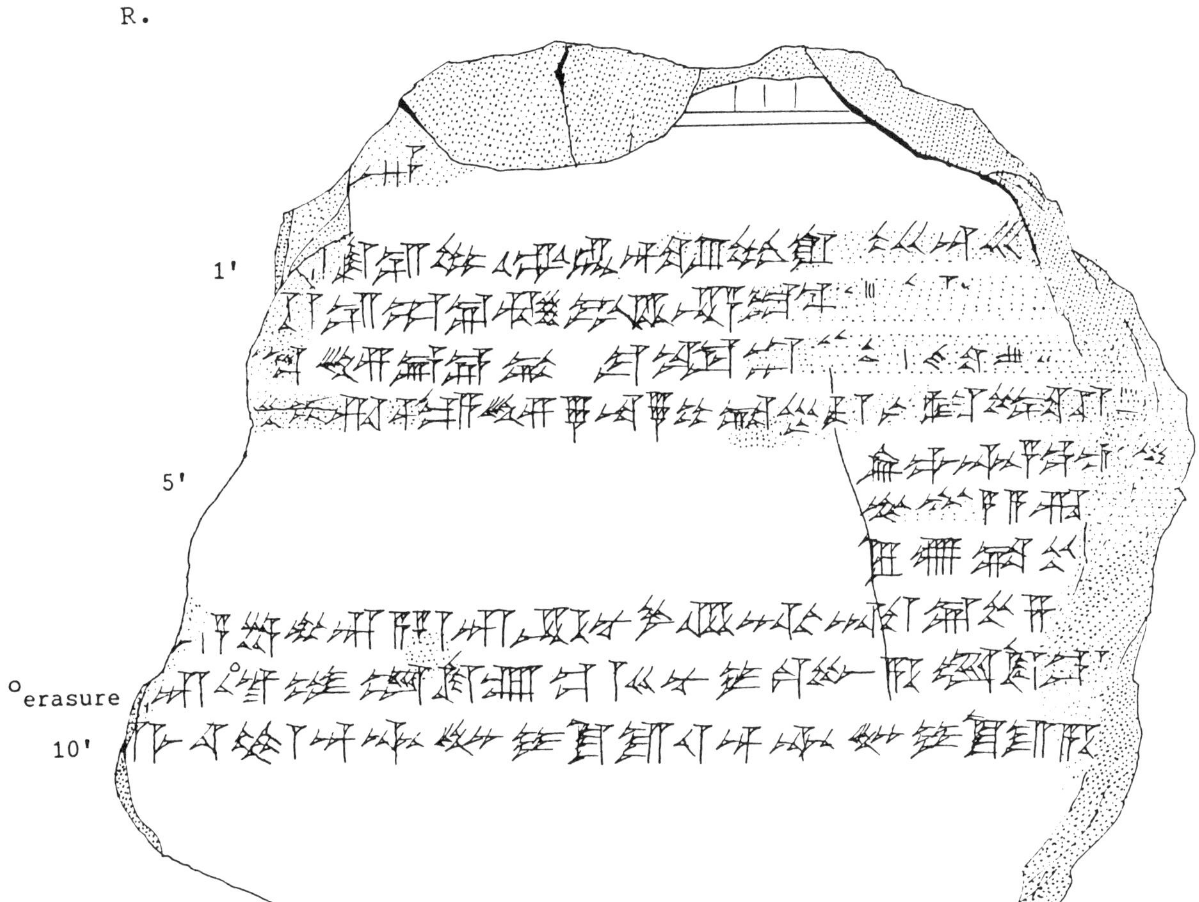

PLATE 130

52

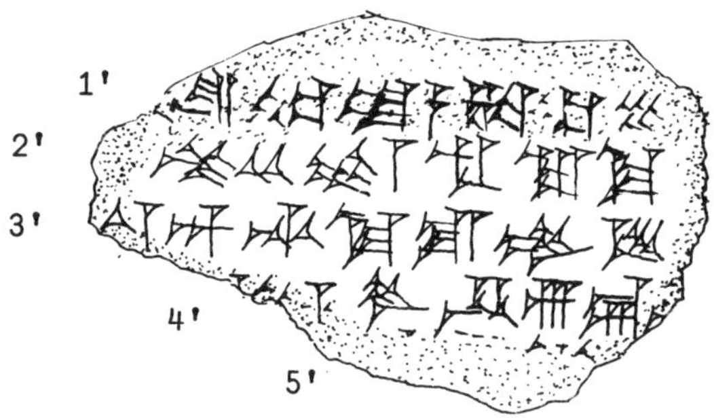

(Rest destroyed)

53

R.

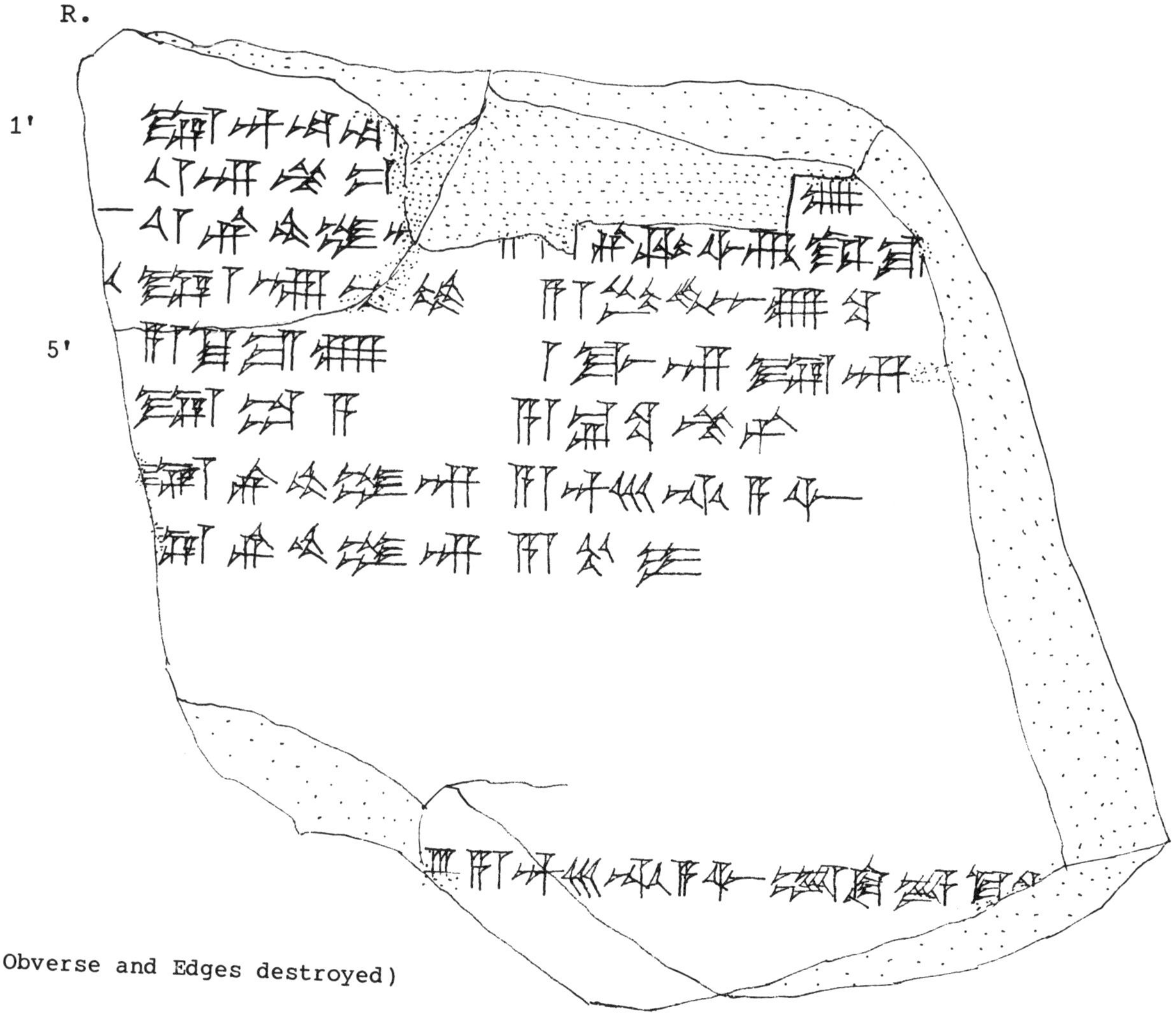

(Obverse and Edges destroyed)

54

O.

1'

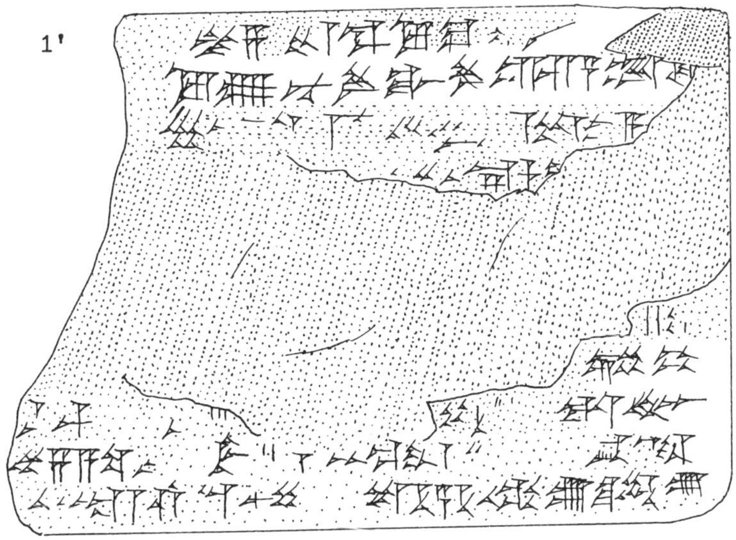

10'

R.

12'

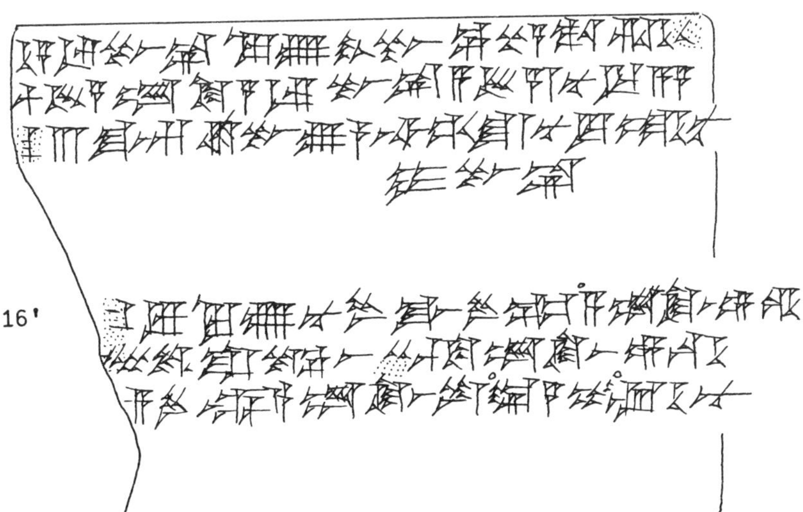

16'

°error for šá?

°over erasures?